Interfaith Marriage

Interfaith Marriage
Share and Respect with Equality

Dilip Amin, Ph.D.

Mount Meru Publishing

Library and Archives Canada Cataloguing in Publication

Amin, Dilip, author
     Interfaith marriage: share and respect with equality
/ Dilip Amin, Ph.D.

Includes bibliographical references and index.
Issued in print and electronic formats.
ISBN 978-1-988207-20-9 (softcover).--ISBN 978-1-988207-19-3 (Kindle)
     1.   Interfaith   marriage.   2.   Interfaith   marriage--Anecdotes.
I. Title.

HQ1031.A48 2017   306.84'3   C2017-901813-2
                                                C2017-901814-0

Published in 2017 by:
Mount Meru publishing
P.O. Box 30026, Cityside Postal Outlet PO
Mississauga, Ontario
Canada   L4Z 0B6
Email: mountmerupublishing@gmail.com
Web: http://www.mountmerupublishing.com/

ISBN 978-1-988207-20-9

Cover design by Ashley Moore (http://www.ashley-moore.com/)

Contents

Preface

For most of my early life, religion was the least of my interests, but all that changed when my children approached marriageable age. Being raised with completely pluralistic[1] beliefs, it is difficult for me to comprehend others' exclusivist thinking.

I discovered that some proud Hindu relatives and friends had gotten married to Muslims by Islamic nikaah marriage after religious conversion or married in Catholic churches after signing a prenuptial agreement to raise children only in the Christian faith. They were reluctant to disclose more details to me and probably found my inquiries an invasion of their privacy. In search of truth, instead of trying to learn locally, I decided to reach out internationally and set up a non-profit web forum Interfaith Marriage with Equality (InterfaithShaadi.org) in 2009.

The website grew in popularity and today has a collection of more than 23,000 comments, which reflect the opinion, mindset and trend of the present generation. Though youths in interfaith relationships will not talk to their parents or best friends about their issues, they gladly disclosed many minute details to me (under alias "Admin"). This gave me the opportunity to understand the complexities of interfaith marriages and the pain people are suffering due to exclusivist religious ideology.

While advising more than 900 new adults[2] in the midst of their interfaith love relationships, I conveyed a basic message of interfaith marriages with religious equality. Endorsements[3] of my views from people in love have assured me that I am on the right path. With this book, I now wish to reach out to the rest of world to promote religious pluralism in marriage and true mutual respect for each other's faith.

There are many direct and indirect contributors to this book. First the author would like to thank some 5000 individuals who shared their views on interfaith marriage with equality (or in-equality) on the Interfaithshaadi.org forum. The author also appreciates more than 900 people in interfaith love relationships that shared their personal experiences. Such experiences and viewpoints helped shape the messages in this book. Many of these real life experiences are included in this book.

---

[1] See Appendix A: Glossary.
[2] Age 18-30.
[3] See Appendix B.

The author also provided draft version of this book to the following individuals from different faiths: Dr. Ashok Kuber, Debbie Motto, Deepak Chandani, Deepak Kotwal, Pastor Connie Winter-Eulberg, Hanah Khan, Dr. Lok Shandilya, Manu Patel, Nainan Desai, Rajiv Varma, Richard Heiman, Sonal Mann, Tushar Pandya and Vickie Sherman. This book has benefitted from their comments and feedback. The views expressed in this book are author's own views. The above reviewers may or may not be in agreement with the views presented in this book.

The author wishes to thank Ashley Moore for cover design, Ekta Patel for Mehndi design, Janki Patel for Mehndi artwork, Aditya Patel for photography and my wife Raju Amin for providing her support throughout this project over past 12 years.

—Dilip Amin, Ph.D.

Disclosures

It is not the author's objective to criticize any religion. However, in order to guide youths in interfaith relationships about potential issues arising out of different religious upbringing, major differences between different faiths are highlighted.

In this book, reference has been made to Dharmic (Hinduism, Jainism, Sikhism and Buddhism) faiths and Abrahamic (Christianity, Judaism and Islam) faiths. However, these two terms are not commonly used or known by the general public. In this book, the word Hindu may include Jains, Sikhs and Buddhists, and vice versa. However, the author acknowledges that all these are different religions with distinct identities.

The term God has been loosely used in this book to convey messages to dating new adults, including when referring to Jesus (Son of God), Buddha, Devas and Devis. Further, the term idol-worshipping and polytheist are used to describe viewpoints of some Abrahamics towards Dharmic religious practices.

The author has used 81 real life experiences of interfaith dating or married couples from the non-profit public forum InterfaithShaadi.org. Their names have been changed for their privacy. The author has not validated commenter's identity nor authenticated information provided by them on the forum. Considering that their information is already in the public domain, the author has used the information in this book for educational purpose.

Information cited in this book is taken from different sources and the author has provided proper references. Most of the research for this book is web based and many web links (URLs) have been cited. It is beyond the author's control if the web links no longer work at a later date.

The author intends to use all royalty received from the sales of this book for promoting pluralism and well being of others.

Chapter I. Introduction

This book is written to promote interfaith marriage with equality. It highlights complexities of interfaith relationships for the benefit of interfaith couples and their parents. Using interfaith marriages as a tool, the author wishes to promote religious pluralism and tolerance in this world.

This book is more than "Interfaith Marriage for Dummies." It provides relevant texts from scriptures, historic perspectives, practical issues, laws governing interfaith marriages, and real-life experiences from hundreds of youths.

As the world is getting smaller, there is greater personal interaction between people with diverse backgrounds. This results in an increasing number of interfaith marriages, and, this trend is expected to increase over the coming years.

Most interfaith conflicts appear only a few months before marriage or in worst cases, just a few days before the birth of a child. The objective of this book is to help educate new adults so that they make fully informed decisions before committing to long-lasting married life.

It is easy for a religious leader to give grand sermons on interfaith harmony but quite difficult in the day-to-day life of an interfaith couple to find middle ground between conflicting religious beliefs. Unfortunately, most interfaith dating couples don't have sufficient knowledge about the intended spouse's faith, or even about their own faith. Further, in the early dating period, it is difficult to bring up sensitive topics like religion for fear of disturbing the fragile romantic relationship. However, couples would be better off discussing critical issues now rather than later. Relevant guidance and talking points are provided in this book.

Historically, interfaith marriages between **Dharmics** (Hindu, Jain, Sikh and Buddhist) and **Abrahamics** (Christian, Jew and Muslim) were rare, but now they are becoming common and increasing in numbers. Table 1 shows the important differences between the belief systems of Dharmics and Abrahamics. The author's marriage survey in 2009 found that 38% of Dharmics got married to Abrahamics in America.[4] About the same

---

[4] Section 2.4.

percentages of interfaith marriages have been reported for Christians, Muslims[5] and Jews.

Table 1: Abrahamic verses Dharmic Faiths*

	Abrahamic	**Dharmic**
Religions	Judaism Christianity Islam	Hinduism Buddhism Jainism Sikhism
Core Belief Style	Exclusivism	Pluralism
Circumcision	Yes	No
End Ceremony	Burial	Cremation
After life	Judgment Day	Incarnation

* This is a high level general guidance. Not all religions follow these beliefs equally.

The main focus of this book is to help navigate a Dharmic-Abrahamic couple from conflicting religious issues. However, the author would like to warn interfaith dating readers and their parents that the journey is not going to be easy.

It is not the objective of this book to criticize any particular faith or religion, but to highlight potential conflicts and major differences. The author expects readers of this book to be educated intellectuals and thus be able to objectively navigate through the difficult-to-swallow information provided in this book. It is hoped that the readers will appreciate the objective of the work in promoting the equality of partners in an interfaith marriage.

Ideally, it would be better if an interfaith couple believes that religious scriptures were written by apostles/sages in earlier times and should be interpreted within its context. However, if one member of the couple believes that the scripture is a direct message from God and must be followed literally, then the other member should know how that will impact their planned married life.

---

[5] Section 2.5.

It is fashionable to talk of being secular and tolerant in colleges, and thus not always easy to recognize an exclusivist. To help readers learn to spot exclusivist thinking in the intended spouse, simple lists of questions are provided in this book.

For the most part, Abrahamic faiths are monotheistic, exclusivist and believe in the superiority of their faith over each other's and others'. Dharmic faiths, on the other hand, are relatively more pluralistic. Abrahamics are expected to identify themselves by clear association with their religious institution and must "formally" accept a particular faith by certain religious ceremony, like **B**aptism, **B**ris, bar mitzvah, **S**hahadah, sunat, khitan, etc. (referred to in this book as "BBS") These exclusivist ceremonies have certainly created problems for even interfaith marriages within Abrahamics, because dual ceremonies (like baptism and bar mitzvah) for a child are not accepted by either of the two faith leaders. Such religious labelings are also present in Dharmic faiths, but are not enforced as much by religious institutions or the Dharmic communities.

In most cases, it is not the couple's religious scriptures, but what that person has learned from it is important. It is hoped that this book will help discuss critical topics that a Dharmic-Abrahamic couple may have overlooked and will help them achieve an ever lasting and loving marriage with clear understanding. Although it may be uncomfortable to read certain chapters, it is hoped that interfaith dating couples will read this book together to gain maximum benefit.

Everyone likes to have equality in many aspects of life. Religious equality in an interfaith marriage should not be any different, though it is difficult to define. Further, tolerance toward religious differences may be high during the dating period but these differences may become a major point of conflict later in married life. The author's objective here is not to define for readers what is right and wrong, but to provide dating couples with talking points to help them make fully "informed" decision. The author wishes you all everlasting happiness in your inter-faith or within-faith married life, irrespective of how you define equality.

While guiding the interfaith couples during the last 9 years, the author wrote many articles (covered in Chapter II) based on common questions raised by youths in love. Other chapters (Chapters III–XI) are directed to couples from two specific faiths. Chapter XII covers conflicting points among scriptures. Eighty-one real life experiences out of more than 900 youths that the author consulted are also described in this book.

In author's experience, initially, most youths were tolerant and accommodating to their intended spouse's faith but later changed their minds to please their parents and religious institutions. In the end, the author felt, most couples were not ready for an interfaith marriage with equality.

With this book, the author is hoping to raise awareness about the potential conflicts due to religious exclusivity, which may lead to pain and suffering among dating and married interfaith couples. It is author's wish to promote religious harmony and pluralism.

EQUALITY
"Why does equality even matter, you might ask?
Well, we know that in an abusive relationship, one partner
maintains power and control over the other. This type of
relationship is extremely unbalanced and unequal."
—Love is Respect.org

Chapter II: Interfaith Marriages

Section 2.1: Interfaith Marriages Are Part of Our New Life

In the Western world, new adults have the opportunity to date individuals from other faiths during their college years. Therefore it should come as no surprise that in North America about a third[6] of the young generation of Dharmics (Hindus, Jains, Buddhists and Sikhs) marry Abrahamics (Christians, Jews and Muslims). This trend is expected to rise in the years ahead.

There is often a large gap between the expectations of parents and children about the child's choice of a life partner, at least initially. Thus, when an Abrahamic life partner is selected, Dharmic new adults will frequently make decisions without prior advice, guidance, or consultation with their parents and vice versa.

It is safe to say that most youths are not sufficiently knowledgeable about others' faiths and how they differ from their own faith. Further, parents are often ill equipped to guide their new adults in this critical transition, resulting in irrational arguments between generations.

In the predominantly first-generation immigrant Hindu and Muslim communities, some parents with unmarried children may look smugly at others whose child has an interfaith spouse without realizing that it could happen in their own home a few years down the road.

We need to recognize that interfaith marriages are a matter of chance, regardless of the religious training given in childhood. Parents of interfaith married couples also need to learn to live with a new reality of life.

Parents who have children in interfaith marriages are reluctant to publicly share their experience, resulting in a loss of critical knowledge for the benefit of each community. It is hoped that wealth of knowledge collected at InterfaithShaadi.org about complexities in interfaith marriages will be of value to many communities.

Interfaith marriages are a part of our modern life and we need to learn to be prepared for it. Several interfaith marriage issues need to be addressed such as:

1) What will be the religion of children?
2) A Dharmic must ask: is there any expectation of a religious "label" to be placed on the child(ren) by BBS (Baptism (Christian), Bris (Jewish) or Sunat (Islamic))?

---

[6] Section 2.4.

7

3) An Abrahamic must ask: will they have to be a part of the Hindu worship practice of puja and the display of Hindu Ishvara icons in the home?
4) Will there be expectation of religious conversion of the groom/bride before marriage?
5) What will be the names of children?
6) Will there be circumcision for religious reason?
7) Which religion will be followed for the funeral rites of the spouse and children by this marriage?

Not all interfaith spouses try to impose their religious beliefs/practices on their counterpart in marriage, but it is critical to find out the facts sooner rather than later. It is also important to recognize that despite all the potential marital pitfalls, a successful and fulfilling inter-religious marriage is possible. One effective way to achieve this is by not imposing one's religious beliefs on the other partner.

> *I will never ask my wife to do something that I know I could not do. If I cannot change my faith, who am I to ask her to do the same? That's hypocrisy. She is Sikh and will remain Sikh and I am still Muslim.*
> —Azad (Section 6.1)

Section 2.2: Ten Points of Interfaith Dating

In next two Sections, some talking points for interfaith dating couples are discussed.

More and more new adults are making friends and engaging in interfaith relationships leading to marriage, sometimes without realizing the complexities associated with their decision. No one is perfect, but one can improve the chances of a happy and long lasting marriage by making informed decisions. Here are some pointers in the order of ascending importance:

10) Face Value: It is very important to look at how he or she dresses, speaks, and interacts with others, as well as his/her compatibility with you. Here, it is also important to learn to differentiate between an inexperienced dater who may be genuinely interested in you from a "professional" dater who knows how to impress you. Some professional daters may have an evangelical objective for engaging you in a friendship.

9) Upbringing: It is important to learn much more about a person than the "face value." A person is defined by what he or she has learned during their lifetime, especially during childhood. Pay special attention to childhood activities, especially religious ones, and think about how his/her experiences will impact your life.

8) Divorces in family: According to research done at Rutgers University[7] divorce risk triples if one marries someone who comes from a family that has experienced divorce.

7) Family background: In this day and age, it would be a good idea to check out your new friend's information from web searches[8,9] and find out what type of family and background this person comes from.

6) Novelty: Remember that novelty, by its very nature, is short lived. Be honest and decide whether you find the religious practices of your partner interesting as a novelty or really understand and accept the reasons and meaning behind the rituals?

5) Opinion of family members: Before you are too deep into a relationship, consult your best friends and older siblings or cousins. Keep an open mind to their comments and advice, and think about their

---

[7] http://www.valfarmer.com/getdoc.asp?docid=808.
[8] http://www.publicrecordsnow.com/.
[9] http://www.google.com/.

implications and relevance to your new relationship now and in the future. Also, involve your parents now, before it is too late to reverse your decision.

4) Roots: People tend to return to their roots as they age. Ponder how your life mate will remain compatible and tolerant of your religious faith, culture, lifestyle and food habits as you grow older and raise your children.

3) Compatibility of your communities: Remember, a marriage is not only a union of two individuals, but to some extent, a union of two extended families and communities. If two sets of parents/in-laws cannot stand each other for even two hours in one room, or if the two communities are at odds, it will bring aggravation and tension later in life.

2) Ability to follow religious vows: Promise only what you mean. For example, do not take shahadah oath for nikaah (Islamic marriage) or accept baptism ritual before a Christian wedding just to please your spouse's parents without fully understanding the meaning of the oath. Be prepared to follow it. Do not lie. A married life based on misleading promises or vows will face serious challenges later in life.

1) Religion of children: This is the most important point to consider for any interfaith relationship. Discuss the expectations of which one of the two religions the children will follow, especially any insistence on **B**aptism, **B**ris, bar/bat mitzvah or **S**hahadah/sunat (**BBS**). Even if you have a secular outlook without any religious preference, you should be alarmed by an expectation that your children will follow your spouse's religion, not yours. You must be wary of whether the person has a fundamentalist streak.

We are responsible for what we are and whatever we wish to be. We have the power to make ourselves. If what we are now has been the result of our own past actions, if certainly follows that whatever we wish to be in future can be produced by our present actions. So we have to know how to act.
—Swami Vivekananda

Section 2.3: FAQ on Interfaith Marriage

To further prepare new adults in interfaith love relationship, here are some frequently asked questions (FAQ) to help make fully informed decisions.

What is the main message here?
Interfaith relationships should be based on mutual respect for both faiths, and marriage should be solemnized without imposing religious conversion on a spouse. After marriage, both spouse's faiths should get equal respect and consideration at home and in raising children.

Is religious conversion for marriage wrong?
Not if it is discussed early on in the relationship and agreed to by both parties, without coercion. Some conservative Islamic and Christian families still believe in the superiority of their faiths, thus forcing the spouse-to-be of any other faith to convert to their faith before an Islamic nikaah or a church wedding can take place. Such expectations should be discussed upfront before getting into an intimate relationship. After years of romantic relationship, to ask an intended spouse to give up his or her religion just before the wedding is not only HIGHLY UNETHICAL, but also will surely lead to marital discord. In such cases, the coerced spouse will surely feel cheated at a time when he/she is expected to experience some of the sweetest memories of his/her life. It may sow doubt in their heart about whether their spouse deceptively practiced proselytism under the guise of love.

What is wrong if one converts to a new faith for the sake of a marriage, but is allowed to practice his/her own faith after the marriage?
Be careful—religious conversion is not a hollow ritual devoid of any meaning or consequences. Let's take a Christian-Muslim marriage as an example. As per the shahadah oath to convert to Islam for nikaah, you accept and declare that there is no God but Allah and Mohammad is His messenger. Further, you acknowledge that associating others (like Jesus) with Allah is the greatest of all sins. Similarly, baptism before a church wedding means conversion to Christianity and a commitment to repudiate former practices (of Islam) and to live with Christ forever. You must ask yourself what is your true intention.

What religion my children will follow?
This should be the MOST CRITICAL question in an interfaith relationship, even if there was no conversion required for the marriage ceremony. Ask if your intended spouse expects your sons and daughters

to have baptism, bris, bar/bat mitzvah or sunat (BBS) to declare their faith for life.

How is the decision to select a faith usually made?

In most cases, the decision for selection of the faith for the spouse and children is made to please the more rigid and intolerant spouse, or the more stubborn parents/community. If one spouse feels that he/she is giving in to coercion, it will sow the seeds of future marital discord.

Are the above questions relevant to Hindus?

The "Dharmic" religions (Hindus, Jains, Sikhs and Buddhists) are not normally accepted or tolerated by the Abrahamic ("People of the Book") in a marriage. Hindus believe in one Supreme Being, but they are free to worship His/Her manifestations in many forms, including female forms. However, this practice is forbidden in Christianity, Judaism and Islam and can pose a serious issue when it comes to "puja" of various Hindu forms of God. According to the Ten Commandments[10]: "I am the Lord your God. You shall have no other gods before me. You shall not make for yourself an idol, whether in the form of any thing that is in heaven above, or that is on the earth beneath, or that is in the water under the earth. You shall not bow down to them or worship them; for I the Lord your God am a jealous God... punishing children for the inequity of parents, to the third and fourth generations of those who reject me."

Can we teach our children both religions?

It is difficult. Young children may get confused with mixed and often conflicting messages. For example, when you take them to a Hindu or Jain temple, you ask them to believe in, respect and bow to several forms of God, essentially a pluralistic message. But when you take them to a mosque or church, they hear just the opposite and exclusive messages. When confronted with such contradiction, children may lose faith in any God or religion.

If my spouse is open-minded, can we get around these religious expectations?

Remember, a marriage is not just the union of two individuals but, believe it or not, a union of two families and two communities. It is ethical to be upfront and honest about your intentions with your new family rather than building life-long relationships based on deception and lies (by fake-conversion).

---

[10] Exodus 20:4-5. The Holy Bible (The Gideons International).

I'm not so religious. What if I don't mind religious conversion for the marriage to please my spouse?

Life is full of changes. In general, people tend to return to their roots as they age, especially when they have children. How will you feel if you find yourself irreversibly locked into onerous practices?

Conversion is only a formality; why not do it just to please my spouse and his/her family?

The religious conversion is not a onetime deal; you are setting a new tone for your life. If you feed a shark, it will come back again for more. Similarly, religious conversion for marriage will be followed by the expectation of a declaration of faith for your children via BBS. Later, you may be forbidden to practice your own religion so that your children will not learn about it and follow it. Also, your spouse or his/her family may not like to be part of religious activities while at your parents' home. Your spouse may insult your parents' religious practices, and may force you to denounce them in front of your family and friends. When your fantasy honeymoon period ends and transforms into a routine married life, these issues may become sore points in your life.

What if my spouse claims he/she didn't know beforehand but is asking for it now to please his/her parents?

Do not be convinced by the commonly used old trick of playing innocent. After living with the same parents and community for most of their life, he/she should have known of his/her parents' and community's expectations. If he/she did not, then you have the right to question his/her intelligence and honesty.

What is the true test that my intended spouse is not a religious fanatic?

Simple! Just ask for two promises, the second one being the more important:

1) No religious conversion before or after marriage; and

2) No religious labeling (BBS or namasanskara) for your children until they are old enough to decide for themselves.

But what if he or she does not agree?

If someone you are dating lacks tolerance for what you believe in and expects you to forsake your own religion for marriage, even just as a meaningless ritual, you must ask yourself if you are prepared to tolerate the intolerance that is being practiced against you.

Why do so many marriages end in divorce?
Some of the major reasons include expectations that were not fully discussed and the resulting complaints that my "spouse changed" after the marriage. Before entering into an interfaith relationship, find out if he or she has true tolerance for what you are and for your beliefs.

Is a fulfilling relationship possible in an interfaith marriage?
Yes, if the interfaith relationship is based on true mutual respect for religious diversity and both parties are willing to continually work toward a lasting relationship that sometimes includes compromises.

Ekam sat vipra bahudha vadanti —Rigveda 1.164.46

Hindus believe there is absolutely one ultimate reality (Brahman) but they have liberty to express the Almighty by different names and forms.

Section 2.4: 38% of Dharmics Marry Abrahamics in America

There was no information available about interfaith marriages between the second generation of Dharmics to Abrahamics in the West. The author conducted the first such survey and published in 2008.[11]

The landmark 2008 Pew Forum survey[12] found that only 10% of Hindus in America married outside their faith. Although the survey covered 257 Hindu families, 86% of them were immigrants and 58% between the ages of 30-49. Thus, it focused on the first generation Hindu immigrants from India and reflects the norms of interfaith marriages in India. It does not provide information on the much higher rate of interfaith marriages that American-born, second generation Hindus are entering into. The author conducted an independent survey showing 38% of the marriages of young Hindus, Jains and Sikhs are to people of Abrahamic faiths (Christians, Jews and Muslims) as shown in Table 2.

Common family names of Hindus, Jains and Sikhs (followers of Dharmic traditions) were picked from the Macy's marriage registry[13] for our data analysis. Non Hindu-sounding first names (like Fatima Patel or Anthony Reddy) were removed. Though individuals' religious preferences were not verified, the consistency of results across these common family names gives some validity to our conclusions. The results clearly show that at least a third of the young Dharmics have selected an Abrahamic partner as their life mate. The outcome was similar for males and females in analysis of subgroups.

Table 2: Interfaith Marriages of Dharmics to Abrahamics

	Patel	Reddy	Jain	Singh	Total
Total Marriages	494	47	45	324	910
To Abrahamic	170	22	15	143	350
%	34	47	33	44	38

Historically in India, interfaith marriages among Hindus, Jains and Sikhs are common, but not with Muslims or Christians because there are fundamental differences between the beliefs and practices of the two major groups of religions—the Dharmic and the Abrahamic. Now in

---

[11] http://www.prlog.org/10139529.
[12] http://commons.trincoll.edu/aris/files/2011/08/ARIS_Report_2008.pdf.
[13] https://www.theknot.com/registry.

America, interfaith marriages between these groups are taking place in larger numbers.

In reality, a marriage is not only between two individuals, but also to some extent, between two extended families. Many times, major difficulties may arise when subtle pressure is applied by the extended family for religious conversion before a church wedding or Islamic nikaah takes place. The challenges may get harder as years go by, especially when time comes to decide the religious fate of the children from the marriage. For example, Islam requires that children of mixed marriages must be raised in the Islamic faith. The Catholic Church strongly advocates that the Catholic parent should do everything possible to insure that a child is baptized and raised as a Catholic.

It remains to be seen how followers of Dharmic and Abrahamic faiths manage their fundamental religious differences in the interfaith marriages.

> *Your religion is like your mother. Just because your mother is less attractive than your friend's mother you can't abandon your mother and adopt a new one.*
> —Mahatma Gandhi
>
> In reference to interfaith marriages, someone may rewrite it as: *Your religion is like your mother. Just because your intended spouse is demanding that you adopt your mother-in-law as your dear mother, you are not going to abandon your biological mother!*

Section 2.5: 45% of Muslims Marry Outside Their Faith in America

Following information is based on an article co-authored[14] with Shafaq Mayet, a proud Muslim girl and a new adult from America.

Interfaith marriages have been increasing among all faiths in America. Interfaith marriages accounted for 58% of Jewish marriages between 2005 and 2013.[15] More than 40 percent of marriages in the Catholic Church were interfaith marriages according to another survey.[16] In the previous section, it has been reported that 38% of Dharmics (Hindus, Jains, Sikhs and Buddhists) are married to Abrahamics (Muslims, Christians and Jews) in America.[17] According to one report, more than 91% Muslims in the West were married to Muslims.[18] This may be a result of either survey sample consisting of mostly immigrant Muslims or counting of non-Muslim spouses as Muslims due to their conversion to Islam before the marriage. A majority of Muslim Americans (62%) says that it is acceptable for a Muslim to marry a non-Muslim according to a 2007 Pew Research Center poll.[19]

A marriage survey was conducted by Dilip Amin (author of this book) and Shafaq Mayet using common family names of Muslims.[20] These names were picked from the Macy's marriage registry.[21] The results showed that 45% of the Muslims in America were married to non-Muslims as shown in Table 3.

Table 3: Interfaith Marriage of Muslims to non-Muslims

	Khan	Ali	Ahmed	Total
Total Marriages	238	149	109	496
To non-Muslims	108	72	44	224
%	45	48	40	45

---

[14] http://www.prlog.org/10369465.
[15] http://www.pewforum.org/2013/10/01/jewish-american-beliefs-attitudes-culture-survey/.
[16] http://www.catholic.org/hf/love/story.php?id=22208.
[17] http://www.prlog.org/10139529 (Section 2.4).
[18] http://www.catholic.org/news/hf/family/story.php?id=22208.
[19] http://pewresearch.org/assets/pdf/muslim-americans.pdf.
[20] http://www.prlog.org/10369465.
[21] https://www.theknot.com/registry.

One surprising result was the marriage of Muslim women to non-Muslims (45.1%). This was nearly same as the marriage of Muslim men to non-Muslims (45.2%). The high interfaith marriage rate of Muslim women is seemingly inconsistent with the Islamic law[22] that prohibits a Muslim woman—but not a man—from marrying outside the faith. The reason for this inconsistency could be that the survey samples probably consisted of new adult Muslims who were well-educated second-generation immigrants. These second generation immigrant Muslims in America are more inclined to go against the normal practices in the home countries of their parents. Spread of globalization and secularism has contributed to the growth in the number of interfaith marriages among the new adults.[23]

---

[22] https://en.wikipedia.org/wiki/Interfaith_marriage_in_Islam.
[23] http://www.interfaithmarriage.org.uk/resource_packs/Resourcepack.pdf.

Section 2.6: Interfaith Marriages: A Message to Dharmics

This article is written to convey a message to Dharmics about interfaith marriages.

As the former president of a Balvihar (Sunday school), the author only regrets one point of our collective inaction: though we taught our kids about our religion, we failed to teach them the practical aspects of interacting with young people from other faiths. In the Western world, it is quite common for new adults to date those from other faiths during their college years, and consequently it should come as no surprise that about a third[24] of our young generation of Hindus, Jains, Sikhs, and Buddhists marry a person from outside of these Dharmic faith traditions. In almost all cases where a non-Dharmic life partner is selected, the decision is made by Dharmic new adults without pre-emptive advice, guidance, or consultation with their parents.

As cited in this article, religious differences could bring complexities to their married life, starting with an "unintended" religious conversion of Dharmic and their progeny to the faith of their spouse. Further, divorce rates in interfaith marriages are higher compared to within the same faith marriages.[25] For these reasons, it is increasingly important for new adults to understand potential complications before entering into a serious relationship.

While interfaith relationships should develop based on a mutual respect for religious diversity, sometimes major differences in fundamental beliefs pose difficulties in finding a common ground. Dharmics carry a pluralistic and tolerant attitude that all faiths help you attain God, and everyone should respect not only their own religion, but other religions as well. But this tolerant attitude is not universal. Many families belonging to Christianity, Islam, and Judaism (Abrahamics) believe in the supremacy of their monotheistic dogma. Their holy books reject what they consider polytheistic beliefs. For example, Hindus believe that the Ultimate Reality can be worshiped in many forms (Saguna Brahman), but this recognition and practice is forbidden in Christianity, Judaism, and Islam, and poses a serious issue when it comes to puja or worship (which is considered very bad idol-worship[26] by Abrahamics).

---

[24] Section 2.4.
[25] http://www.religioustolerance.org/ifm_divo.htm.
[26] Section 2.11.

In another example, Islam forbids marriage with a non-believer (in Allah). Non-believers are expected to convert to Islam by taking the shahadah oath; the declaration that there is no God but Allah and Mohammad is his apostle. A similar practice also exists in some Christian sects where there is often intense pressure from family members and the clergy to perform a religious conversion of a Dharmic by baptism before the church wedding. An uninformed Dharmic will only discover the oftentimes unmentioned expectation of religious conversion after years of being in a romantic relationship. At this point, reluctantly accepting the religious conversion may be the only way of averting a marital gridlock.

Religious conversion may be a matter of just a brief ceremony, but do not underestimate this ritual as a trivial matter. Taking this oath will set a tone for your life and your children's lives. You will soon find out that the conversion was not just a matter of satisfying the sentimental obsession of the parents-in-law, but a binding commitment guarded by every member of the new community. As per the shahadah oath, you will be forbidden to display an image of Goddess Laxmi or Lord Ganesh, or any other deity in your own home since associating partners with Allah is the greatest of all sins. Offering prayers or supplications to anyone, living or dead, is an unpardonable sin. Furthermore, attempting to later reclaim yourself as a Dharmic, even after talaak (divorce), could be punishable by death[27] or life imprisonment by some Middle Eastern countries' laws. Therefore, one should be prepared to accept conversion to a new religion as a serious and irreversible process.

Most conflicts in inter-religious marriages will surface after you have children. For Abrahamics, it is vital that children from their marriage follow only the rules of their individual holy book. A Muslim spouse and the community may demand your kids have sunat (religious circumcision) and bear only an Arabic name. A Jewish person may not ask for a religious conversion for the spouse but may want bris circumcision to declare the Jewish faith for the child. A Christian spouse may require baptism of children and require them (and you too) to attend church every Sunday, while you may wish to take your child to the Mandir or Balvihar. Another major consideration is about the expectation for family planning. The author learned of a case where an Ahmedabadi young woman already had five children because her Catholic husband

---

[27] Mohammad said, "Whoever changes his Islamic religion, then kill him." (Bukhari 9:84:57).

did not believe in birth control. Did she know and realize the consequences of her interfaith relationship while dating in college?

One may want to believe that marriage is a secular act and not a religious one. Unfortunately, some religious leaders and communities would like to use the wedding as a tool for their ambition of religious expansion. This author learned of a case in Boston where without the shahadah and Islamic wedding (nikaah), a local imam denounced the wedding and most Muslim relatives did not attend the wedding reception party. In almost all cases of a Hindu-Muslim marriage in which both Muslim and Hindu ceremonies are performed, the religious conversion to Islam (shahadah) is performed first. Then it is followed by the Muslim wedding ceremony (nikaah) and after that by the Hindu ceremony (vivaha).

Similarly, in many church weddings declaration of faith to Christianity is a mandatory requirement. Therefore, technically speaking, after conversion to Islam or Christian faith has been performed, the Hindu ceremony is totally superfluous oxymoron because it is a Muslim-to-Muslim or Christian-to-Christian wedding performed by a Hindu priest! In such a wedding, do celebrating Hindus really know what they are celebrating?

While investigating the possibility of a relationship with those from other religions, be sure to find out if there is going to be any pressure on you to convert by performing BBS (Baptism, Bris, Shahadah/Sunat) and raise your future kids as Abrahamics from not just your future life partner, but also from his or her family members and religious community. The BBS as shown in Figure 1 and used throughout this book is not a hollow ritual devoid of meaning. It is an affirmation of conversion to an Abrahmic religion. If a couple is looking for an interfaith marriage with equality, it is a good idea not to put a religious label on the children from such marriage.

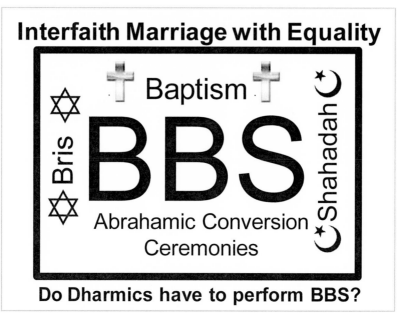

Figure 1: Abrahamic Conversion Ceremonies[28]

Not all Abrahamics impose their religious beliefs and practices on their spouse, but it is very important to find out the facts sooner than later. It is also important to note that despite all the potential marital pitfalls, a successful and fulfilling inter-religious marriage is possible, ideally by not imposing one's religious beliefs on the other partner. A similar message has been given in Jodhaa Akbar, Gadar,[29] and Namastey London[30] movies. Bollywood stars Kareena Kapoor and Saif Ali Khan kept the religions out and got married by a civil wedding,[31] and it is an admirable act. If someone you are dating cannot show you this same respect and expects you to forsake your own religion for marriage, even just in name sake, you must ask yourself if you are prepared to tolerate the intolerance being practiced against you.

Before entering into a relationship, one should have an open dialogue about religious expectations (especially regarding conversion) and

---

[28] For detailed explanation, view this video:
https://www.youtube.com/watch?v=hlAuY85RlcE.
[29] http://www.youtube.com/watch?v=NIPVwnvhojE.
[30] http://www.youtube.com/watch?v=ELguePfC_qM.
[31] Section 2.12.

recognize the far-reaching consequences. Though dealing with this issue early on will obviously be important for the well being of the couple, it will also be a significant issue for their children, not to mention the couple's extended families who take pride in preserving their religious and cultural traditions that have been passed down through many generations. Well-informed and well thought out decisions for selecting a life mate will certainly bring long lasting happiness in a married life, even if it is an interfaith marriage. Most importantly, you want to make sure you will have the freedom to follow your traditions and raise your children to do the same without threats to this liberty from your spouse and his or her relatives.

> *Eastern parents should let their children, who are in the West or are living and working outside their home town, have dating experiences, considering many of them end up marrying outside their faith anyways.*

Section 2.7: Religious Conversions for Marriage

This article is directed to proud Hindu parents and youths.

Proselytism and religious conversion of poor and less fortunate Hindus in India is of major concern to many, but the silent religious conversions of educated and blessed Hindu new adults and their children in the West has not raised the eyebrows of most.

Thirty eight percent of marriages of Hindus, Jains and Sikhs (Dharmics) in America are to Christians, Jews and Muslims (Abrahamics).[32] Forty five percent of Muslims in America marry to non-Muslims.[33] However, there is a limited tolerance for Hindus and Hindu practices of praying to multiple forms of God in Abrahamics' exclusivist religious beliefs.[34,35, 36, 37] Maybe for this reason they expect conversion of the Hindu spouse. Many marriages in Christian churches or in mosques require religious conversion of Hindus by baptism or shahadah respectively, to the faith of intended spouse. In some cases, a Christian or Jew may not ask for a religious conversion for marriage but will expect to declare the interfaith child as a Christian by christening/baptism or Jew by bar/bat mitzvah ceremony, respectively.

Considering that the divorce rate in interfaith marriages is estimated to be quite high,[38] why would any one give up his/her birth religion under pressure? If Mahatma Gandhi had to rewrite his famous statement today, he would probably say, "Your religion is like your mother. Just because your intended spouse is demanding that you adopt your mother-in-law as your dear mother, you are not going to abandon your birth mother!"

In many cases, the partner will start by telling that "I don't care for religious conversion," "It is only a formality," and "Do it just to please my parents or grandmother" but don't underestimate the inner desire of your partner. If your doctor tells you that you have a high cholesterol or blood pressure, would you not be concerned about a future heart attack or stroke? As a Hindu, a request for performing BBS for marriage should be considered an alarming sign for major trouble coming soon to your marriage.

---

[32] Section 2.4.
[33] Section 2.5.
[34] http://www.religioustolerance.org/chr_savs.htm.
[35] Section 2.9.
[36] Section 12.6.
[37] http://www.zawaj.com/articles/interfaith_marriage_iv.html.
[38] http://www.religioustolerance.org/ifm_divo.htm.

If your intended spouse or in-laws are expecting the BBS religious conversion, especially for your children, then you have one of two choices: 1) accept his or her Abrahamic faith and be prepared to give up your birth religion and cultural heritage or 2) clarify that you have pride in your religion and ensure equality by not accepting the BBS religious labeling request. Promise only what you mean. A married life based on misleading assurances or lies will have serious consequences later for both. Married life is a long journey which you should not start without clear understanding.

Without realizing long-term consequences, Hindu youths may opt to accept a new religion just to please their intended spouse and in-laws. In some cases, Hindu parents allow Hindu children to convert to the other religion just to please child's future in-laws or for the happiness of the child.

These days, most Abrahamics are not religious fanatics, but instead are open-minded and will not expect the performance of BBS from the intended Hindu spouse. However, ensuring that the person you are dealing with is tolerant to your identity is a proactive measure to reduce conflicts later. Keep in mind that "tolerance" and "open mindedness" are not measurable characteristics and can change with the wind. Not acceding to performing BBS is a simple litmus test to find out the "true colors" of the intended spouse. Thus, Hindu youths and parents need to learn to ask a simple question: is there any expectation for the children of this marriage to accede to baptism, bris/bar mitzvah or sunat?

Love is often an unplanned event. Love is said to be blind to religion. If so, then why are Hindus expected to be blind? Hindus should check whether their partner's love of their Abrahamic faith or their love for their partner comes first. It is the Dharmic parents' responsibility to guide their love-blinded children for the equality of both faiths. The BBS has no place in an interfaith marriage with equality.

In many cases, when a Hindu adamantly denies the conversion for marriage and for their progeny, the other party considers it and understands. When there are other options available, why not ask for them? If the BBS, which is a religious conversion, is an absolute requirement from your potential Abrahamic in-law, why will you want to tolerate some one's intolerance for what you are? By submitting to the BBS request, Abrahamic's intolerant practices against others are nurtured and propagated.

Marriages may be made in heaven; however a high percent of interfaith marriages end in divorce.[39] With such a high failure rate, why would anyone want to give up their birth religion? In many cases, divorce costs a lot more than a marriage. The BBS promise may have legal consequences, and after the BBS, the Hindu may find it difficult to win a child custody case against an Abrahamic. Check with your lawyer before submitting to the BBS request.

When it comes to college education, most Hindu parents will do anything possible to make sure their children have nothing but the best. For example, if their son or daughter gives up a medical career for a bar tender job and finds a real joy of life, the Hindu parent will be sure to give hell until the child changes his or her mind. Similarly, if a Hindu new adult becomes a cocaine addict, the parents will not support it by saying that "we want to see you happy and you decide what ever is right for you." Yet when it comes to religious conversion for marriage, many Dharmic parents lack the conviction or courage to guide their children and face the Abrahamic in-law. Now it is time, in this supposedly tolerant nation of America and world, to say NO to the BBS and expand tolerance and equality in interfaith marriages.

In general Hindu parents are great bargainers when it comes to purchasing a car or a house. Those same negotiation skills can be used when a son or daughter selects an Abrahamic interfaith marriage mate. One needs to respectfully deny the request for conversion by stating that we are what we are and wish to remain so after the marriage. Tolerant potential in-laws will surely consider this request. At least one should ask, just to learn of their "true colors."

If a Hindu daughter found a handsome and well educated Hindu and that intended spouse later asked for a $5,000 dowry as a pre-condition for the marriage, that parent would probably ask their daughter to reconsider her decision, fearing that this *junwani* (old timer) may bring more troubles later in her life. Similarly, why should anyone tolerate it if a *junwani* Abrahamic asks for religious pride as dowry for the marriage?

Many parents tolerate the intolerance and accept the thought of religious conversion for their children, thinking this is an easy fix to the marital gridlock. Further, there is no risk to their prestige in the Hindu community since no one will find out. However, the time will come when these proud Hindus, now grandparents, will feel guilty seeing their grandchildren following a different faith. It will not be pleasant for these

---

[39] http://www.religioustolerance.org/ifm_divo.htm.

proud Hindu grandparents to drive their Abrahamic grandchildren to a church, synagogues or mosque/madrasas for religious education. This guilty feeling will be worse when the time comes to pass your hard earned life estate for the benefit of the believers of the Abrahamic faiths. At that time grandparents may wish that the grandchildren had the option of being Hindus.

The BBS is a social evil for interfaith couples. In our experience, most Abrahamic youth don't intend to impose the BBS on their interfaith spouse; however many end up doing so because of pressure from their community and religious institutions. Instead of enjoying the most quality time, the couple has to resolve the BBS issue by uncomfortably discussing it just before their marriage. It is hoped that soon there will be an end to the BBS religious conversion practices in interfaith married life.

Well-informed and well thought out decisions for selecting a life mate will be more likely to bring long lasting happiness in a married life. It is important however that one makes sure there is the freedom to follow one's traditions with the ability to raise their children to do the same, without threats to this liberty created by the Abrahamic in-laws and his or her religious institutions. One of the most important things Hindu, Jain, Sikh or Buddhist parents and youths need to do is to proactively say "NO" to the BBS religious conversion practices of Christians, Jews and Muslims.

Rose or Carnation?

Let a rose be a rose and a carnation be a carnation.

If you are looking for a carnation, why bother with a rose?

Do not expect a rose to convert to carnation. Even if you managed to convert a rose to carnation, it will never be like a real carnation.

Learn to love both, rose and carnation, equally. Together rose and carnation will increase beauty and complement each other.

Section 2.8: Ten Points for Dating a Hindu

The previous two sections covered what a Dharmic should know about an Abrahamic in a love relationship. It is also not going to be easy for an Abrahamic to marry and adjust to a Hindu (or Jain, Sikh, Buddhist). Here points are raised that may be objectionable to the Abrahamic belief system (also read The Geeta on Abrahamic?[40]).

Approximately 38% of Hindus marry to an Abrahamic in America. Hindus are pluralist in general, and thus may be more open minded in terms of accepting Jesus as a savior and Allah as One God. In addition, they may not have hesitation visiting a church, synagogue or a mosque to explore more about different faiths. Further, the Hindu lover may accept teaching their future children about other faiths and even may agree to baptism, bris/bar mitzvah or sunat rituals for children. Though this openness, tolerance to other faiths and to some extent the novelty of a different culture may attract you to consider a Hindu as your life-mate, awareness of the following pointers about Hindus is advised.

10) Food habits: A Hindu may be a vegetarian and may prefer that others in the family not consume meat. Regular alcohol consumption may also be considered bad.

9) Weddings: A Hindu may not have concerns about being a part of an Abrahamic marriage ceremony, but a Hindu will insist on having the Hindu vivaha ceremony where multiple Devas and Devis (commonly described as specific energies of the Ultimate Supreme Brahman or Gods) will be invoked from heaven, earth and water. Will the Abrahamic community be comfortable being a part of such polytheist ritual? Check with your rabbi, imam or priest/paster to see if he/she is agreeable to dual marriage ceremonies.

8) Novelty: Indian costumes, food and culture may be attractive before marriage but afterward the novelty may wear off. Conversely a Hindu spouse may be very sympathetic to one's Abrahamic history (e.g. holocaust or discrimination of Muslims in the West) but after marriage they may complain about hearing the same stories again and again.

7) Close-knit families: Hindus in general believe in an extended family, which includes distant relatives. After marriage, many visitations to and from these relatives should be expected. While these relatives may not

---

[40] Section 12.2.

openly say so, they might be skeptical about whether this Abrahaimc is out proselytizing Hindus.

6) Idol-worshipping: Participation in extensive Hindu rituals of praying to various deities may be expected at one time or another at Hindu in-laws' home or at a Hindu temple (e.g. Garba dance). One can only decline these invitations so many times. Additionally, a Hindu spouse may insist on having his or her own altar with Hindu deities in the house. Conflict may arise if the Abrahamic spouse opposes worshipping God this way, especially if the Hindu participated in Abrahamic worshipping practices.

5) Circumcision: The Hindu spouse may not accept religious circumcision for their male children, because it denotes Himsa (violence) against a newborn son. Justifications for circumcision on medical grounds may be challenged based on current available scientific facts.

4) Spiritual meaning: The Hindu may agree to be a part of his or her spouse's religious rituals but may do so just for social reasons or to please that spouse without having the same core spiritual feelings toward that form of worship (e.g. during the Sabbath time the Hindu spouse may meditate or pray to Lord Krishna!).

3) Reversal in attitude: Though the Hindu spouse may have agreed to raise children in the Abrahamic faith, later they may conclude that church sermons are boring, madrasa teachings are offensive or that children spend too much time in synagogues versus fun trips, adventures or other learning experiences.

2) False conversion: Though the Hindu spouse may have had the baptism or shahadah religious conversion necessary for the church or nikaah wedding, he/she continues to remain Hindu in belief. For them, the conversion may have been just a hollow ritual devoid of true religious meaning.

1) Pluralism: In general, Hindus are inclusive and pluralist in their beliefs and for that reason may accept the Abrahamic faith but will do so without understanding core Abrahamic exclusivist belief. It will be easy to convince a Hindu to ADD a God (e.g. Lord God, God the Father, Jesus or Allah), but the Hindu will get furious when asked to REMOVE Hindu Gods from their home. A Hindu spouse may only see the Abrahamic God as one of many manifestations of God but not the ONE God. The possibility exists that after years into a marriage the exclusivist Abrahamic will realize that his or her children are pluralists or atheists.

The issues brought up in these ten points deserve serious consideration by couples planning Hindu/Abrahamic marriages. Adequate forethought about the differences may prevent the potential disagreement, heartbreak and stress from occurring or even dissuade the prospective couple from entering into a marriage in the first place. The issue of exclusivity of one's beliefs versus pluralism and in which faith future children will be raised may in fact be deal breakers. On the other hand, awareness, understanding and acceptance of these differences can contribute to a long and satisfying marriage.

Like going for a backpacking trip, go light. If you burden your interfaith spouse with your faith, your spouse may ultimately get tired and cut short the relationship.

Section 2.9: Hindus, Abrahamics and Intolerants

At least in public, most people claim to be tolerant of others. This article was written as a rebuttal to a question raised at Patheos[41] and covers who is tolerant and who is not.

Tathagata Roy had serious objections to painting Muslims, Christians and Jews with the same coarse brush called "Abrahamic." These three traditions are very different in some ways; for example: Jews do not proselytize, whereas Christians and Muslims do. Then again, Christians in present time do it by persuasion, while extreme Islamists may do it by force. Thus, he (Roy) implied that these three are very different.

Someone could counter this argument by saying that these three Abrahamic traditions are more or less the same. All three are monotheist, exclusivist and supremacist faiths. All three believe that salvation is possible only through their version of faith or that they are the "chosen" people. All three believe in their own version of God and have not accepted each other's vision of God. Further, all three believe that Hindus are "idol worshipers" and, two of these traditions believe that on the Judgment Day, the idol worshipers will get the "Hell of Fire" while they will be "saved." All three traditions have based their scriptures on some variations of the Second of the Ten Commandments that are supposed to be the stern injunctions from their God.

Being raised as a Hindu, the author was taught *"Ishvara Allah tero nam"* (both Ishvara and Allah are equally valid names of One God). Further, all those who have good karma will achieve moksha (salvation), regardless of which path they follow. It is your karma, not the specific religion, or name of God, that is important. Hindu Dharma teaches that there is only One Absolute Supreme power and thus it is a truly monotheistic religion. But Hindu Dharma allows abundant freedom of expression for the forms of God; therefore Hindus in general, have no problem with someone praying to God in the name of Buddha, Jesus or Allah.

As a child, the author was never confused by this all inclusive, pluralistic view. In contrast, leaders of all three Abrahamic monotheist religions believe that a child will get confused with teachings of two different faiths; therefore, parents in an interfaith marriage must pick one of the

---

[41] Originally published at http://www.patheos.com/Resources/Additional-Resources/Hindus-Abrahamics-and-Intolerants.

two faiths for their children.[42,43,44] Religious fanatics of all faiths argue that a child cannot be raised in two faiths. If so, then whose god will win? Followers of all three Abrahamic faiths usually expect a Hindu spouse and/or their children to undergo baptism, bris or shahadah/sunat to publicly announce that their God will rule in their married life.

Jews may not proselytize but they consider interfaith marriages a "Silent Holocaust."[45] In a Hindu-Jew marriage, the Jewish partner may do anything possible, including giving "conditional" love, to have their children go through the bris ceremony and raise them in the Jewish faith only. To a Hindu spouse and their children in an interfaith marriage, does it matter what method—force, persuasion or conditional love—is used when the ultimate result is the same: baptism, bris or shahadah/sunat?

As Lisa Miller[46] (writer and journalist) has explained, a Hindu believes there are many paths to God. Jesus is one way, the Qur'an is another, and yoga practice is a third. None is better than any other; all are equal. Most traditional, conservative Christians have not been taught to think like this. They learn in Sunday school that their religion is true, and others are false. Jesus said (John 14:6), "I am the way, the truth, and the life. No one comes to the Father (God) except through me."

Fortunately, these days, most Abrahamics are no longer exclusivists and are happily tolerating spouses from other faiths in their married life. According to a 2008 Pew Forum survey, 65 percent of Americans believe that "many religions can lead to eternal life"—including 37 percent of white evangelicals, the group most likely to believe that salvation is theirs alone. As Lisa Miller has further stated, conceptually at least, we are slowly becoming more like Hindus and less like traditional Christians in the ways we think about God, ourselves, each other, and eternity. Stephen Prothero, religion professor at Boston University, has long framed the American propensity for "the divine-deli-cafeteria religion" as "very much in the spirit of Hinduism. You are not picking and choosing from different religions, because they're all the same."

---

[42] http://www.patheos.com/Resources/Additional-Resources/Bindis-and-Baptism.html.

[43] http://www.patheos.com/Resources/Additional-Resources/When-Your-Father-Is-Not-a-Christian.html.

[44] http://www.thejewishweek.com/features/first_person/interfaith_couple_baptism_fire.

[45] http://en.wikipedia.org/wiki/Silent_Holocaust.

[46] http://www.newsweek.com/us-views-god-and-life-are-turning-hindu-79073.

Are all religions the same? It depends. Religious scripture may say one thing but an individual may interpret it differently based on current understanding of their scriptures. In reality, for an interfaith couple, it is not the spouse's scriptures but an individual's personal faith and beliefs that count. If so, then there are only two types of Abrahamics, and for that matter Hindus too: those that are tolerant and respect others the way they are, and those that are intolerant and wish to transform their spouse (and children) from other faiths to acquiesce to their intolerant view of the world.

> *A mother will breast feed her just born son with relentless love, without thinking that one day the same son could run away with his wife deserting her. The mother is simply doing her duty without expectation of fruits.*

Section 2.10: Can Allah Be the Father God?

This article is written to show that religious exclusivity has no place in today's tolerant world.

Exclusivist monotheist faiths teach that there is only one way to heaven and of course, it is their own. Exclusivists claim non-believers will get the "Hell of Fire" or will not be "saved." Such intolerant teachings about other faiths create many problems in interfaith relationships, not to mention the world at large.

Allah literally means God in the Arabic language. In that respect yes, Allah can be the God the Father as described by Christians, or Ishvara as described by Hindus. However in Malaysia, non-Muslims are banned from using the word "Allah" to refer to God.[47] Likewise, Reverend Franklin Graham[48,49] clarified that "Muslims do not worship the same God the Father I worship." Further, he stated: "I don't believe that you can get to heaven through a Buddhist or Hindu faith. I think Mohammad only leads to the grave." Such intolerant statements from some faith leaders clearly show that their fight is not about the literary meaning of the word "Allah," but about the exclusivist thinking behind their dogma which states that one can achieve salvation only through their own version of the faith.

Where did this exclusivist thinking originate? All three Abrahamic faiths accept the teachings of the Second[50] of the "Ten Commandments." It states "I am the Lord your God. You shall have no other gods before me. You shall not make for yourself an idol, whether in the form of anything that is in heaven above, or that is on the earth beneath, or that is in the water under the earth. You shall not bow down to them or worship them; for I the Lord your God am a jealous God punishing children for the inequity of parents, to the third and fourth generations of those who reject me." Successive Abrahamic scriptures have tried to perfect this jealous God's message.

Most Christians believe that Jesus is the Son of God and that faith in Jesus is the only way to achieve salvation and to enter heaven. Jesus said:

---

[47] http://news.yahoo.com/malaysias-top-court-allah-muslims-only-060945018.html.

[48] http://www.newsweek.com/franklin-graham-his-pentagon-disinvitation-72643.

[49] The author acknowledges that Franklin Graham is an evangelist and most Christians do not carry such belief.

[50] Exodus 20:4-5 (also see Subsection 12.3.1).

"I am the way, the truth, and the life. No one comes to the Father except through Me."[51] However, quite contrary to that belief, Koran teaches to have faith only in Allah. According to the Koran, Jesus, the son of Mary, was no more than God's apostle. Allah forbids that He Himself should beget a son! Further, those who say, "the Lord of Mercy has begotten a son" preach a monstrous falsehood.[52]

Why do Mohammad, Jesus and other apostles interpret THE GOD's direct message differently? Alternatively, are Allah, God the Father and Ishvara different Gods? For an exclusivist monotheist this is a very difficult question to address; for a pluralist, it is not a relevant question and an atheist may simply smile at this discussion.

The exclusivist concept creates a major issue for an interfaith Abrahamic couple. Let's take a Christian-Muslim couple, for example. As per the shahadah (oath) to convert to Islam before the nikaah (the Islamic wedding), one must accept and declare that there is no God but Allah and Mohammad is his apostle. One also acknowledges that associating others (like Jesus) with Allah is the greatest of all sins. Similarly, baptism before a church wedding means conversion to Christianity and a commitment to repudiate former practices (of Islam) and to live with Christ forever. Obviously, in theory there cannot be a theologically accepted middle ground for a Christian-Muslim couple.

A pluralist Hindu, who believes that all faiths can lead to Eternal Life, will not have a problem accepting Allah and God the Father as different names and forms of the One Supreme Being called "Ishvara" by Hindus. However, a Christian-Muslim couple wishing to have a modicum of equality in their relationship may have major problem resolving the fundamental question: is Jesus the Son of God and the Savior, or just an apostle?

Conflicting religious scriptures certainly create a major problem for an interfaith couple. The BBS (Baptism, Bris, or Shahadah/Sunat) religious ceremonies are the most fundamental core practices of believers of Abrahamic faiths. It helps clarify significantly which camp one belongs to. In an exclusivist intolerant concept, a clear decision has to be made: are you with us, or are you a non-believer? Is it black or white? A child of an interfaith couple can have only one of three choices: Sunat, baptism or bris circumcision. The inclusive thinking has no place in an

---

[51] Bible (John 14:6).
[52] Section 12.7.

Abrahamic's life i.e. you cannot have two of the BBS rituals, like sunat+baptism or bris+sunat rituals!

Can a child be taught that Allah is the same as God the Father or Ishvara? Most Abrahamics believe that a child cannot be raised in two faiths because the child will get confused and lose interest in both faiths. In a Hindu-Abrahamic marriage, can the couple take their child to a Hindu temple every Saturday for murti puja (idol worship?) of multiple Gods and Goddess and on Sunday to a monotheist church? How will they manage such fundamental conflicting beliefs and justify it to their Abrahamic family and church members? The issue posed here confronts mainly the exclusivist Abrahamic partner, not the all-inclusive pluralist partner. Most Hindus are probably okay happily singing "*Ishvara Allah tero nam*" meaning both Ishvara and Allah are equally valid names of One God.

The monotheist concept that "my way is the only way" is an exclusivist fundamentalist interpretation of religious scriptures. Suhag Shukla has stated,[53] "(Reverend Franklin) Graham fails to recognize the role that his brand of narrow-minded Christianity as well as other fundamentalist interpretations of the world's religions have played in not only many of our nation's problems but those of the world, including terrorism, wars, violation of civil rights, human rights, atrocities and annihilation of entire cultures and communities."

Only when a pluralistic thinking emerges that Allah, God the Father and Ishvara are all equally valid names of One God, and prevails in the world, can peace and harmony among different faiths and communities be established.

> *You are not here to please your lover on a short run but to make a long lasting happy married life. Promise less but produce more.*

---

[53] http://news.rediff.com/report/2010/may/07/american-evangelist-attacks-hinduism.htm.

Section 2.11: Idol-worshipper: Who Is and Who Is Not?

Abrahamic faiths have strict codes against idol-worshipping, however it is not clear how one defines idol-worshipping. The author wrote this article to stimulate discussion on this topic, including the author's personal life experiences.

Padma Kuppa[54] in her Patheos article wishes Hindus to distance themselves from the terms "polytheist" and "idol-worships." Her concern is to find a proper fit with monotheist exclusivist Christians, Jews and Muslims (Abrahamics) in America.

As per descriptions in the Bible[55] and Koran[56] and also in a practical sense, Hindus are polytheist, idol-worshippers and pray to "other gods." Actually, in the author's view, Christians are also polytheist (believing in the trinity; LORD God, Jesus as a Son-God and the Holy Spirit) and idol-worshippers (wood and gold crosses, idols of baby Jesus, Mary, John, Paul, Peter, Santa and so on). If so, how are Christians different from Hindus? Why it is bad to use an "idol" to help us focus on God? Who is to decide that it is wrong to see God in different forms?

Just like anyone else, the author is a man with a wandering mind and he needs a focus point to pray to God. When the author visits any Hindu temple, he expects to take "darshan" (vision of the divine) of multiple idols (deities) and will bow to every one of them. If this is not enough "idolatry" for the author, he also visits Jain and Buddhist temples and bows to many more "idols." Further, the author has bowed to Jesus and Mary's "idols" and has eaten Jesus' body (bread)! The author has also prayed in a mosque and in the direction of the Islamic "idol," the Kaaba (Black Cube). The author was disappointed by not finding a focus point in synagogues. However, the author later learned that Jewish people use a candle or Star of David (idol) to pray at the Sabbath time.

The word idol can be defined very broadly. A Christian radio described "idolatry" as being "idle," praying to the cross without faith, being alcoholic and drug addict and so on. If so, the author is absolutely not an idol-worshipper. He rarely watches television and loves to live a very active life. The author prefers to spend time for the betterment of society rather than spend time in religious institutions trying to please God.

---

[54] http://www.patheos.com/Resources/Additional-Resources/Language-Matters-Padman-Kuppa-11-17-2011.html.
[55] See Section 12.5.
[56] See Section 12.6.

However, to an intolerant Abrahamic who is allergic to the word idolatry, the author would gladly profess that he is a proud idol-worshipper.

Hindus have the complete liberty to pray to God in any and every which way that works for them. Mount Kailash, the river Ganges, the monkey God Hanuman, the elephant God Ganesh, the Sun and Moon, the Mother Earth and many plants and animals are all sacred to Hindus. It is the feeling of reverence for creation that counts, not the names and forms or their labels.

During his childhood, the author has seen his mother go every morning to several temples, put flowers on some sacred stones, tighten a red thread around a Pipala tree trunk, water a holy Tulsi shrub and when returning, bow and feed a cow. Whatever her approach may have been to connect to God, the author certainly learned from her to respect any and every one, including Mother Nature and animals.

The Hindu greeting of "Namaste" means "I see the divine in you and bow to it." How beautiful! The author is so proud to have been taught the Hindu philosophy of seeing God in every one, be that my boss or servant. Respect for others and nature around us will certainly make this world a better place to live, rather than being exclusivist and human-centric.

By the law of association, the material image calls up the mental idea and vice versa. That is the way we ALL use an external symbol when we worship. If someone can realize his divine nature with the help of an idol, would it be right to call that sin?

Swami Vivekananda had no reservation associating with the word idol. He has stated, "If such (his guru) Ramakrishna Paramahamsas are produced by idol-worship, what will you have—the reformer's creed or any number of idols? Yes idolatry is condemned! Why? Nobody knows. Because some hundreds of years ago some man of Jewish blood happened to condemn it? That is, he happened to condemn everybody else's idols except his own."

By reading the Bible and Koran, the author learned that Abrahamic faith scriptures provided no or less tolerance for the believers in "other gods." It is basically a war of "us" against "them." The first of two of the Ten Commandments state that there is no god other than LORD God and if you pray to other gods, the LORD God will punish you for several generations.[57] The Bible states, "Our God is greater than all gods."[58] Jesus said, "Who is not with me is against me."[59] Further, He added, "No one comes to the Father except through Me."[60]

As discussed in earlier sections, Jesus claimed that he is the Son of God,[61] while Allah (God) forbids that He Himself should beget a son![62] Allah said, "believers take neither Jews nor the Christians for your friends."[63] Reverend Franklin Graham[64] claimed, "Muslims do not worship the same God the Father I worship. I think Mohammad only leads to the grave. I don't believe that you can get to heaven through a Buddhist or Hindu faith." Richard Land[65] called the Mormon religion a cult. So, where will these "us against them" debates end?

To add to the debate, Lord Krishna also stated "I am the beginning, the middle and also the end of all beings,"[66] and "those who are devotees of other gods and who worship them with faith actually worship only Me, but they do so in a wrong way"[67] and "As all surrender unto Me, I reward them accordingly. Everyone follows My path in all respects."[68] In this case, is Krishna's message any less exclusivist[69] than that of Christ and Allah?

Scriptures cannot be changed now, but we have to learn to interpret the scripture in its context and historical significance. It is possible that Jesus may have made a few exclusivist statements but others may have over-interpreted him. Actually, Jesus himself never used the word "idol" or "other gods" in any of his direct messages. It is difficult to believe that Jesus, who changed the Second Commandment of jealousy and anger

---

[57] Exodus 20:3-5.

[58] II Chronicles 2:5.

[59] Matthews 12:30.

[60] John 14:6.

[61] Luke 22:70.

[62] Koran 19:34.

[63] Koran 5:51.

[64] http://content.time.com/time/world/article/0,8599,1952497,00.html.

[65] http://content.time.com/time/nation/article/0,8599,1675308,00.html.

[66] Geeta 10:20 (also see Section 12.2).

[67] Geeta 9:23.

[68] Geeta 4:11.

[69] The author expects Hindus to counter by saying Lord Krishna's message was not exclusivist. Likewise, an Abrahamic may claim that their scriptures are not exclusivist but it should be interpreted with its context. The author will let our readers be the judge for both sides of the argument.

to—"Love thy neighbor"[70]—would ever recommend sending Mahatma Gandhi to hell just because Gandhi was not baptized or did not endorse Jesus as the true savior.

Are LORD God, God the Father, Jesus as the Son of God, Allah, Krishna, Goddess Laxmi, Buddha, the Golden-Calf and many more deities just different forms of the SAME God, or are they different super powers? Whose claim on God is right and true?

Is my idol better than yours? Is my Barbie doll better than yours? Instead of fighting, why not go and play with all dolls, if allowed to? It is time to give up childish talk and be a true pluralist.

> The religious labeling (BBS including namasanskara) is a social evil for interfaith couples.

---

[70] Matthew 22:39.

Section 2.12: Saif and Kareena: Interfaith Marriage

Many of celebrities' life details are in public domain. Here, the author has used Bollywood celebrities Saif and Kareena's published information to show that in spite of their different backgrounds a Hindu-Muslim marriage with equality is possible.

Kareena Kapoor and Saif Ali Khan's romance was a hot subject for Bollywood. Saif's mother, renowned actress Sharmila Tagore, converted to Islam for her marriage to Mansoor Ali Khan in 1969, changed her name to Begum Ayesha Sultana, gave Muslim names to all three of their children and raised them solely in the Islamic faith. Saif's first wife Amrita Singh, a Sikh, converted to Islam in 1991 to marry him. They gave Arabic names to their kids. In 2004, she got talaak (divorce). In 2012, Saif married Kareena, a Hindu, without her converting to Islam.

Sharmila Tagore started her Bollywood career as a Bengali Indian film actress. She was also the head of the Indian film censorship board. Sharmila was born in a Bengali family in Hyderabad, India to Gitindranath Tagore who was then Deputy General Manager of the British India Company, owner of Elgin Mills. She is the great-granddaughter of Nobel laureate Rabindranath Tagore. On 27 December 1969, Sharmila Tagore married Mansoor Ali Khan Pataudi, Nawab of Pataudi and converted to Islam.

Mansoor Ali Khan Pataudi, nicknamed Tiger, was a former captain of the Indian cricket team. He was the 9th and last Nawab of Pataudi until 1971, when India abolished royal entitlements through the 26th Amendment to the Constitution of India. They are the parents of three children: Saif Ali Khan, a Bollywood actor, Soha Ali Khan, a Bollywood actress and Saba Ali Khan a jewelry designer.

Saif grew up in Bhopal at the family estate at Pataudi. Since his mother had converted to Islam, his childhood was spent in a Muslim atmosphere. Even with his maternal Hindu grandparents, he never discussed religion. His paternal grandmother was the center for all his religious education and theological experience. She had him read the Koran in his childhood. Their servants were all devout Muslims. When Saif went to study in England at Winchester College, his grandmother was worried that he would become a Christian. At the school he had to go to chapel for half an hour before he went to class. Saif went to the headmaster and said that he was a Muslim, so he refused to go to chapel. The headmaster organized a Maulvi Saheb for the two Muslims in the school. Apparently, Saif Ali Khan was a proud Muslim.

In 1991, Saif Ali Khan had nikaah, the Islamic wedding, with 12-year-older actress Amrita Singh. For his marriage preference, it has been quoted, "Saif had clearly told Amrita that she had to fall in line and go through only a nikaah. Very nawabi when it comes to the crux."[71] A nikaah for a Hindu or Sikh requires religious conversion to Islam by shahadah oath and one is then given a Muslim name. In 2004, Amrita and Saif separated and eventually had a talaak. It is not clear if religion played any role in the disagreements that led to their divorce. Their children had Abrahamic names—Sara and Ibrahim—and are with their mother while Saif started courting an Italian girlfriend, Rosa Catalano.

Kareena Randhir Kapoor was born to Sindhi-speaking Babita and Punjabi-speaking Randhir Kapoor on 21 September, 1977 in Mumbai, India. She has an elder sister, Karishma. The Kapoor family have been actors for generations, including her paternal great-grandfather, Prithviraj Kapoor; her grandfather, Raj Kapoor; her paternal uncles, Shammi, Shashi, Rishi, and Rajiv; as well as aunt, Neetu Singh and Jennifer Kendall, the wives of Rishi and Shashi respectively. Prithviraj Kapoor, Raj Kapoor, Randhir Kapoor and her mother Babita Shivdasani—all of them—had been driven from Islamic Pakistan at the time of partition because they were Hindus.[72]

Randhir Kapoor was very protective of his daughters and wanted both of them to keep away from acting, get married and settle down, as per the Kapoor family tradition. This led to irreconcilable differences between her parents, which ultimately led to a divorce. Both sisters left Randhir to live with their mother.

For her man, Kareena said, "I want a man I can keep for myself. I wouldn't ever share my man with anyone else. If I found out that my man is unfaithful, there'd be no tears, no shor-sharaba, I'd just slaughter him." Apparently, Kareena is a person with high self-esteem and personal pride. She lived secretly with Saif and at the Lakme Fashion Awards in October 2007 they made their liaison official.

Kareena, raised in a proud Hindu family, is mostly a vegetarian and enjoys yoga. On the other side, Saif is a proud Muslim. Normally, a Muslim would expect the non-Muslim spouse to convert to Islam before a nikaah, the Islamic wedding ceremony. Saif is now different and does not believe in imposing his religious beliefs on others. A similar message

---

[71] http://www.telegraphindia.com/1090705/jsp/7days/story_11198177.jsp.
[72] http://narainkataria.blogspot.com/2008/03/indian-american-intellectuals-forum-41.html.

has been given in the movies like Jodhaa Akbar, Gadar and Namastey London. Bollywood stars Hrithik Roshan (with Suzanne Khan; now divorced), Fardeen Feroz Khan (with Natasha Madhvani) and Aamir Khan (with Kiran Rao) did not require that their intended spouses change their religion for marriage. They got married by a civil wedding. Even Saif's sister Soha Ali Khan got married to Kunal Khemu, a Hindu, without any one changing their religion. These are admirable acts.

Although Saif is a proud Muslim, he is "massively open-minded" about religious matters.[73] He has stated, "I've been brought up to believe in the oneness of God. In some places, He is known as Jesus. In other places He is known as Bhagawan or Allah."[74] Saif also said, "I would never want her (Kareena) to change her religion. That is the trouble with religion; really it expects conversion. I don't buy or believe that any more. If and when we do get married no one has to change his or her religion."[75] Saif and Kareena got married in 2012 by civil wedding.

Saif and Kareena have set the tone for a new generation of youths in India and around the world by displaying interfaith marriages with equality and true mutual respect for each other's faith.[76] Now with their son's name being Taimur Ali Khan, it remains to be seen if they will expose Taimur to both faiths. Will Saif and Kareena put real religious tolerance into practice rather than merely preaching on Bollywood screens?

Religion is all about faith, and faith has no logic.

---

[73] http://www.sabrang.com/cc/comold/august98/saif.htm.

[74] http://saifamrita.blogspot.com/.

[75] http://zeenews.india.com/exclusive/what-sharmila-couldnt-do-in-her-time-kareena-manages-easily_5725.html.

[76] http://indianexpress.com/article/opinion/columns/intermarriage-is-not-jihad-it-is-india/.

Section 2.13: Circumcision: Science or Superstition?

Circumcision for religious reason is an irreversible religious label on a child and thus this topic deserves discussion.

"There is my covenant, which you shall keep, between me and you and your descendants after you: Every male among you shall be circumcised," God commands Abraham,[77] the Jewish patriarch. "Any uncircumcised male who is not circumcised in the flesh of his foreskin shall be cut off from his people; he has broken my covenant." Later, Jesus revised this guidance by saying circumcision is of no avail.[78]

All three Abrahamic faiths (less so for Christianity) believe in circumcision. It is believed that if the male child is not circumcised, something negative would happen to the boy and the child would not be "saved." Contrary to such beliefs, circumcision is not a practice in Dharmic traditions. Hindu sages would probably have labeled it *himsa* (violence).

The American Pediatric Association[79] has not recommended universal newborn circumcision, though they have cited benefits over risks. They have stated that the medical benefits alone may not outweigh these other considerations for individual families and that circumcision is an elective procedure.[80] Most other international health authorities also have not recommended routine circumcision.

There is no major medical issue noted for uncircumcised Japanese individuals.[81] Further, personally the author has not heard no-circumcision as an issue with Hindus, especially those who are living in reasonably hygienic conditions. In the USA, the overall rate of circumcision is declining. For example, in the western US, the rate of circumcision in newborns has dropped in the last 32 years from 64% to 40%.[82]

---

[77] Genesis 17:11. Also see Subsection 12.3.6.
[78] Romans 2:25-29.
[79] http://www.aap.org/en-us/about-the-aap/aap-press-room/pages/Newborn-Male-Circumcision.aspx.
[80] http://pediatrics.aappublications.org/content/130/3/e756.
[81] Circumcision rate less than 1%.
http://www.photius.com/rankings/circumcised_men_country_ranks.html.
[82]
https://www.cdc.gov/nchs/data/hestat/circumcision_2013/circumcision_2013.htm.

To have foreskin on the penis is not a birth defect to be surgically corrected, rather the foreskin has abundant nerve endings designed to increase sexual sensation. One study using 5,552 men found that circumcision was associated with frequent orgasm difficulties (11% versus 4%) and women with circumcised spouses more often reported incomplete fulfillment of sexual needs (38% versus 28%).[83] When in doubt, why give pain to a newborn child? Why create doubt on God's creation of skin over the penis?

One needs to keep in mind that the painful procedure of circumcision done to a child (1) is done without his consent, (2) is a violation of his human right according to some people, and (3) may have negative psychological and emotional consequences. If in doubt about scientific merits, parents should let the child decide at an adult age about the circumcision.

The bottom line for scientific merit is that the jury is still out. If it is a matter of faith, an interfaith couple should decide whose faith would rule their married life.

The difference between LIKE and LOVE

When you like a flower, you just pluck it. But when you love a flower, you water it daily.
—Buddha

If your lover "likes" you, he/she will pluck you and put you in a completely different culture and faith but if he/she truly "loves" you, will nurture you and care for who you are.

---

[83] http://www.ncbi.nlm.nih.gov/pubmed/21672947.

Section 2.14: Meera versus Margaret: Discrimination of Own Type

In earlier sections the author discussed issues in interfaith marriages. Here, issues in withinfaith marriages are highlighted. It is human nature to discriminate and, to some extent, to be intolerant of others. However if we learn to love and respect others, it will be a win-win for all.

Interfaith marriages have many issues, but intra or withinfaith marriages are not without their own issues either. The withinfaith divorce rates and gravity of problems are also significant. Some of the root causes of problems in withinfaith marriages in Eastern culture are unusually high expectations, ingrained social customs, discrimination against women in some cases, and sometimes the paradoxical human nature to discriminate against one's own type. It is time for an attitude change. In this article, some of the main issues related to withinfaith marriages of people from Eastern cultures are highlighted using hypothetical names, Meera (Hindu) and Margaret (Western Christian).

As a new fiancée in a Hindu family, Meera may be expected from the start to help her mother-in-law-to-be in the kitchen frying samosas (Indian dumplings) while the same Indian mother-in-law-to-be will be joyous if Margaret just eats the samosas she has fried for her. Any gift from Meera's parents may not be sufficient to please the Hindu boy's parents, while the same parents may gladly buy many Indian costumes for Margaret and her entire family at their own expense.

In many cultures, women have traditionally been housewives and have been expected to be responsible for household chores and for maintaining social relationships. In this day and age the new generation of educated Eastern women are expected to take on additional responsibilities such as earning for the family. Unfortunately, some Eastern men and their families have not fully adapted to the reality of this social change. Meera may work outside the home but when she returns home after work, she is expected to carry out all household chores, including taking care of children and cooking. Her husband may decide to help where he feels appropriate or may just relax. The same Eastern man, if married to Margaret, will gladly take over many household chores including cleaning dishes and bathrooms.

Eastern parents are not used to seeing men working in the kitchen or folding the laundry. When Eastern parents visit their son in the West, normally they wish to relax during their vacation. When they see their son going into the kitchen to help Meera, the parents will immediately intervene and offer to take over their son's chores, not Meera's. The same Eastern parents do not realize that they are much less likely to have a chance of living with Margaret for a significant time during their visit.

The author knows of a case where a Hindu-American girl married a Pakistani after religious conversion to Islam. The (former) Hindu is treated like a queen by Muslim in-laws whenever she visits Pakistan. In contrast, her Muslim sister-in-law from Pakistan gets rude treatment from the same Muslim in-laws in spite of her doing all the daily chores. These Pakistani parents do not realize that the (former) Hindu daughter-in-law, in her mind, underwent a fake-conversion ceremony (shahadah oath) necessary for the Islamic nikaah wedding. The Pakistani parents are still unaware today that this couple also had a Hindu wedding ceremony (prohibited in Islam) and that their Hindu daughter-in-law is performing Ganesh puja every day in America.

When there is a withinfaith marriage, parents expect to maintain traditions coming from generations. In another example,[84] Bangladeshi Raquib's Muslim-Muslim engagement is in trouble because of the expectations that he purchase certain gifts (clothes) of sufficient value for his wife's parents in Pakistan. While the dowry system is still prevalent in the East, the parents would not even dream of a dowry if the engagement was to Margaret.

It is normal for Eastern parents to micro-analyze a potential fiancé(e) when it is a withinfaith marriage. For example, a Patel-Hindu contemplating marriage to another Patel-Hindu has to answer if the selected Patel is Kadva or Leuva Patel and whether they are Swaminarayan, Shaivites or Vaishnav. However the same parents will not know about Margaret beyond the label of German-French.

During the engagement process, the withinfaith fiancé(e) undergoes strict scrutiny and background checks. Even if there were some un-authenticated information that Meera was flirting with boys in college, it could become a big moral issue. It is a practice in some Muslim communities to display a bloody bed sheet after the honeymoon night as proof of the bride's virginity and if the new bride does not come through, it could be grounds for a divorce on the first day. Would they follow the same practice if the wife was Margaret?

Many Eastern boys and girls in Western colleges purposely date friends from a different faith. One of the main reasons is that in the early 20's, withinfaith dating often escalates to talk of marriage that they have no

---

[84] https://www.interfaithshaadi.org/blog/?p=5382.

interest in now. Muslim and Hindu girls will not consider sleeping with a boyfriend of their own faith due to the social stigma; these girls may be less reluctant with a boyfriend from another faith. Likewise, an Eastern boy may start dating Margaret just for the romance but may end up marrying her.

Due to the issues mentioned above, should Eastern boys and girls consider interfaith marriage over withinfaith marriage? That is certainly not the message here. Interfaith marriages have their own issues. In general, divorce rates in interfaith marriages are higher compared to withinfaith marriages.[85] Most interfaith issues surface after children reach the ages of 5-13, when it becomes time to decide the children's "formal" religion.

Cultural issues could also add to complexities at a later age. As an Eastern man enters late middle age (i.e. 50+ years) he would tend to go back to his own roots and may find that there is less of common interest left with the menopausal-Margatet.

Compared to interfaith marriages, the gravity of issues is higher in the early years for withinfaith married couples. If Meera wishes to be successful in a withinfaith marriage, she needs to learn to deal sternly with her in-laws. From the start, Meera has to start teaching the Eastern husband about the more contemporary rules of married life. If Meera deals with the issues early on, her marriage may improve over the years. In contrast, many interfaith marriage issues tend to resurface about ten years into the marriage. These religious conflicts may continue even until it is time to perform the final rites.

The time has come for Eastern parents to adapt to the new realities of life. Typically Hindu parents will always have something to complain about with Meera's choices, whether she is in an interfaith or withinfaith marriage. Those parents should be reminded that the situation could potentially be worse if Meera decides to get into a relationship with Margaret!

Parents should know that they don't "own" their child; rather the child has come into this world through them. If parents start respecting their children like they respect their friends and boss at work, the parent-child relationship will blossom and both will benefit.

The grass is always greener on the other side. Instead of getting stuck on issues in your planned married life, one needs to learn to deal with issues

---

[85] http://www.religioustolerance.org/ifm_divo.htm.

at hand. For example, if a person raised in the Dharmic faith fell in love with a religious person from an Abrahamic faith, the most critical questions to address upfront are the decisions whether or not to convert to the spouse's religion and what the formal religion of any future children would be. Dharmic couples considering a withinfaith marriage would be advised to evaluate real compatability with each other and potential negative influences of in-laws.

Life is never like a rose garden; and even if it is, roses always have thorns. Learn to live and let others live.

> Interfaith marriage should be like a salad bowl where tomato and celery can fully express their characters and compliment each other.

Section 2.15: Interfaith Marriage and Divorce Laws

Interfaith dating couples must clearly understand all applicable marriage, divorce and child custody laws before committing to an interfaith marriage. Such couples may face mainly two types of laws: Religious Institutional Rules and Regulations, and Governmental Laws.

Almost all religious institutions have strict codes against interfaith marriages. For Dharmic faiths, generally the community does not strictly enforce such rules or there are alternate choices available. In some Christian faiths, for example Catholics, the non-Catholic party will have to convert or sign a prenuptial agreement[86] to raise children as Catholics. Some churches will not allow one to do the last rites of parents and excommunicate them for an interfaith marriage in the family.[87] In Islam, no Imam will perform a Hindu-Muslim marriage and the Hindu must convert to Islam before the Islamic nikaah wedding. Nikaah with an Abrahamic ("People of the Book") may be possible without conversion but children must be raised only in the Islamic faith.

The formal religious conversion (even fake-conversion just for marriage) or signing of any prenuptial agreement may have serious legal consequences, especially during a child custody battle in the event of a divorce.

In the west and most Christian majority nations, only secular laws apply to all marriages and divorces. In most Muslim majority countries, laws influenced by Islamic Sharia[88] apply. In India, complex marriage laws are designed to appease different religions. Hiddush[89] conducted Freedom of Marriage survey and found severe marriage restrictions in Israel and also in Muslim (62%; 33/53) and Christian (7%; 8/120) majority nations, but not in Hindu/Buddhist (0%; 0/14) majority nations. In this section, marriage and divorce laws from United Kingdom as representative western laws, a Jewish state Israel, from a moderate and secular but Muslim majority country Malaysia and Indian marriage and divorce laws are highlighted.

Information presented here is for educational purpose only. An interfaith couple must explore all laws applicable in their own country. One should

---

[86] Section 3.4.
[87] https://www.interfaithshaadi.org/blog/?p=10573.
[88] https://www.youtube.com/watch?v=RiWLGEKusIg.
[89] http://marriage.hiddush.org.

not take this information as a legal advice but instead consult with an attorney with expertise in interfaith marriages.

2.15.1: Western Marriage and Divorce Laws

Marriage between people in the UK is governed by Marriage Act 1949[90] and Marriage Causes Act 1973.[91] As far as the British law is concerned the couple needs only to be of an appropriate age and have the capacity to marry. Religion is not a limiting factor. In short, interfaith marriage is okay in UK and conversion to another faith is more of a personal choice. This same freedom is also guaranteed through the European Convention of Human Rights.[92,93]

2.15.2: Israel Marriage Laws

Israeli law permits only religious marriages held by religious testimony, and does not allow civil marriages. Among the Jewish population, the Chief Rabbinate, which operates according to Orthodox Jewish standards, has a monopoly over marriage. Only those who are recognized as Jews according to Orthodox Jewish law can get married in Israel. Members of other religions can only marry spouses of the same religion and only by their own recognized religious authority. The result is that no interfaith or non-religious marriages are allowed in Israel. However, the Ministry of Interior registers and accepts civil marriages held abroad.[94]

2.15.3: Malaysian Marriage Laws

The Malaysian constitution grants freedom of religion and makes it an officially secular state, while establishing Islam as the "religion of the Federation" to symbolize its importance to Malaysian society.[95] Interfaith love with a Malay[96] is one of the most popular themes at

---

[90] http://www.legislation.gov.uk/ukpga/Geo6/12-13-14/76/contents.

[91] http://www.legislation.gov.uk/ukpga/1973/18.

[92] http://www.echr.coe.int/Documents/Convention_ENG.pdf.

[93] The author would like to thank Jimmy (https://www.interfaithshaadi.org/blog/?p=8828) for providing valuable legal information. This material is used all over in this Section.

[94] http://marriage.hiddush.org.

[95] https://en.wikipedia.org/wiki/Islam_in_Malaysia.

[96] As defined by the Constitution of Malaysia, Malays must be Muslim, regardless of their ethnic heritage; otherwise, legally, they are not Malay (https://en.wikipedia.org/wiki/Islam_in_Malaysia).

InterfaithShaadi.[97] The question raised below by Sameer is a typical question by such youths.

Sameer says:

My fiancée *is a Chinese Malaysian (non-Muslim) and I am (non-Malaysian) Muslim. I don't want my* fiancée *to convert (to Islam). What are our chances to marry in Singapore*[98] *and apply for a long term visa in Malaysia? What will happen if I say I am not Muslim?* —Sameer

It gave great pain to the author to disclose to these innocent lovers that only option left for them is to 1) give up this love relationship or 2) unwillingly convert the non-Muslim intended spouse to Islam if they want to settle in Malaysia. Let's look at Malaysian marriage laws to understand the complexity there.

In Malaysia, the Federal Constitution is supreme and the freedom of religion is something that is guaranteed by the constitution under Article 11.[99] When it comes to Family Law (namely marriage), there are two primary statutes, the Law Reform (marriage and divorce) Act 1976 (Civil Marriage) and the Islamic Family Law (Federal Territories) Act 1984[100] (Muslim Marriage). The Civil Marriage Act of 1976 specifically states, "This Act shall not apply to a Muslim."[101] Hence, in Malaysia there is no means for a Muslim to marry a non-Muslim under the Civil law. In fact, the Muslim who goes through a marriage or even cohabits with non-Muslim runs the risk of falling foul of a number of offences under State Syariah (the Malay spelling of "Sharia") Criminal Law prohibiting fornication (zina) and close proximity (khalwat).[102,103]

---

[97] https://www.interfaithshaadi.org/blog/?cat=112.

[98] A secular marriage is possible in Singapore, read details here
https://en.wikipedia.org/wiki/Matrimonial_law_of_Singapore.

[99] http://confinder.richmond.edu/admin/docs/malaysia.pdf.

[100]

http://www2.esyariah.gov.my/esyariah/mal/portalv1/enakmen2011/Eng_act_lib.nsf/858a0729306dc24748257651000e16c5/1d314361e275004248256981 0025f0fc?OpenDocument.

[101] Laws of Malaysia, Act 164
(https://unstats.un.org/unsd/vitalstatkb/KnowledgebaseArticle50620.aspx).

[102] **Dr. Zakir Naik** explained Koran (24:30) as when a Muslim man sees a woman the Muslim man has to "lower his gaze" and show his modesty. View details here https://www.youtube.com/watch?v=foLbqR6fBf8.

[103] http://www.themalaymailonline.com/malaysia/article/what-happens-during-khalwat-raids-uk-broadcaster-joins-malaysias-religious.

A Muslim must register his/her marriage under Islamic Family Law Act 1984. A marriage between Muslims and non-Muslims is prohibited under Islamic law,[104] except in certain limited circumstances. A Muslim Man is allowed to marry a Kitabayah (People of the Book). A Kitabayah is a Christian woman whose ancestors were Christians before the prophethood of the Prophet Mohammad; or a Jewess whose ancestors were Jews before the prophethood of Jesus. With many other restrictions in place, in most cases, the non-Muslim needs to convert to Islam to register a marriage in Malaysia.

It is said that there is no compulsion in Islam,[105] but here in all practical senses interfaith couples must know that there is compulsion to convert or give up the love after years into relationship.

Malaysian citizens are given an identity card (MyKad[106]), of which Muslims' MyKad states religion as "Islam."[107] As stated above Muslims can marry only to a Muslim; this means the non-Muslim spouse must convert and make appropriate changes in the MyKad.

A marriage registered under the laws of a foreign country must be re-registered at the Malaysian Representative Office within 6 months of the date of marriage. A couple married outside Malaysia will not be able to register a Muslim to non-Muslim marriage in Malaysia and their children will not have the benefit of Malaysian citizenship.[108] If the Muslim/non-Muslim couple married overseas comes to Malaysia, and someone calls the authorities on them, the Syariah authority will likely arrest the Muslim partner for zina and khalwat (since the marriage is not recognized in Malaysia).[109]

Parallel to the civil courts, there are Syariah Courts that conduct legal matters related to the Muslim family sphere. Legal issues like Muslim divorce and Muslim apostasy are conducted in the Syariah Courts. Syariah laws do not apply to non-Muslims.

---

[104] Koran 2:221; also the Malaysian Islamic Family Law (Federal Territories) Act 1984- Section 10. Persons of other religions: (1) No man shall marry a non-Muslim except a Kitabiyah and (2) No woman shall marry a non-Muslim.
[105] Koran 2:256.
[106] https://en.wikipedia.org/wiki/Malaysian_identity_card.
[107] http://www.jpn.gov.my/en/informasi/aplikasi-utama/.
[108] Details at http://www.jpn.gov.my/en/perkhidmatan/pendaftaran-semula-perkahwinan-bagi-pasangan-bukan-islam-yang-telah-didaftarkan-mengikut-undang-undang-negara-asing-pada-atau-selepas-01-03-1982/.
[109] Read Loyarburuk at http://www.loyarburok.com/2008/07/10/muslim-non-muslim-marriages-in-malaysia/.

It is important for an interfaith dating person to know that conversion to Islam is a one-way street. It is impossible to convert to any other faith for a Muslim.[110] It is even impossible to change a name in MyKad to a non-Muslim in Malaysia (read practicing Hindu Revathi Massosai's case[111]). A person having a Muslim registered name but practicing another faith has no right to marry but in Islam (read Zarinah's case[112] where a practicing Hindu girl was arrested for marrying a Hindu man). Even after years of practicing another faith, the Syariah Police will enforce that a former Muslim (even practicing another faith for most of later life) be given only Muslim final rites (read Mr. Moorthy case[113] where a practicing Hindu's body was taken away from his Hindu wife).

---

[110] **Mohammad** said, "Whoever changes his Islamic religion, then kill him." (Bukhari 9.84.57) Read more at http://www.jihadwatch.org/2010/12/malaysia-islamic-agency-vows-to-enforce-islamic-apostasy-law and http://www.wikiislam.net/wiki/Persecution_of_Ex-Muslims. Even a former non-Muslim's marriage with a Muslim ends with him uttering talaak, talaak, talaak, the divorcee has no right to marry a non-Muslim later in life.

[111] **Miss Revathi Massosai** was born to Muslim converts and given a Muslim name, but she was raised as a Hindu by her grandmother and has always practiced Hindu faith. However, under Malaysia's Islamic law, having Muslim parents makes one a Muslim and, as such, one is not allowed to change one's faith or marry a non-Muslim. But Miss Massosai married a Hindu man in 2004 and the couple has a young daughter. When in January 2007 she asked a court to officially designate her a Hindu she was detained and taken to an Islamic rehabilitation center. Her detention was twice extended to six months, during which time she says religious officials tried to make her pray as a Muslim and wear a headscarf. She is adamant that she will remain a Hindu. In the meantime, Miss Revathi and her daughter have been placed in the custody of her Muslim parents. (taken from http://news.bbc.co.uk/2/hi/asia-pacific/6278568.stm)

[112] **Zarinah** had Hindu father and mother. Later the father converted to Islam and changed children's name to Islamic, but in all practical matters Zarinah was raised as Hindu. Now she decided to marry her Hindu lover, but Malaysian police came and arrested her in the middle of the Hindu wedding. Zarinah said there was a possibility that she could be charged with insulting Islam if the problem was not solved quickly. (taken from http://www.themalaymailonline.com/malaysia/article/path-to-leave-islam-simple-but-far-from-easy)

[113] **M Moorthy**, a Malaysian mountaineering hero was buried as a Muslim, against the wishes of his Hindu wife, who denied he had converted to Islam before his death. The decision follows a Malaysian High Court ruling that it cannot override the country's Islamic Courts in matters of religious conversion. An Islamic Syariah Court subsequently upheld a claim by his former colleagues in the army that he had become a Muslim last year. However his family, who wanted him to have a Hindu funeral, was not allowed to appear before the court

The author feels Muslim majority countries apply interfaith marriage laws favoring Islam only and are unfair and unjust to minorities. To the best of the author's knowledge, there is no Christian or Hindu majority country that has made interfaith marriage laws favoring only their majority. If it is a matter of following Koran, then any Muslim getting into a romantic love relationship before marriage should be severely punished for khalwat.[114] The Malay government should do more to educate non-Muslim and Muslim youths about the serious consequences after interfaith love. Interfaith dating youths have to do their homework and fully understand all the legal and other consequences of their actions.

2.15.4: Indian Marriage and Divorce Laws

India has a dual system of matrimonial laws. Personal laws ordinarily govern various communities or groups of communities, although individuals can opt out of the community-specific family-law regime and voluntarily subject themselves to the national laws on civil marriages.[115]

2.15.4.1 Indian personal marriage laws:

Hindus (includes Jain, Sikh, Buddhist) are governed by the Hindu Marriage Act, 1955.[116,117] Each of the parties shall belong to and profess the Hindu (Jain, Sikh, Buddhist) faith or religion. Sikh couples may be able to get their marriages registered under the Anand Marriage 1909 Act (amended in 2012) instead of the Hindu Marriage Act.

Muslims are governed by their personal laws under which nikaah (i.e. marriage) is a contract and may be permanent or temporary and permits a man to have four wives if he treats all of them equally. To have a valid nikaah under the Muslim Law, presence of a qazi (priest) is not necessary. Merely a proposal in the presence and hearing of two sane

---

to dispute his conversion because they are not Muslims. The family went to the civil court and argued that Mr. Moorthy was a practicing Hindu. They say he was even interviewed for local television two months ago about his preparations for the Hindu festival of Diwali. But the High Court agreed with government lawyers who argued the Civil Court had no jurisdiction. Taken from http://news.bbc.co.uk/2/hi/asia-pacific/4563452.stm.

[114] Koran (24:30); see details earlier about "lowering gaze" by Dr. Zakir Naik.

[115] This information is a summary based on material found at Legalight.in, SudhirLaw, Wikipedia, Indiankanoon.org and other sources. Information presented here is for educational purpose only. Interfaith couples should check with an attorney for legal consultation in their own country.

[116] http://indiankanoon.org/doc/590166/.

[117] http://en.wikipedia.org/wiki/Hindu_Marriage_Act.

males (or one sane male and two sane female adults) who are all Muslims and acceptance of the said proposals at the same time constitutes a valid "nikaah." Under Indian laws, a Muslim husband can divorce his wife without any reason merely by pronouncing three times the word "Talaak." However for a Muslim woman to obtain divorce certain conditions are necessary.[118]

Parsees are governed under the Parsee Marriage & Divorce Act, 1939[119] which outlines the provisions of their marriage and law.

Christians are governed by the Indian Christian Marriage Act, 1872.[120] If one party thereto alone is a Christian, such a marriage becomes valid only if the personal law of the non-Christian party treats such marriage as valid. Where the wife is a Christian woman and the husband is a Hindu, there is no prohibition under Hindu law for such a marriage. Where one of the parties to a marriage in India is a Christian and the other party is a non-Christian the best course to adopt is to solemnize the marriage under the Special Marriage Act, 1954.

2.15.4.2 Indian civil marriages:

Persons of any religion (Hindu, Muslim, Christian or Parsee) who get married under the Special Marriage Act, 1954 (also called "Civil Marriage") are governed by the said act.

Special Marriage Act, 1954 (General Marriage Law):
The Special Marriage Act, 1954[121] provides for a special form of marriage in certain cases and for the registration of such and certain other marriages and also for divorce available to all citizens of India married under the Act. A marriage between any two persons (Muslim, Christian, Hindu and others) may be solemnized after giving notice thereof under the Act. After the marriage has been solemnized, the Marriage Officer shall enter a certificate thereof and the parties to the marriage and three witnesses shall sign the certificate of marriage. The effect of registration of Marriage is that all children born after the date of ceremony of marriage shall in all respects be deemed to be the legitimate children of their parents. The marriage of any member of an undivided family belonging to Hindu, Buddhist, Sikh or Jain religion, solemnized under this Act shall be deemed to affect his severance from the family. The Act provides for remedies like restitution of conjugal rights, judicial

---

[118] http://indiankanoon.org/doc/1458498/.
[119] http://indiankanoon.org/doc/122564/.
[120] http://indiankanoon.org/doc/1166543/.
[121] http://indiankanoon.org/doc/4234/.

separation, nullity of marriage and divorce. There is provision made in the Act for the grant of alimony pendente-lite and permanent alimony to the wife.

2.15.4.3 Multiple marriage ceremonies in India:

Sometimes a couple goes through multiple marriage ceremonies to please two sets of parents or for personal preferences. Legally, only the first registered marriage ceremony and laws relating to it will apply to that marriage.

Messages to all parents

- ➤ Parents must realize that their children are not their property.
- ➤ Parents don't own children. Children just came to this world through parents, that's all.
- ➤ Treat your children like guests.
- ➤ Talk to your children like you would do to your best friend or a boss at work.
- ➤ Do not suppress your children (like a spring), one day they will bounce back with disaster.
- ➤ Treat your children like a wet soap in your hand, if you hold too hard or too soft, it will slide out. You have to learn to hold them with just right pressure.
- ➤ Trust them, respect them, give them good practical education and hope for the best.
- ➤ Give them education about sex and interfaith marriage assuming they could potentially do it. Proper teaching and trust will go a long way.

Chapter III: Hindu-Christian Marriages

Couples in Christian-Hindu relationship are requested to read/view:
- Section 2.2: Ten Points of Interfaith Dating
- Section 2.3: FAQ on Interfaith Marriages
- Section 2.8: Ten Points of Dating a Hindu
- Section 2.11: Idol-worshippers: Who Is and Who Is Not
- Section 12.5: The Bible on Hindus?
- Watch this video prepared by InterfaithShaadi: https://www.youtube.com/watch?v=hlAuY85RlcE.

Section 3.1: Hindu-Christian Marriages

About a third of Hindu youths in America get married to Christians.[122] Most Hindu youths in the West however take pride in their religious traditions and insist on going through Hindu vivaha (marriage). Most Christian significant others take part in the Hindu wedding out of curiosity, fascination for colorful rituals, out of respect for the intended spouse and/or because they find a spiritual meaning from the all inclusive pluralistic Hindu way of praying to God. In some cases, the Hindu and Christian ceremonies are performed on the same day, sometimes in the same wedding hall.

In one case, the Christian spouse requested the Hindu priest to put a picture of Lord Jesus into the Hindu ceremony and the request was applauded by all attending pluralistic Hindus. However in another case, a Hindu youth interviewed a Hindu priest and requested on behalf of her Christian fiancée that the Hindu wedding be performed without putting a forehead dot (kum kum) on the Christian, without the Christian praying to Hindu Gods, and without taking any prasad (offering from Gods). The proud Hindu priest simply declined to be part of such wedding.

While there are Christians who marry Hindus that are ready to live married life with equality of both faiths and without imposing his or her Christian dogmas on the Hindu spouse, there are other Christians who are not ready to tolerate Dharmic traditions and expect the Hindu spouse and children by this marriage to accept "unintended" religious conversion by baptism. After a Hindu to Christian conversion, a Hindu marriage is simply a Christian-Christian marriage performed by a Hindu priest. In most cases, the Hindu priest and all celebrating Hindus at the Hindu marriage have no clue about the conversion of the former Hindu. Such Hindu weddings are shams, and probably performed simply to save face for the Hindu parents in the Hindu community.

Two themes found throughout the Bible are religious exclusivity and religious intolerance to others.[123] Christianity's core belief is that salvation exists only through faith in Jesus Christ. Jesus said: "I am the way, the truth, and the life. No one comes to the Father (God) except through me."[124] The Gospel of John and Peter gave frequent messages that the followers of other religions held invalid beliefs, which were

---

[122] Section 2.4.
[123] Section 12.5.
[124] John 14:6.

wrong, deluded, immoral, and/or heretical.[125] Some of the acts of intolerance cited were actually ordered by God, i.e. "When the Lord your God brings you into the land you are entering to possess and drive out before you many nations… then you must destroy them totally. Make no treaty with them and show them no mercy"[126] and "do not leave alive anything that breathes. Completely destroy them… as the Lord your God has commanded you."[127]

Even today, no major Christian church holds a pluralist theology that each person is "saved" through his or her own religion. Does this mean that Mahatma Gandhi will not achieve salvation because he was never baptized? Many churches will expect a religious conversion of a Hindu before marriage, a sign that they do not approve a marriage between a Christian and a Hindu. Some other churches will ask the Hindu spouse to sign a prenuptial[128] that the children from this marriage will be raised only as Christians. After divorce, this one sided affidavit will have serious legal consequences.[129] For this reason, a request for a wedding involving a Hindu in a church should be considered as a very serious matter.

Baptism is the act to cleanse former (Hindu) sins and practices, and later live with Jesus Christ forever. A Hindu youth should not have the wrong impression that baptism is a hollow ritual devoid of meaning. The most critical test to identify an intolerant Christian intended spouse is to ask "What if I decline baptism/christening of our children?" If ultimately only a Christian heritage is expected, then the Hindu should wonder why you are willing to tolerate someone's intolerance for your identity and culture.

If your intended spouse (or in-law) is expecting you and/or your children to undergo baptism, then you have one of two choices: 1) accept his or her Christian faith and be prepared to give up your birth religion and cultural heritage completely or 2) clarify that you have a pride in your birth religion and ask for equality by denying the baptism religious labeling, especially for your children.

As per several surveys,[130] it is estimated that more than half of interfaith marriages end in divorce. A frequent reason given for divorce is that "the

---

[125] http://www.religioustolerance.org/excl_bibl.htm.
[126] Deuteronomy 7:1-3.
[127] Deuteronomy 20:16-17.
[128] Section 3.4.
[129] http://www.youtube.com/watch?v=wllEAoQEk74.
[130] http://www.religioustolerance.org/ifm_divo.htm.

person changed" after the marriage. It is not that anyone really changes, but that the other person failed to recognize the actuality. It is critical that a Hindu considering interfaith relationships with a Christian gets to know the "real" him or her sooner rather than later.

Fundamental religious differences can bring unexpected complexities to a marriage. Ideally both faiths and traditions should be respected and followed without imposing one's intolerant religious beliefs on their spouse. Increased awareness of these complexities and better foresight and preparation will increase the odds of a long and happy interfaith marriage.

FAQ: Christian-Dharmic Marriage

➤ Does the Christian intended spouse believe that "salvation" is possible only through Jesus?

➤ Are your Hindu parents not going to be "saved" on the Judgment Day?

➤ Does he or she believe that Lord Ganesh and Goddess Kali are not incarnations of the same "Lord your God" described in the Bible?

➤ Does the Christian intended spouse have any reservations about coming to a Hindu temple, bowing to Hindu Gods and taking offering (prasad) from the Gods? Is the Christian going to be afraid of the "jealous" God if he or she has to take part in a prayer (puja) to God in the form of Goddess Durga? Will the Hindu intended spouse have the same spiritual meaning for Jesus as it was taught in your church?

➤ Do you have to get married in a church? Do you have to have a Hindu vivaha where multiple Gods will be invoked?

➤ Do you have to change your religion by baptism before marriage?

➤ Do your children have to have baptism/christening to announce the child as a Christian? Do your children have to have namasanskara and other Hindu rituals? What are the consequences if you decline it?

➤ The American Academy of Pediatrics stated benefits are not compelling enough to recommend universal newborn circumcision. Do your sons have to be circumcised in accordance with your spouse's religious belief?

➤ Name is everything, as it reflects the tradition and culture the parents are proud of and would like the child to continue. Are the children going to have Dharmic or Christian first names and your current last name?

➤ A membership in a church may cost from 3-12% of your gross family income. Are you planning to be a member of a church, especially after children? Are you planning to spend the same amount of money supporting Hindu religious institutions?

➤ In case of your or your child's death, will there be a Christian burial or the Hindu cremation and final rites?

Section 3.2: Follow Jesus, Not the Church

Jesus[131] was a progressive thinker and believed in adapting to time. Several points are raised to support this assertion.

The Second Commandment[132] describes the jealous and angry[133] God's stern message against praying to "other" gods and warning to punish your innocent grandchildren to the third and fourth generations if this commandment is not followed. In contrast when asked, Jesus stated the Second Commandment as "love thy neighbor."[134] How beautiful!

Jesus was inclusivist and accepted Jews and Gentiles alike. Jesus himself never used the words "idol gods" or "other gods." His teachings were more concerned with being a good person rather than criticizing "other" gods as emphasized in the rest of Bible[135] or church sermons.[136] Regarding tolerance of others, many churches teach that Jews, Muslims and the non-baptized Mahatma Gandhi[137] will not be saved. This certainly is not in line with the inclusivist and tolerant message that Jesus gave us.

Jesus was not dogmatic. There was an old tradition of not doing any work on the Sabbath day.[138] Jesus clarified however, that it was lawful to

---

[131] Also read http://www.newsweek.com/andrew-sullivan-christianity-crisis-64025.

[132] God gave the Ten Commandments to Moses on Mount Sinai (around year 1593 BC). The Second commandment states, "You shall not make for yourself an idol, whether in the form of anything that is in heaven above, or that is on the earth beneath, or that is in the water under the earth. You shall not bow down to them or worship them; for I the Lord your God am a jealous God... punishing children for the iniquity of parents, to the third and fourth generations of those who reject me." (Exodus 20:4-5)

[133] God is described as a "Jealous God" 31 times, as an "Angry God" 238 times and "fear" word is used 455 times in the Bible, many of these citations are by God Himself.

[134] "And the Second (commandment) is like it: You shall love your neighbor as yourself." (Matthew 22:39) "There is no commandment greater than these." (Mark 12:31)

[135] Section 12.5.

[136] Currently, no major Christian church holds pluralist theology (each person is saved by his or her own religion, independent of Christ) or liberal concept of salvation.

[137] http://www.hinduismtoday.com/modules/smartsection/item.php?itemid=5129.

[138] And LORD spoke to Moses, saying: "Tell the people of Israel to keep my Sabbath day, for the Sabbath is a sign of the covenant between Me and you

do good on the Sabbath.[139,140] Similarly regarding the tradition of washing hands before eating bread, Jesus said[141] it is more important to be a good human being than to strictly follow certain traditions. God asked to make a covenant to circumcise all males.[142] Jesus explained that circumcision was of no avail.[143] It was said that God loved burned animal offerings and animal sacrifices.[144] Jesus clarified "...to love one's neighbor as oneself is more than all the whole burnt offerings and sacrifices."[145] Apparently Jesus was a reformist and more interested in karma, not dogmas.

---

forever. It helps you to remember that I am the LORD, who makes you holy. Yes, keep the Sabbath day, for it is holy. Anyone who desecrates it must die; anyone who works on that day will be cut off from the community. Work six days only, but the seventh day must be a day of total rest. I repeat: Because the LORD considers it a holy day, anyone who works on the Sabbath must be put to death." (Exodus 31:12-15)

[139] Matthew 12:12.

[140] Jesus said: "What man is there among you who has one sheep, and if it falls into a pit on the Sabbath, will not lay hold of it and lift it out?" (Matthew 12:11) "The Sabbath was made for man, and not man for the Sabbath." (Mark 2:27)

[141] Not wash their hands when they eat bread is not that important as to transgress commandment of God. "Why do you also transgress the commandment of God because of your tradition?" (Matthew 15:2-3) "For out of the heart proceed evil thoughts, murders, adulteries, fornications, thefts, false witness, and blasphemies. These are the things which defile a man, but to eat with unwashed hands does not defile a man." (Matthew 15:19-20)

[142] "There is My covenant, which you shall keep, between Me and you and your descendants after you and your descendants after you. Every male among you shall be circumcised. And you shall be circumcised in the flesh of your foreskins, and it shall be a sign of the covenant between Me and you," God commands Abraham (Genesis 17:10-11), the Jewish patriarch. "Any uncircumcised male who is not circumcised in the flesh of his foreskin shall be cut off from his people; he has broken My covenant." (Genesis 16:14)

[143] "For circumcision is indeed profitable if you keep the law; but if you are a breaker of the law, your circumcision has become uncircumcision. Therefore, if an uncircumcised man keeps the righteous requirements of the law, will not his uncircumcision be counted as circumcision? And will not the physically uncircumcised, if he fulfills the law, judge you who, even with your written code and circumcision, are a transgressor of the law? For he is not a Jew who is one outwardly, nor is circumcision that which is outward in the flesh; but he is a Jew who is one inwardly; and circumcision is that of the heart, in the Spirit, not in the letter; whose praise is not from men but from God." (Romans 2:25-29)

[144] Leviticus 6:25; I Kings 8:63; II Chronicles 7:5, II Chronicles 15:11-12, II Chronicles 29:32-33, Psalms 66:15, Ezekiel 43:19-25.

[145] Mark 12:33.

For enemies, LORD said,[146] "Now go and attack Amalek, and utterly destroy all that they have, and do not spare them. But kill both man and woman, infant and nursing child, ox and sheep, camel and donkey." Jesus gave exactly opposite message,[147] "love your enemies, bless those who curse you, do good to those who hate you, and pray for those who spitefully use you and persecute you."

Jesus said, "Whoever slaps you on your right cheek, turn the other to him."[148] The person of such a tolerant spirit would probably never endorse the Christian crusades where millions of innocent people were killed in His name. How is it logical that killing millions of innocent people is not sin, but a newborn child carries sin so as to require cleansing with baptism?

On the matter of baptism,[149] John the Baptist baptized Jesus[150] but Jesus never baptized anyone.[151] For an interfaith marriage, the church will insist on baptism of the intended spouse. It is interesting that a Catholic Church will insist on re-baptism of already baptized Mormons or Protestant Christians (and vice a versa). Apparently baptism is not as much about Jesus but for the church.

Are the leaders of today's churches progressive thinkers and believers of adapting to the times, as Jesus was in his time?

If a couple were looking for an interfaith marriage with equality, it would be easier to follow Jesus but not the church. If you love Jesus, have a Christmas tree[152] in your home and follow His messages. In line with Jesus' inclusive teachings, also respect your spouse's faith and celebrate ALL holidays but do not agree to baptize the children as an obligation to

---

[146] Samuel 15:3.

[147] Matthew 5:44.

[148] Matthew 5:39.

[149] Conversion to cleanse from former practices and later live with Christ forever.

[150] Matthew 3:13.

[151] Father Kenneth Doyle: "The synoptic writers—Matthew, Mark and Luke—offer no clarity on this, because they are silent on the question of Jesus baptizing." (http://catholicphilly.com/2013/03/think-tank/catholic-spirituality/did-jesus-baptize-anyone-lectors-and-the-shehe-problem/) This book's author focused on Jesus' direct messages (in Matthew, Mark and Luke) but acknowledges John's (3:22) message, "After these things Jesus and His desciples came into the land of Judea, and there He remained with them and baptized."

[152] Not a Christian religious symbol.

the church. It is just fair to let an interfaith child decide his or her own faith as an adult—that is progressive thinking.

I do not seek redemption from the consequences of my sin. I seek to be redeemed from sin itself, or rather from the very thought of sin.
—Mahatma Gandhi

Section 3.3: A Jealous and Angry God

The Abrahamic God is described in the Bible as a "Jealous God" 31 times and as an "Angry God" 238 times. The word "fear" is used 455 times in the Bible; many of these citations are by God Himself. An example of how do Christians justify a Jealous God and reconcile Him with a loving God is provided in a blog written by **Jason**[153] titled "**I, The Lord your God, Am A Jealous God.**" The blog begins by quotations from Bible depicting a jealous God as follows:

Exodus 20:5: "You shall not bow down to them or worship them; for I, the LORD your God, am a jealous God, punishing the children for the sin of the fathers to the third and fourth generation of those who hate Me…"

Exodus 34:14: "Do not worship any other god, for the LORD, whose name is Jealous, is a jealous God."

Deuteronomy 4:24: "For the LORD your God is a consuming fire, a jealous God."

Joshua 24:19: "Joshua said to the people, 'You are not able to serve the LORD. He is a holy God; He is a jealous God. He will not forgive your rebellion and your sins.'"

Nahum 1:2: "The LORD is a jealous and avenging God;…"

Jason then asks if God is a jealous God, then how can it be reconciled with 1 Corinthians 13:4 which says, "love…is not jealous"? Surely if love is not jealous, and God is jealous, then God cannot be considered loving. Jason argues that jealousy is not always bad and can be a good thing depending on the situation. He further argues that the word "jealous" is translated in the New Testament from the Greek word zelos, which has a good connotation. Jason then continues that human beings are spiritually married to God and jealousy in marriage is a good thing. Jason concludes by saying that he is very comfortable with the idea of God being jealous.

This is not the right approach and the author has responded as follows:[154]

---

[153] http://jaytheophilos.blogspot.com/2004/12/i-lord-your-god-am-jealous-god.html.
[154] These views appeared on InterfaithShaadi.org.

"Jason, you found it very comforting knowing your God is a jealous— and for you! If your God was not "jealous" and "angry," and instead was a loving God, why will you not feel comfortable?

Mahatma Gandhi spent plenty of time in churches to learn about Christianity,[155] but he found "love" in Lord Krishna. Is your God going to be jealous of Gandhi's God? On the Judgment Day, what will be the fate of Gandhi? Tell me what is more important… Gandhi's good work (karma) or which God he prayed to?

Amongst the different Gods (or Godlike figures) such as the LORD God of Israel, God the Father, Allah, Jehovah, Krishna, Goddess Lakshmi, elephant God-Ganesh, Mahavir and Buddha, which of these listed God(s) are "other gods" or "idols" will your God be jealous from?

What is wrong in having liberty to pray to God as one desires? Jews feel holy in Israel and not in Saudi Arabia. Muslims pray only in the direction of the Kaaba (Black Cube) to reach Allah, even though Allah is in all directions. Christians have a little more liberty and believe in the Holy Trinity, 3 forms of God. Catholic churches are full of manly and womanly figures, photos and wooden or Golden Crosses… are these not "idols" or "graven images?" Even Hindus, who believe that there is one absolutely Supreme Reality, have the liberty to express God in whatever form they wish to see Him/Her. Why would (any) God want to take away the liberty of praying to Him or Her in any way one desires?"

> *We are all originally divine (sat-chit-ananda) and not originally sinners. There is no such thing as original sin. We simply do not have the problem that Christianity offers to solve.*
> —Rajiv Malhotra

---

[155]http://www.cyberspacei.com/jesusi/authors/gandhi/autobiography/mgbio2_01 1.htm.

Section 3.4: Church Marriage Contract

To hold a Hindu-Christian marriage in a church most likely means the couple must sign a contract for marriage. The church will want to make sure the next generation of this family will be Christians.

PROMISES REGARDING CHILDREN

Catholic Party:

I, ___, reaffirm my faith in Jesus Christ and, with God's help, I intend to continue living that faith as a practicing member of the Catholic church. In addition, I promise to do all that I can to share this faith with our children and children that have already been born by having them baptized in the Catholic church and raising them as Catholics. — Signature

Non-Catholic Party:

I, ___, recognize that my future spouse has promised to live out the Catholic Faith as a practicing member of the Catholic church and raise our children in the Faith of the Catholic church and I do not have opposition to this. —Signature

Additional information about such contracts can be found from the web site of the selected church for an intended wedding. See reference for sample documents for the USA[156] and India.[157]

The non-Christian party should understand the grave implications of signing such one-sided prenuptial agreement. Basically, one is ending his/her religious heritage of birth and accepting Christianity as his/her future heritage. Such a signed affidavit will have major implications if there were to be a child custody battle after divorce. One should consult with one's own lawyer and parents before signing such legal documents.

---

[156] https://www.interfaithshaadi.org/index.php/literature/108-catholic-church-marriage-registration-form-usa or
http://www.diocs.org/Portals/2/Documents/Chancellor/MA%20MB%20MC_7_12_.pdf.
[157] https://www.interfaithshaadi.org/index.php/literature/100-pre-nuptial-with-roman-catholic-church.

Section 3.5: A Christian and Hindu Interfaith Marriage of 24 Years in the States

In this book, the author has presented personal life experiences from 81 interfaith couples and their parents as appeared on InterfaithShaadi.org (names have been changed for their privacy).

Approximately 200 people shared their Christian-Dharmic interfaith dating/marriage experiences at InterfaithShaadi.org. The author has selected 14 representative cases for readers of this book. In a few cases, the author (Admin)'s views are also included. Let's see what Ashwini has to say.

Ashwini says:

Well... I am going to comment briefly and share our experience of a Christian and Hindu interfaith marriage of 24 years. We have definitely evolved in our viewpoints with each decade of marriage, and as life has given us more experience. Fortunately, we have a similar viewpoint on religions, in that they are human constructs with plenty of flaws, often with political purpose. I think my core beliefs are:

1. No religion has a monopoly on reaching God and the divine. We reject this wholeheartedly. We reject exclusivity found in the Abrahamic religions. By their standards, I am a pagan, a kafir, and the "unchosen;" not very flattering names for child of God.

Baptism, which 2 of my kids went thru, was presented as more of starting a spiritual life, rather than a commitment to Jesus and Christianity, when the Methodist pastor performed it. We explicitly stated we embraced both religions during this time. Since then, we have gone more towards the Dharmic tradition, as worshipping Jesus as the only messenger of God was too restrictive.

2. Every religious tradition when you dig deep, tries to address the fundamental challenge of how to live, why are we here, what is mortality. If you get past the superficial names of god, the rituals, the stories, they are the same issues. The answers, however, are somewhat different.

3. Polytheism vs. Monotheism—let's see. How can the Christians really claim monotheism being somehow superior to the other... they themselves need the Holy Trinity to describe God. Then throw in the Saints and Popes and Mother Mary, the Apostles and it sounds polytheistic, doesn't it? How about the Muslims worshipping Mohammed as well as the concept of a God? Why have both?

Perhaps we humans just need multiple characters to describe the Divine.

4. We try to pick the best values of each religion as the values we concentrate on: for Christianity, it is love, charity and forgiveness. From Hinduism, the concept of Karma, Dharma, Bhakti and controlling ones desires. We have tried to strip away the dogma that has little to do with living a spiritual and righteous life.

I can say raising children in both traditions has been challenging, but it has hopefully made our kids critical thinkers. They have embraced the values of human decency, kindness to animals (they are all vegetarians) and an appreciation of both cultures. My worry is that what we have given them, especially the Dharmic viewpoint will get lost or diluted out with the next few generations. However, I remind myself that this is happening in kids from same-religion families. We cannot control the future; just influence it. —Ashwini

> *You cannot believe in God until you believe in yourself.*
> —Swami Vivekananda

Section 3.6: I Chose to Be Baptized when I Was Pregnant

Bharti says:

I think religion is something that is very personal. In different phases of my life, I have felt different pulls. I chose to be baptized when I was pregnant with my child, to incorporate my husband's ancestry. However, I refused to let my child be baptized, because I felt I was not in a position to make a commitment for her. Since then, she speaks our language, does puja daily and has brought our way of life back into our home. —Bharti

Bharti added:

Raising interfaith and or multiracial Desi kids is a unique experience. There are not very many such marriages in my community, so advice is rather sparse.

It would be nice to get the perspective of couples who have raised interfaith and multiracial children. I especially want to hear form Indian ladies married to non-Desis. How do you deal with festivals, in-laws, etc? If there are values in the other culture/family that you consider harmful to your child, how do you protect him or her from it?

While nobody has been mean to my face about my marriage or my child, I have heard things through the grapevines. Is there a way to protect your child from hearing this stuff or feeling bad? —Bharti

Bharti added (a month later):

Hay Niti!

This is my personal experience, so it is one of my perspectives:

I got baptized because I felt that my child should be exposed to and have a sense of belonging in both religions. In order to be part of church life and community, my husband and I chose to be baptized. Shortly after our child was born, we were contacted by the church to have our child baptized. We did not feel that we could make that decision for her. In fact, in hindsight, we both realized that even getting baptized ourselves was completely unnecessary for the purpose of making our child belong. She has to confront the fact that she is different and find her natural religious balance. Her (our daughter) relationship with God is her own. As parents, we have the unique privilege of guiding her, but it is up to God to call her.

Secondly, many aspects of traditional Christianity were incompatible with our belief system as a family and here's why:

(1) The Life of Christ is very inspiring to us, and it is undeniable that if a person could live as he did, it is most definitely a successful life. However, the church spends the vast majority of time (in my perspective) on his death. I think you can say this about the Christian religion as a whole—remember, the resurrection gave birth to Christianity.

(2) The concept that those who have not accepted Christ go to hell, and in the alternative—those who truly accept Christ can be forgiven of their sins by that very acceptance.

(3) "I like your Christ, I do not like your Christians. Your Christians are so unlike your Christ." —Mahatma Gandhi

If you are in the US, church is about politics too.[158] We disagreed with much of the church's conservative views and agenda—on homosexuality, on abortion, on birth control, on its view of the role of women etc.

However, this is just a personal experience. It is up to you to choose the right balance for your family. Please feel free to ask any questions to me and I will do my best to answer.

Thanks! —Bharti

If you are in an interfaith love relationship, please do not make your love a battleground of whose God is a right one! Be a pluralist.

---

[158] Progressive Christians in the U.S. do not manipulate politics as the fundamentalist Christians do.

Section 3.7: We Agreed to Have Our Children Baptized

Neelam, says:

Hello,

I'm a Hindu woman engaged to a Christian man. We have agreed to have our children baptized but we have agreed that this will not define them as Christians. I grew up learning the Vedas and teaching Balvihar in the USA. My fiancé has agreed to participate in doing pujas, taking kids to Balvihar, and chanting mantras with me. His only condition is we celebrate Easter and Christmas with his parents. Do you have any words of wisdom? I'm still struggling on how to preserve our Hindu heritage. Any thoughts would be appreciated. —Neelam

Admin says:[159]

Dear Neelam,

You know your situation the best, however we will provide you with some tips to critically evaluate your situation.

Our recommendation to anyone dealing with an Abrahamic is NO BBS (in your case, no baptism). It is not that 10 minutes of a dip in water is an issue but the thought process behind asking for it is a concern. The BBS will set a tone for your married life. Your children will have to go through different confirmatory stages, including attending church during their teenage years for knowledge required for baptism. You are a pluralist, meaning *Ishvara Allah tero nam*, while Christianity is an absolutely exclusivist religion. The teaching in churches may not match with the teachings in your Balvihar (read McKenna versus Pooja[160]). Your children will get confused for who is God. You will be better off making up your mind about which one of two faiths will be good for your children. Best would be to let children decide their own faith when they become 21 year old.

If you don't have the intention of making your children Christians (you said, "we have agreed that this will not define them as Christians"), why

---

[159] "Admin" refers to administrator of the website InterfaithShaadi.org. Author has been the sole administrator of this website.

[160] http://www.hinduismtoday.com/modules/smartsection/item.php?itemid=5129 and
https://interfaithshaadi.org/index.php?option=com_content&view=category&id=106:will-gandhi-go-to-hell-since-he-was-not-baptized&Itemid=78&layout=default.

would you want to lie to his parents, his religious institutions and to God the Father and baptize them? Why make lies and deceptions a foundation of your married life?

Have you read the Bible? We love Jesus' messages and for that reason we highly recommend following Jesus, not the church.[161] Tell your fiancé that your children will follow Jesus but will not be baptized. Explain to him that following Jesus' teachings is more important to you than 10 minutes of a baptism ritual. Is that not true?

Tell him that you agree 100% with "His only condition is we celebrate Easter and Christmas with his parents." Yes, go for all Christian holidays, exchange lots of gifts, feed his big family with delicious food and enjoy. Be even a better Christian that most others in his church. In addition, tell him that children will (unless kids don't want to) spend more time reading Christian scriptures than Hindu scriptures and you will take children to church every Sunday, however you wish to skip that baptism labeling now because you don't want to lie or you want to take more time to think it over. For now keep all your options open and after having children, if you feel like it, you will agree to baptize the children.

If he and/or his parents are religious fanatics, he will not accept the "no baptism clause" and will walk away from the relationship. For his family, it may be vital that their grandchildren are sin free (it only takes 10 min of baptism ritual to wash sins!).

Neelam, according to Christian doctrine, it is possible that his parents may think you are still carrying original sin from your birth. In this case, the Christian family will reluctantly tolerate you, the sinner. They may wish you to be "saved" but will feel bad and sad that they could not convince you to follow the right path. On the Judgment Day, Jesus and God the Father will "save" your baptized children, your husband and in-laws; while you, your Hindu parents and Gandhiji will be sent to hell. What an absurd teaching if that is what his parents learned from Christianity. However, we do not feel this will be an issue considering he told you that he has agreed to participate in doing pujas, taking kids to Balvihar, and chanting mantras with you.

Stealing salt (*Dandi Kutch*) was not the objective of Gandhiji, but to fight injustice. Likewise, Rosa Parks did not fight for that bus seat, but for the thought process behind asking to go to the back of the bus. If Rosa Parks did not say "NO" on that day, there would not be a "President" Barack Obama. If you, a Balvihar student, will not stand up

---

[161] Section 3.2.

to this injustice, who else will? Do we have to wait for Mahatma Gandhi to resurrect and plan a Dandi Kutch to teach Christians that Muslims, Jews and Hindus are not sinners? In so many cases, Hindus marrying Christians in America are submitting to this request for baptism; when can we expect your Balvihar to produce a Rosa Parks?

In any dealing, there are measurable items and there are others you cannot measure it. The baptism is clearly a very specific measurable event and your child will have that "label" for his/her life. The others, like "pujas, taking kids to Balvihar, and chanting mantras with me" are not measurable. What if he joins you for pujas two times, take kids to Balvihar for a few times and chant mantras 10 times; and in the end he decides that this is not working out for him? He may say he has fulfilled his promises and now he does not want any part of it. You will be stuck with him.

If one is smart, he or she would simply say adamantly "no BBS," then wait and see their reactions over the next few months. At the very least, this is one good way to learn the truth.

Are we anti-Christian? We hope you don't read it that way. We are talking about interfaith marriage with equality; we do not see baptism as an equality of two faiths. Yours is not a within-faith marriage and he should not get stuck on a baptism ritual for interfaith children.

We truly believe that your boyfriend is a pluralist and not at all a religious fanatic. He may truly believe and respect Hinduism. Maybe all we have written is not at all applicable to him. Quite possibly, your planned fake-baptism for your children will not have any effect on your marriage or your children's lives. In spite of all these, we still like you to buy an insurance; no BBS.

If you go out to buy a house and hire a home inspector, what would you expect him/her to tell you? If he/she just tells you how wonderful the flowers are there in front of the house, and does not mention the cracks in the basement foundation, you will certainly be hurt. Like a good home inspector, we are just pointing out that this BBS issue will be a major crack in your marriage foundation, and will remain with you even after 40 years. It is worth your while to seriously think these issues through, before coming to a decision that can impact the rest of your life.

Neelam, we want you to think through all potential practical issues and know the other family well. We hope we helped you make an "informed" decision, whatever that is. We wish you the best. —Admin

Section 3.8: I Am a Christian Getting Married to a Hindu

Equality in an interfaith marriage is difficult to define. Here, Cathy is trying to find a good balance between two conflicting religious practices and ready for dual religious labeling (namasanskara and baptism) for their children. The author challenges her on some of her statements to better prepare her for planned happy Christian-Hindu married life.

Cathy says:

I am a Christian (Lutheran) getting married to a Hindu fiancé. We will celebrate a Hindu shaadi in India and receive blessings from a Christian priest in my home country (in the West), and we are happy to accommodate both traditions without expecting the conversion of the other. We both fell in love with the other as the whole person, created by their cultural and religious upbringing as well.

However, I wish to comment on what you (Admin) said about Christians and baptism. I find it an intolerant statement that we both (myself included) could not celebrate the rituals involved in naming a child. I want to baptize our children, not for religious reasons but for the reason that not accepting the rituals of my heritage implies not accepting my identity and equal parenthood. For the same reason I heartfully wish to celebrate namakarana sanskara so as to not leave out the other parents' background and raise children who are comfortable with a unique blend of backgrounds and a duality of religion. The same goes for the yearly celebrations of Diwali, Saraswati puja as well as the first haircut of a child, etc.

But to me, it seems you have defined religious tolerance as refusing or belittling the other partner's tradition when it involves Christian rites. Would you not agree that it would be entirely unjust to demand the other parent to let go of their Hindu, Muslim, Sikh or Buddhist rites—that, effectively, also produce religious identity? Do you not see the discrepancy? What is your reason for thinking that it is the unilateral right of the other spouse to deny the performance of rite XYZ on their children, because whether you see it or not, this is what you are suggesting?

More importantly, in an interfaith marriage, I find the best advice to be "always 'in addition to', never 'instead of'." Rejection is the one surefire way to generate cleavages, inequality and resentment in a relationship. I wholly agree with Nancy who says we can all be just as defensive, and this comes out when both partner's backgrounds are not allowed to be expressed to the fullest. For this reason I do not feel that your advice is equally based or even productive.

I hope we can have an enlightening discussion on the topic. It should be noted that we might have very different conceptions of the definition of "baptism" as a rite. I do not consider it a rite that is exclusive and binding children to a single religion only. On the other hand, I do not consider Hindu rites neutral. We should appreciate both to their fullest.

I should also note that we have been living together, have had numerous discussions about our beliefs ending on "agree to disagree" and have a puja altar in the house. I take full part in festivals and he visits church with me, on the rare occasion that I do so.

As a parent I consider it my duty to ensure the children feel at home in both of their parents' traditions. To not teach them about Hinduism as well as Christianity would be to hurt their future growth to balanced adults. However, I am not going to teach them that "there are multiple forms of THE GOD, be that Allah, Jesus or Krishna" —to require a person to teach this would be equivalent to requiring them teach the Hindu concept of Vishnu, Shiva and Brahma, and I am not or ever will be Hindu, neither will my husband be Christian. Instead, we both are going to teach them what Mom believes and what Dad believes, and that people with different beliefs can get along, both within a family and in a society.

I feel like it is necessary to state all this, because it seems to me that you have profound mistrust towards "Abrahamic" spouses and have grouped them under a label of suspicion—as if there is always a fundamentalist in them waiting to come out that requires monitoring. This is not to deny that many spouses become increasingly conservative after having children, regardless of their faith.

I also deeply respect your quest for religious tolerance. Still, I ask you to look at how, just maybe, your way of defining a tolerant spouse has affinities to Hinduism and is therefore not the ideal place to begin a dialogue in an interfaith marriage. —Cathy

Admin says:

Dear Cathy,

It is great that you are willing to respect two religions and traditions and looking for EQUALITY for both faiths. With such a beautiful thought, you will have a happy and ever lasting interfaith marriage.

Let's evaluate some of your statements for reality checks.

You mentioned that "I want to baptize our children" and "I heartfully wish to celebrate namakarana sanskara... " This is a beautiful polytheist pluralistic thought. However, such religious labeling has no place in an interfaith marriage with equality for the following reasons:

RELIGIOUS LABELING: Baptism is the act to cleanse former (Hindu?) sins and practices, and later live with Jesus Christ forever. It is not fair to give such an irreversible religious label on an interfaith child. If namakarana sanskara is also considered a religious label, keep both out. Let the child decide his or her own religion at his or her 21 years of age, fair?

NO DUAL LABELING: All Christians and Jews know that a child cannot have baptism (to announce the child Christian) as well as bris (to announce the child Jew) circumcision ceremonies. Watch videos here.[162] The same is true for baptism and sunat (to announce a child Muslim). Further, even within Christian faiths, a Mormon may not tolerate a Catholic, Greek-orthodox or Lutheran baptism for the marriage! To ask any non-Mormon, i.e. a Sikh or Jehovah's Witness, a Mormon-baptism is not fair. We believe, it is better to keep the religious labeling out of the interfaith marriages with equality.

You want baptism just as a rite, because you believe it is not exclusive and binding. However, your religious leaders will correct you on that— baptism is not a hollow ritual devoid of meaning. It is not the ritual but the thought process behind asking for baptism and the rigid dogmas to follow is a concern.

Now let's look at a deeper question... who is THE God? Is Jesus the only savior? Or, in addition can Allah, LORD God of Israel, Buddha and Krishna could also lead to salvation? Why you disagreed to have a puja altar in the house, but you are willing to do the Saraswati puja? Is Saraswati puja not idol worship as described in the Bible? If you don't believe in the Second Commandment and Christian exclusivity, then we do not see any issue marrying a Hindu or for children's baptism.

If you are not an exclusivist Christian, why are you saying, "I am not going to teach them (my kids) that "there are multiple forms of THE GOD..."? If so, then who are Krishna, Goddess Laxmi and Allah... fake or other gods?

---

[162] http://www.youtube.com/watch?v=wllEAoQEk74.

Cathy, for your knowledge, Hindus are not idol worshippers and are 100% monotheists believing in only one Supreme Reality; however liberty is provided to Hindus to express THE God in multiple forms. Actually, Catholics do exactly the same—The Father, Son and Holy Spirit, the wood-cross, baby Jesus, black Jesus, white Jesus, idols of Mary, St. Paul, St. John, the Pope... on and on. Likewise, Muslims pray to the (direction of) black-cube, Kaaba, hang some Arabic writings on wall in their homes and consider it holy and glorify their religious leaders, like Mohammad and Ayatollah. So, what is wrong in having liberty to express THE God (or godly things and people) however way one pleases?

You said, "I am not or ever will be Hindu, neither will my husband be Christian." That's the way it should be. You are more tolerant than some other Abrahamics. However, how about your kids? Are they going to be Hindus, Christians, both or atheists? Are they going to be: 1) multi Gods idol worshipper polytheist Hindus on Saturdays and 2) monotheist and exclusivist Christians on Sundays? Are you going to be okay when your baptized daughter will sit down every day with her dad to do Saraswati and Ganesh puja in the altar in your own home? Let's hope it will never bother you and your parents. Consider putting Jesus' and Mary's symbols into your (future) husband's altar and whole family join for praying. In your own words, this is called "always 'in addition to', never 'instead of'." Pluralism is the only way for any interfaith couple seeking equality.

Cathy, sit down with your fiancé and clarify these as true or false points below to find out how much you truly love each other over certain religious dogmas:

Q: Is "salvation" possible only through Jesus Christ?
Q: Are your fiancé and billions of other Hindus not going to be "saved" on the Judgment Day (unless they get baptized)?
Q: Are Lord Buddha and Goddess Saraswati not incarnations of the same "Lord your God" described in the Bible?
Q: Cathy, do you have any reservations about going to a Hindu temple, bowing to Hindu Gods and taking offering (prasad) from Gods? During a Hindu wedding ceremony the Hindu priest will invoke many Gods from heaven and earth. Are you going to be okay being part of such a wedding?
Q: Do you have to get married in a church? Did you check with your Christian priest to see if it will be okay to have a polytheist Hindu wedding and not a (or in addition to a) monotheist Christian wedding?

Q: Does the child just born carry sin? Is your intended husband carrying sin?

Q: Do your children have to have christening/baptism to announce the child as a Christian and to wipe away their sin?

Q: Name is everything. Are the children going to have Dharmic or Abrahamic names?

Q: A membership in a church could cost from 3-12% of your gross family income. Are you planning to be a member of a church, especially after children? Are you planning to spend the same amounts supporting Hindu religious institutions?

Q: In case of a child's death in your family; will he/she get a Christian burial or the Hindu cremation final rites?

Note that on most of above points, you cannot have both ways.

Most new adults fail to recognize what you have stated, "many spouses become increasingly conservative after having children, regardless of their faith." During dating, talks of "tolerance" and "open mindedness" are not constant or immutable characteristics and could change over time. For this reason, it is important to dig deeper to learn the "true color" of the fiancé by asking certain critical questions. Any decision made after the above reality checks will be a good decision.

Cathy, do not be afraid of these religious complexities created 1000's of years ago. It is best is to let your love rule, not Hindu and Christian religious dogmas. Trust each other fully. Teach children to respect both (all) God(s) and scriptures and when they are 21 let them make their own religious choices. Is this not fair? —Admin

Religion is a man made process of life, whereas humanity and mankind are morals of Almighty.
—Sabana (https://www.interfaithshaadi.org/blog/?p=1835)

Section 3.9: I Am a Christian Mother and My Son Is Marrying a Hindu

Marie says:

I am a Christian mother (Catholic) of a son who is planning to marry a Hindu girl. I have struggled with the exclusivity of Christianity for quite some time. I consider myself liberal and tolerant, and I am still searching for an explanation of "only one way to the Father." Having said that, I still feel somewhat uncomfortable praying to other Gods. My son wants a Hindu ceremony in which his parents are part of. I am hoping for a ceremony that blends both cultures and is truly reflective of who we are. Who we all are? I would be fine with anything my son decides, but I was educated that I am very much a part of the ceremony… I just want to be authentic. My faith has always been important to me, and a guiding light in my life. —Marie

Admin says:

Dear Marie,

So, your concern is… in the Hindu wedding, the Hindu priest will invoke multiple male and female Gods from the heaven, earth, water and all directions. The Hindu ceremony will begin with praying to an elephant head God Ganesh. There will be multiple idols (deities) and extensive puja rituals. There may be a religious Garba dance and you will have to eat offerings from Gods, prasad. All non-baptized-new relatives will surround you; who do not believe that Jesus is the only savior. Further, the new Hindu wife may not wish your grandchildren to be baptized in the Catholic church to remove the original sin. If you do literally believe in what is said in the Bible, you will be committing so many sins. Your LORD God will surely punish you for three to four generations.[163]

Relax! It is normal that an interfaith marriage gives anxiety to parents. Avoid negative thinking; no horror is going to happen by your son marrying a Hindu. You seem to be educated, intelligent and an independent thinker. It is time to look at this new world with love for everyone. Jesus will be proud of you for being a good human being. If you could show your true love for your new Hindu relatives, it will be a win-win for all. So, go buy a sari and bindi and be ready to enjoy the colorful Hindu wedding.

---

[163] The 2nd of the Ten Commandments.

Hopefully your son has done his homework and he knows what he is getting into. If he is not a true pluralist, this newlywed will have the same horrible fate as Rima[164] who has gone through many hardships and ultimately got separated.

Jesus in his direct messages never mentioned "idol worship" and "other gods." Please confirm it for us. Further, He changed the second of the Ten Commandments of "jealous god" to love thy neighbors. We love Jesus and his messages.[165] It is beyond our comprehension to think that Jesus will send Mahatma Gandhi and your soon to be Hindu-daughter-in-law to hell on the Judgment Day.

Catholics and Hindus have many similarities. Like all Abrahamics, Hindus believe that there is one absolute Ultimate Reality. Catholics are polytheist and believe in three forms of God; Hindus believe in a few more forms of the same God. Like the marble statue of Mary and the wood cross are not idols, in the same way, Hindus' Gods are not idols. Catholics don't pray to two pieces of wood but see Jesus' sacrifice through the wooden cross. Likewise, Hindu Gods are not idols but a way to see the Ultimate Reality.

You want to blend both cultures, so ask your new Hindu relatives to put a Jesus' cross into the Hindu wedding rituals and they will be happy to accommodate you. Christ and Krishna will be happy to bless the newlywed. Later your Hindu daughter-in-law will be glad to visit your church and eat Jesus' body/bread while you reciprocate by visiting a Hindu temple and eating prasad. You can also have a Catholic wedding in your church for this couple, except that do not ask the Hindu to sign the one sided prenuptial child-rearing contract.[166] Further, teach your grandchildren that Jesus is dad's God and Goddess Lakshmi is mom's God. How beautiful!

The word "tolerant" can have a negative meaning and implies that you are willing to "put up" with her beliefs. Instead of being "tolerant," create true mutual respect for each other.

Regarding your grandchildren, Hindus believe that a child is born divine. It is one's karma that will determine the ultimate fate. If you want to show your genuine love for this new Hindu daughter-in-law, please do not ask for baptism of the children and let your son and daughter-in-law enjoy their Interfaith Marriage with EQUALITY.

---

[164] Section 3.12.
[165] Section 3.2.
[166] Section 3.4.

Now you have an opportunity to learn Jesus' real message of love for all. Show it in true spirit. Enjoy the Hindu Vivaha ceremony and a Hindu in your life. —Admin

Marie says:

I appreciate Admin's response because you answered some questions for me. I will have to look within, and to God for the answers I need. I see my future daughter in law as a precious gift, and I will continue to try to be a better human being. —Marie

---

I refused to let my child be baptized, because I felt I was not in a position to make a commitment for her.
—Bharti (Section 3.6)

Section 3.10: I Am a Hindu and My Ex-boyfriend a Christian

Neena says:

This is really a very crucial topic. I am a Hindu and my ex-boyfriend Christian. We were madly in love and wanted to get married but he said he could marry only if I am able to accept his Christian faith and before marriage I will have to be baptized. I loved him truly and so I studied about it a lot... prayed a lot... tried my level best and then said that I will marry and accept his faith but with consent of my parents as running and getting married is against my principles of life. So I spoke at my home and my parents also did not agree for simple reason that if he loves you truly then why he is asking you to change what you are as a person. He always asked me to talk to parents or go against and get married. I was confused so much what to do... as I loved him so much... however things didn't work out... My love was at stake for faith! And finally it didn't happen and now he is engaged to a Christian girl.

What is all this... I am so messed up now... what is above Love, I still can't figure out... why was it necessary to convert or accept any other faith and become Christian! Does God accept this that you fall in love and later don't agree to marry if the girl doesn't change religion!

This is just not justified. —Neena

> *I really don't believe that love is enough to sustain a marriage. Once frustration crops in, love will go out of the window.*
> *—Agnostic (Section 5.6)*

Section 3.11: Can I Convert Just for One Day to Get Married?

Hindus are used to many forms of God(s) and rituals. Sometimes they do not have a problem adding another God/ritual/religion to please their intended spouse and their parents. In the next two sections, unintended consequences of "fake-conversion" are covered.

Rohit says:

I have a Christian girlfriend and I am a Hindu. We want to get married but the problem is that her family is asking me to convert to baptism by taking a dip in holy water. I am fine with it but I want to know that once we get married we both will follow our own religion and the girl's family would not come to know about it. My question is that if I convert myself and from the next day I start following my own religion so that my God is happy and she will follow her own religion so that her God is also happy. Is it possible? I hope it's not a sin to get married to a person you can't live without and converting just for one day to get married? Please help! —Rohit

Admin says:

Dear Rohit,

"Conversion to Christianity for just one day" is an absolute sin. Christ and Krishna will never forgive you. You will be lying to and insulting Jesus, the church, the girl's parents, all your Hindu relatives, and most importantly, yourself. Unless other Christians tell us differently, baptism is not a hollow ritual devoid of meaning. Would you convert to Islam for one day if she were a Muslim? Does your self-esteem really allow you to do this? Why would you want to start your marriage journey in the wrong direction? Why would you make lies and deception the foundation of your marriage?

Instead of "Baptism for One Day" option above, we recommend one of three below:

1) Go to her church and learn more about Christianity. If you find out that Christianity is a better religion than Hinduism, yes, then convert and proudly announce it to all.

2) An alternative is to take the Christian girl to a Swamiji or guru or give her Holy Geeta and teach her about Hinduism. Maybe she will find Hinduism a better religion (like Julia Roberts) and maybe want to

convert. At least let her experience first hand the difficulty you are having, when asked to abandon your religion and choose another. Or...

3) Forget about this conversion business (#1 and 2 above). You remain 100% who you are and let her be 100% who she is. Go to a court and get married. Make sure you do exactly the same for your children too. Teach them about both faiths without any formal religious label on them. When children reach age 21, let them choose one of the two religions by their own free will.

Baptism may be a 10 minute ritual, but it may have major legal implications for you: A) Let's say in the event of your death following baptism, your parents want to give you the Hindu cremation final rites. Your wife wants you to have a Christian burial. In all likelihood, the court will approve the Christian burial because you are (were) legally a Christian. B) The church may ask you to sign a prenuptial agreement[167] for your children, meaning you are ending your Hindu heritage now. Is that your intention? C) Let's say after 10 years of marriage there is a divorce. In the custody battle for the children, the court may give a judgment in favor of the Christian spouse and may ban you from teaching them Hindu religion, because these children are Christians and both parents are (were) also Christians.

Rohit, you seem to be educated and intelligent and hope the Christian fiancé is the same. Make a decision today that will make you proud of yourself even when you reach 80 years old. We wish you the best. — Admin

---

Don't Drink & Drive advertisements are neither about not drinking nor about not driving. If you mix the two, it does not mean you will certainly have a car accident or automatically get a Driving Under the Influence (DUI) ticket. It is a matter of probability and making wise decisions.

Likewise, the mission at InterfaithShaadi is to impress new adults that inter-religious complexities are real, encourage them to talk about it "sooner than later" and help them make an "informed" decision for their interfaith relationship, whatever that decision is.

---

[167] Section 3.4.

Section 3.12: I Converted without the Knowledge of My Family

Fake-conversion just for marriage and without true faith could bring disastrous results later in life. Let's read Rima's experience.

Rima says:

My husband and I met during our bachelor degree college and we were best friends. He always told me he loves me more than his life. I talked to my parents that I want to marry him. My parents maturely reacted to me. They made me understand many times that this relationship won't work as he is Christian and don't trust whatever he says.

My husband used to talk big things about the richness of his family and his parents although it was totally lie. He used to make stories and I always believed him because when you are in love with someone you always believe him, moreover you lose the ability to differentiate truth because "love is blind."

We had lots of problem in getting married and my husband even told me once that he might get converted to Hinduism. He was ready to do anything for our marriage. My husband got US visa so he told me that he would go to US only if I marry him so I converted to Christianity. I married him without informing my family and he went to USA.

My elder sister had arranged marriage and married in the same caste. She had problem in her married life. My parents told me that they are totally opposed to allowing me to marry any Christian guy. My sister already had problem in her married life so if I would have problem in married life in future then they will be in lot of pain. Still I was not convinced by them.

My parents got to know that I got married and they didn't tell me anything. When my husband came back from USA, my parents had a little function and I moved to my husband's family.

Now my life changed from here…

I had lots of bad experiences every day. Let me describe some of them.

We had a dance party after our marriage function and at the end of the party my parents requested to me to tell DJ to play garba (Hindu folk dance). I did but my husband got angry that why they played garba. Her mom stood up and walked away as she hates garba. My husband is scared of her mom too much. IF HE LOVED ME MORE THAN HIS

LIFE THEN HOW COME HE DIDN'T TOLERATE GARBA FOR ME?

He took me every Sunday to church and we sat there for almost two hours. Even though I never went to temple and had puja for two hours but still for his love I did everything he said. Once on New Year I asked him to go to temple and he refused. He is scared that if his mom knows then she will feel bad. IF HE LOVED ME MORE THAN HIS LIFE THEN HOW COME HE SAID NO TO JUST SPEND 15 MINUTS IN TEMPLE?

We had Satya Narayan Katha at my mom's home. My mother-in-law told me that don't let his son sit in the puja as it is sin in their culture. We just went to puja for few minutes and my husband even didn't take prasad. I told him to eat it as normal food but he didn't take it as having prasad is sin in Christianity, he said. Before marriage whenever he came to my home and I offered prasad, he always took it. IF HE LOVED ME MORE THAN HIS LIFE THEN HOW COME HE DIDN'T EAT PRASAD, THOUGH ONE DAY HE HAD TOLD ME THAT HE WOULD GET CONVERTED TO HINDUISM?

There are lots of small things that I feel shy to write down. One year I lived with his family and almost each day I cried. He didn't allow me to either go to my friends or my parents' home. I have to go everywhere with him else I am not allowed to go. I never dare to take murti (idol) of Lord to his home. He liked me to wear Western clothes to show off that he is very global and free but his mind is sick.

During fight he told me that he hates Hindus. I asked him why did you marry Hindu girl then he said it's good to convert any Hindu girl into Christianity. During fight if I don't get convinced by him then he would start hitting himself and he even hit me twice. We were to immigrate to Canada so I was waiting for the day to go out of India and get divorce.

Today I'm in the West and whenever I talk to him for divorce, he fights with me and start hitting himself. He asked me to first kill him and then go. I don't want to be a reason for someone's suicide so I am still with him. I don't want kids because by default our kids will be Christian. According to him, its sin in Christianity to take divorce, on the other hand he can hit his wife.

Still my parents don't know anything about my bad life. I always pretend that I am very happy. I don't want to see them sad.

Indian Christians have created their own rules and created their own weird religion that they say is Christianity.

My life is so precious. I was very happy in my life but one sick Christian family has devastated it.

I don't know who is Admin of the site, but thanks for creating this site and giving awesome replies. —Rima

Admin says:

Hello Rima,

We are sorry to hear of your ordeal. Thank you for speaking out! We hope you have someone to help you in this difficult time.

It is not necessarily only religion or an interfaith marriage to be blamed here. Your husband's controlling behaviors extend beyond religion into all areas of your life. Youths do have to learn to look for the warning signs of religious fanaticism early on in their relationships.

Your husband clearly loves to proselytize and is a love-jihadi. He (and his family) had no interest in a "Hindu" wife. If you want to save your marriage and want them to start loving you dearly, you have to: 1) start believing that Hindus are idol-worshippers and that 2) all Muslims, Jews and Hindus—including Mahatma Gandhi—will go to the hell (on the Judgment Day) because they have not accepted that Jesus is the true savior.

If you want to understand the mindset of your husband, you have to read The Bible on Hindus?[168]

He hit you twice. This is against laws of most countries. Tell him not to touch you again otherwise you will report it to the local police who will arrest and deport him to India. Your citation on this web site about hitting you will serve as some proof of his prior behavior.

You have some hard choices to make, including A) truly converting to Christianity to please your husband and his family, B) continuing to endure the abusive and manipulative relationship you are in, in the hope that he will change or C) going through with at least a separation if you cannot initiate a divorce at this time. Let's examine each of these options.

A) To be happy after conversion to Christianity you have to truly believe in it. If you cannot accept giving up your own beliefs, culture and who you feel to be inside, this will not be an option for you. Your comments don't lead us to believe that this would be a comfortable

---

[168] Section 12.5.

choice for you but you are the one to make the decision after all you have been through.

B) Continuing in the relationship as it is, is not safe. He has hit you twice. He needs to work on his own anger and manipulative behavior and see the need to do so. Even if you think you want to work on changing his attitude (understand this will be difficult), you need to first have a back-up plan for abusive situations—a safe place to go until the situation diffuses and you can safely be in his presence again to continue salvaging your marriage. If he would be receptive to marriage counseling, pursue it. This may take a while for him to come around to agreeing to, if ever. Does the church you attend have counseling from the priest or pastor? He might be most receptive to that. Can you use Christian teachings from the New Testament on love and tolerance to remind him of more appropriate and yes, Christian values and behaviors? Can you enlist the support of other Christians you feel comfortable with and or Hindus in your community, for yourself? How much more can you take and how much energy are you willing to invest in saving this marriage?

C) A separation may be necessary which may or may not lead to a divorce. If you must, you leave. You cannot know whether his suicide threats are real and he should be working on his threatening and manipulative behavior if you are to have any chance in plan B above. In the long run, only he is responsible for his actions, not you. If you decide to leave, have a plan. Would you return to India to be with your family? Would you stay in the West? You did not mention whether you have a job and could be self supporting if need be. You might need to be quite removed from him to get any peace; if you do decide to leave—where might this safer, peaceful place be?

There is a lot to think about, with a lot of hard, painful decisions. You have the right to do what is best for you, what keeps you safe and what will provide you with a happier, more satisfying life.

Whatever you decide to do, be honest and tell your parents the facts today. Everyone makes mistakes. Your parents may truly love you and they may be waiting to help you. They may already suspect what is going on. We are guessing they would be happy to have their daughter back and that might even be the safe haven you need for a while to restore your life to some normalcy. You are young and have the rest of your life ahead of you—you want to make the most of that, without chronic pain and turmoil. Best wishes. —Admin

Rima says:

Dear Admin,

I appreciate your reply and your precious time for giving me such a good suggestion. This website is really good source of knowldge and you are doing good. Yes I am well educated (still became fool). I am a software engineer. Could you please tell me that how can I again get converted into Hinduism? Thanks. —Rima

Rima says (18 months later)**:**

Dear Admin,

Just wanted to inform you that I got divorced from my husband. —Rima

---

The author of this book asked a question to Gurumaa (July 3, 2009, New Jersey, USA):
"What are your views on unintended religious conversion for marriage?"

Gurumaa's reply on religious conversion practices for interfaith marriages is summarized in this Video:

One God One Love:
http://www.youtube.com/watch?v=skp09RhUfTY#aid=P6KG-TM4xNA

Section 3.13: Hindu Girl: I Did Not Agree to Baptize Our Children

Preeti says:

I am a born Hindu and my fiancé is a Catholic. We are planning to tie the knot in 2 years' time.

Our relationship grows stronger by appreciating differences of each other and we celebrate the differences together. However we are not in alignment when it comes to raising the kids. We decided and agreed to raise the kids in both faiths. I have a concern and didn't agree to baptize our children. What I understand on baptism is it simply means "You follow Jesus and he is the only God."

He explains that baptism is simply a ceremony for cleansing of mortal sin, it's a blessing and sign of purity. The baby will be blessed and guarded from Evil.

He is ok with my decision of not baptizing the children but not happy with that. I am worried and confused. Please advise. —Preeti

Admin says:

Dear Preeti,

You have raised a very vital question for any interfaith marriage—what will be the formal religion of children? You are on track by declining the baptism (no BBS); be firm with it.

You are not here to please him on a short run but to make a long lasting happy married life. Promise less but produce more.

This is an interfaith marriage and he should not get stuck on Christian dogma (and you on Hindu dogma). You two have to get married and make your own new religion with your own rules and new belief sets.

Do not sign the prenuptial agreement necessary for Catholic church wedding. If necessary, marry without the church.

Tell him that you will give birth to sin-free children (as per Hindu belief). It is the child's karma that will decide if he/she is a sinner. For this reason, you do not see any need to wash sins of a new born.

Tell him that even without baptizing your children, you will respect Christianity, celebrate all holidays, will go to his church, will display Jesus' cross in your home, teach children from the Bible (and Geeta) and will be a better Christian (without baptism) than many others. We are optimistic that he will agree to your reasoning and will appreciate your pluralistic (not exclusivist) thinking.

On his point of "The baby will be blessed and guarded from Evil," is this truth or superstition? Jews believe in circumcision of a male child and believe that one should not work on the Sabbath day. If not followed something negative will happen; again is this truth or superstition? Jesus changed that and accepted all uncircumcised gentiles and further told his followers that it is okay to do good karma even on the Sabbath day; is this not progressive thinking? If Jesus gave such wonderful messages, why are some churches today teaching that Mahatma Gandhi's karma is not important, but his baptism label is? For such reasons, we recommend following Jesus and not necessarily the church.[169] Adapt from Jesus' true teachings but decline baptism from the church.

With reference to superstition mentioned above, some Hindus believe in putting black ash on a child's forehead to guard from evil or in breaking a coconut in front of a new car as blessings from God, while others may see these practices as nothing but superstition. Agree that this is an interfaith marriage and both parties have to give up superstitious beliefs. It is not the 10 minutes ritual of baptism that is of concern, but the thought process behind asking for it. The BBS will set a tone for your newly married life.

Everyone can talk of equality and tolerance, but those are not measurable qualities. If you wish to find out the true tolerant nature of his family, decline the BBS. All of a sudden, reality will come out. We recommend NO BBS as a sort of insurance from a religious fanatic, just to make sure. Best wishes. —Admin

---

[169] Section 3.2.

Section 3.14: A Church Prenuptial Is a Must

Interfaith couples should not underestimate the powers of religious institutions. They could change your life in many ways, including after death.

Maya says:

I am a Hindu girl in love with a Christian. We are both very liberal in our religious faith, so are my parents. However, his parents are ardent practitioners of Christianity.

Although, they have not forced me to convert, they insist on us getting married in the church only and to have Hindu ceremonies in secrecy which is upsetting me and my parents.

I have spoken with the church representatives, and have been informed that though there is no need for me to be baptized, however I would have to sign a pre-nup that our children would be raised in Christian faith.

I have been informed by my boyfriend and the church that if I do not follow up a Christian wedding after our civil marriage (by Special Marriage Act) and do not sign the pre-nup, his parents would be punished by the church and that their rights would be stopped like holy communion and after death burial rights.

I feel pressurized by these circumstances and do not understand what to do? Please guide. —Maya

Admin says:

Maya,

Now you are at a right place for guidance. You will not find similar guidance in any other place. Your's is a typical story for us and that is why we have made this web site. We are working hard to make this world a better place to live for all. Just hang in there with us. Educate yourself here.

We believe in Jesus but not the church, we believe in Allah but not in all of Mohammad's teachings, we believe in LORD God but do not see why a Hindu considering marriage with a Jew has to have bar mitzvah for the interfaith children to announce them Jews. This BBS is a social sin created by religious institutions for their survival, nothing more.

The issue— "his parents would be punished by the church and that their rights would be stopped like Holy Communion and after death burial rights" —is their issue. You have nothing to do with it. Their religious institution is very rigid and controlling. Ask them if they would consider attending other churches in the area they might be comfortable worshipping in.

Maya, we have seen repeatedly on this site that intended spouses claim they are ignorant of their family's dogmatic, even fanatical approach to their religious expectations, even after having lived with those parents and in that community for most of their lives. You have a right to be clear and to stand up firmly in your own beliefs while exploring these issues fully with your fiancé. His parents have their own issues to work out with their church; that is not your fault or responsibility. Your intended husband must decide where he stands, with his family or with you and how he is going to navigate any rift that occurs. Whatever you agree to will set the tone for the rest of your marriage and you want that to be satisfying to both you and your husband. This understanding must come before the marriage, not after, if you want to avoid any future conflict.

Hypothetically, let's assume you loved a rich, handsome and highly educated Hindu man from your community and he asks you for Rupees one lakh dowry as a part of marriage condition just to please his parents. What would you do? Even your parents may pressure you to agree to give this small fund, but will you not be alarmed by the *junwani* (old timer) thinking and terminate this marriage agreement? If you would terminate the engagement in this hypothetical case, why would you agree to give away your some 1000 generations of Hindu heritage and pride as dowry just to please his parents and their church in your current situation?

Tell him that this will be your life: First, you will get married once, in the same location and time, under Jesus and Krishna's photos, by both Hindu and Christian ceremonies, and in the presence of all relatives from both sides. Both the Bible and Geeta will be sitting side by side in your home and children will learn from both. When your children reach age of 21 years, they will declare their own faith, whatever that is. Maya, tell us what is wrong with this? Is this not beautiful?

Read all we have written and come back to us with more questions. Best wishes. —Admin

Maya added:

Dear Admin,

Thank you for giving me confidence to do the right thing. Both of us have this beautiful vision of living a full life without any hindrance from religious fanaticism. However, it seems the religious institutions are holding our parents at ransom here and indirectly black mailing us into falling in line with their ideologies. If I do it now, I fear I would always fall prey to it. I am waiting for my boyfriend to clear things with his church and parents, and if needed take a stand, which would make things clear for me in more than one way.

In any case, I would not take a decision out of guilt or pressure. Regards. —Maya

---

Real life is not clearly black or white, however you will have to make a clearly black or white decision for your planned interfaith married life when it comes to announcing a formal religion of your children. If not sure of it, do not commit to a formal religion for children now.

Section 3.15: It Is a Love Marriage Where We Do Everything except Love

This story is a sad example of what can happen when you have "not done your homework" early in the love relationship phase. It is much easier to get out of an incompatible relationship before marriage, than it is after years, especially after children.

Sushma says:

I am an Arya Samaji Hindu female married to a Roman Catholic male. There was a lot of difference between our backgrounds but I adjusted. After my marriage I have lost myself forever.

I had a daughter and I got busy with her. He has possessive nature and I did not know how to handle our relationship. I got sucked into it. To him I was responsible for everything bad that happened to him. He is 9 years older to me.

Somewhere I have always gone wrong in this relationship. It is a love marriage where we do everything except love.

I am against divorce. I feel guilty that I went against everybody to marry so I cannot subject them (my parents) to my pain. I got thyroid after I had my daughter but he was not very understanding. In temper, he has pulled my hair when he knows I am having hair fall problem. My parents did not interfere. When we fight we want to kill each other.

The day my daughter leaves for college education I won't know what to do with myself or him. I am no more an easy person to live with. In India it's very difficult to walk out of a relationship suddenly.

Over the years I have been living with him because he says I am selfish. I don't like anybody in his family, all they want me to change (to Christianity) including him. I had married him in a hurry. I am stuck for life, still I am doing all my duties as a wife.

My daughter is a Catholic. I and only I am responsible for this mess. My life is spoiled. He is forever judging me in everything. I wish I could just disappear into nowhere from this situation. I always thought, in this religion crazy world, my child would be like a symbol of world peace but I was wrong.

Either I am crazy or I am losing it. My coping skills are zero. I have no confidence left in me, even duffers around me are doing better than me in real world. I am a failure. —Sushma

Section 3.16: I Am Not My Wife's Husband!

Ron says:

Anyone contemplating marriage to a member of an Abrahamic faith is fooling himself or herself if they believe there will not be difficulty. It is a game of "High Stakes Poker." You cannot see which cards are in the hands of in-laws, neighbors, acquaintances, church members etc. Certainly, you cannot see the future and the circumstances that may appear. Eventually, you may find yourself opposed by your spouse with the encouragement of allies within their church. Don't be surprised when your marriage is stressed beyond all prior limitations. After children manifest, the "Stakes" will grow exponentially as others scheme behind your back to get your children into church, Sunday school and Bible camp.

Welcome to my world. My wife and I were married in a civil ceremony in the judge's chambers at a local courthouse. We agreed to not push our beliefs on each other. Eventually, these things changed. We had children. Neighbors, who initially accepted my family, now only speak with my wife. She is a member of their church. My children and I are treated as "Heathens." A church official once told me that I was not recognized as my wife's husband because I was not a church member and as such could not be her spouse. Neighbors have asked our children: "Why don't you go to church?" One man came into our yard when he saw my 10-year-old son alone. This man was upset that my son was not attending church. To my son's credit, he told the man to mind his own business. After years of being pressured to conform to the likes of them, we now ignore their existence as much as they ignore ours. —Ron

Section 3.17: I'm Hindu and She Is Protestant Christian

Hari says:

Hi Admin,

I'm a Hindu guy, and my girlfriend is Protestant Christian.

After 5 years of relationship we've decided to get married, and now issues have started. Her cousin is forcing her to get me converted... what the heck? I am from a typical Hindu family, once I told my dad that I am in love with a Protestant girl and my dad was fine with it. He asked me get my girlfriend to try to adopt the (Hindu) culture during festival times.

Then the issue became serious again. She said being a Protestant she won't be able to adapt to our culture. She told she is brought up not believing praying to statues. Problems kept occurring ever since we started talking about marriage. Please advise me on this. —Hari

Admin says:

Dear Hari,

You are a good citizen of this world. We need to make sure we all live with peace and harmony. Unfortunately, these religious leaders want us to keep fighting among us so they could survive.

The Bible's Second of the Ten Commandments teaches them not to tolerate people from other faiths. Christians (mainly Catholics) have killed millions during their crusades; more than collectively killed by Muslims. Today for an interfaith marriage, a Protestant will not tolerate a Catholic, who will not tolerate a Mormon, who will not tolerate a Muslim, who will not tolerate a Jew, and all these will not (are not supposed to) tolerate idol-worshipper Hindus. So, when will this intolerance end?

Your girlfriend said, "being a Protestant she won't be able to adapt to our culture." While your girlfriend may not adopt your culture for herself, this will be a very difficult and unhappy marriage if she does not allow you to express your beliefs and worship in your own manner, and if you are continuously pressured from her family and church to convert. Is this how you want to live?

Are we saying you should not marry her? Yes and No. You should not marry her if she now believes she cannot tolerate Hindus. On the other hand, YES, marry her if you could educate her before your marriage, that *"Ishvara Allah tero nam."* There is only One God, you may call Her or

Him LORD God, God the Father, Allah or Ishvara. Ask her to forget the church and follow Jesus. Ask her to read all that we have written on God. It is your duty to clarify your stance, help her "see the light" of at least respecting your religion and then, depending on the outcome, make a responsible decision on whether to go forward with this marriage.

You said, "her cousin's forcing her to get me converted." Tell them that you are a Hindu and will remain a Hindu. Make it clear to your girlfriend that, especially for children, NO BBS. A signed agreement, notarized, might be a good idea or even a more detailed prenuptial contract to ward off future conflict.

You said, "my dad was fine with it, and he asked me to get my girlfriend to try to adapt to the Hindu culture during festival times." We bow to your parents. They are so noble and why would you go against them? Tell your girlfriend that you will take your children for Easter parade, have big party for Christmas (and Diwali), will take them to a Mandir on Saturdays and to a church on Sundays, but will not allow the label of baptism to be put on your children. Your children will not be born sinners because you are pure and hence there is no need to wash their sins by baptism. Your interfaith children should decide their own faith when they are 21 year old, whatever that faith is.

You said, "After 5 years of relationship we've decided to get married, and now the issues have started." This is common to many interfaith couples. Hindus go along assuming the Christian/Muslim/Jew is a pluralist but, in many cases, suddenly before marriage the Hindu finds out the requirement of the BBS. This BBS has given much pain to interfaith couples. We believe this BBS is a social-sin for interfaith couples and must go.

Educate her. Free her from the clutches of her church. Untill she has learned the lesson of pluralism, don't think of marrying her. Best wishes.
—Admin

Chapter IV: Jewish-Hindu Marriages

Couples in Jewish-Hindu relationship are requested to first read/view:
- Section 2.3: FAQ on Interfaith Marriages
- Section 2.8: Ten Points of Dating a Hindu
- Section 2.9: Hindu, Abrahamics and Intolerants
- Section 12.2: What Geeta Says for Abrahamics?
- Section 12.3: The Torah on Hindus?
- Section 12.4: Bar Mitzvah for Hindus?
- Watch this video prepared by InterfaithShaadi:
  https://www.youtube.com/watch?v=hlAuY85RlcE.

Section 4.1: Jewish-Hindu Marriages

Jews and Hindus do not proselytize and there is no historic conflict between them. In this regard, a Jew-Hindu marriage may have less religious conflicts compared to a union with a Christian or a Muslim. There are many Jew-Hindu weddings that are performed in the same marriage hall. A Hindu priest performs the routine Hindu ceremony and a Rabbi performs the Jewish wedding. Both participants wear wedding costumes to match the wedding being performed at the time. However, the major issue will come after childbirth when it is a time to circumcise the baby boy, name the child and declare the faith of child.

In some cases, Jews are permitted[170] to marry any adherent of a monotheistic religion (like Christianity and Islam), as long as any children of the marriage are brought up as Jewish. Modern Conservative Judaism does not sanction intermarriage but encourages acceptance of the non-Jewish spouse within the family and hopes that such acceptance will lead to the spouse's conversion to Judaism. Some rabbis from the denominations of modern Judaism (Reform, Reconstructionist, and Renewal), are generally willing to officiate at interfaith marriages; they do, however, still try to persuade interfaith married couples to raise their children as Jews. Unfortunately, many Jewish partners find that these issues or concerns are not present for them while dating, yet parental or personal hopes for Jewish children often arise later in the relationship with a Hindu or other non-Jewish partner.

In the USA between 2005 and 2013, more than half (58%) of marriages involving Jews were intermarriages with non-Jewish partners.[171] The possibility that this might lead to the gradual dying out of Judaism is regarded by most Jewish leaders as precipitating a crisis; some religious conservatives now even speak metaphorically of intermarriage as a silent holocaust.

Most Jewish leaders challenge the notion of raising a child in more than one tradition. This is the most critical question a Dharmic (Sikh, Jain, Hindu or Buddhist) considering relationship with a Jew should ask: are Coming of Age bris/bar mitzvah/bat mitzvah ceremonies of children expected to declare them Jews?

---

[170] Many Jewish leaders still say it is not permissible to marry someone outside of Judaism, and many who say they will perform such weddings often see the choice as less desired.

[171] http://www.pewforum.org/2013/10/01/jewish-american-beliefs-attitudes-culture-survey/.

"This is my covenant, which you shall keep, between me and you and your descendants after you: every male among you shall be circumcised," God commands Abraham (Genesis 17:11), the Jewish patriarch. "Any uncircumcised male who is not circumcised in the flesh of his foreskin shall be cut off from his people; he has broken my covenant." Some traditional Jews believe that if a baby is not circumcised by bris ceremony, something negative would happen to the boy. Some Jewish leaders believe that if a baby boy is not circumcised, the child will not feel a part of the Jewish community and some may not accept him as such.

Earlier the author has discussed if circumcision is science or superstition.[172] Probably it is not the scientific merit, but the religious belief that plays a major role in the decision to cut or not to cut.

Both Jews and Hindus believe that there is only one Ultimate Supreme Reality. However unlike Hindus, Jews are forbidden to express the same God in different forms. The fact that many Gods and Goddesses are worshipped by Hindus is erroneously considered to be polytheistic idol worship by many who do not understand the true nature of Hindu Dharma.

If a Dharmic is considering a lifelong relationship with a Jew, it would be wise to know what kind of interpretations of scriptures[173] your intended spouse has learned during his/her lifetime and believes in. First, ask what does "God" mean to him or her? Is the LORD your God who talked to Abraham, Israel and Moses also the same one who later gave messages through Jesus and talked to Mohammad? Are Hindu Goddess Lakshmi and Lord Krishna incarnations of the same LORD God of Israel? During a Hindu wedding ceremony, the Hindu priest will invoke many Gods from heaven and earth. Jewish men or women planning a marriage to Dharmics must consider: are they willing to take part in such a wedding and will they be comfortable entering Hindu, Jain, Sikh or Buddhist temples, taking prasad (offerings from God) or being part of other Hindu rituals.

Initial impressions of "tolerance" and "open-mindedness" are not concrete and easily shift under pressure. Decisions must be made based on measurable promises.

For many issues listed on the next page, there is only one possible way. If an explanation is given that it is a matter of faith, an interfaith couple

---

[172] Section 2.13.
[173] Chapter XII.

will have to decide whose faith will rule the married life. If a Hindu youth really wants to learn the truth about the intended Jewish spouse, decline the bris circumcision and bar/bat mitzvah for a child and watch the reactions.

It is hoped that today's youths considering interfaith relationships understand that some of the religious commandments are not to be taken literally. Every human being is God's "chosen" person. One should be free to express their belief in God in any form and way one desires. Pluralism is the only way for couples considering interfaith marriage with equality.

FAQ: Jew-Dharmic Marriage

➢ Do you have to sign a Ketubah prenuptial and endorse the Second of the Ten Commandments?

➢ Do your sons have to have religious bris circumcision, an irriversible procedure done without the child's consent and without compelling scientific merit?

➢ Do your children have to have bar- or bat mitzvah label on the children to announce them as Jewish adults?

➢ A name is significant as it reflects the tradition and culture the parents are proud of and would like the child to follow. Are your children going to have Dharmic or Jewish first names?

➢ Do you have to live within a driving distance from a synagogue so your children can attend a Jewish day care and your family can have the benefit of Jewish education? Are you planning to celebrate all Jewish holidays? Are you planning to spend equal time and efforts to celebrate Hindu festivals and visit temples too?

➢ Lisa Miller of Newsweek (July 8, 2010) has stated the cost of being a Jewish could be high (in certain conditions it is estimated to be up to $110,000 per year). Are you planning to spend the same sum of money for Jewish and Hindu causes?

➢ In case of a child's death in your family will he/she get a Jewish burial or the Hindu cremation final rites?

Section 4.2: Ketubah: Jewish Marriage Contract

A ketubah (meaning written thing) is a Jewish prenuptial agreement. It is considered an integral part of a traditional Jewish marriage, and outlines the rights and responsibilities of the groom, in relation to the bride.

The following provides flavor for a traditional Orthodox ketubah. Most Jewish couples today however are signing a new ketubah that speaks directly about their love and commitment. Please review cited references[174] for detailed information.

ORTHODOX KETUBAH
On the ___ day... join each other in ___, before family and friends to make a mutual covenant as husband and wife, partners in marriage.
The groom, ___, promises ___, the bride: "Be my wife according to the practice of Moses and Israel. I shall cherish you and honor you as is customary among the sons of Israel who have cherished and honored their wives in faithfulness and in integrity." And I here present you with the marriage gift..., according to the law of Moses and Israel; and I will also give you your food, clothing and necessities, and live with you as husband and wife...

The bride, ___, promises ___, the groom: "You are my husband according to the tradition of Moses and Israel. I shall cherish you and honor you as is customary among the daughters of Israel who have cherished and honored their husbands in faithfulness and in integrity."

"We, as beloveds and friends, promise each other to strive throughout our lives together to achieve an openness which will enable us to share our thoughts, our feelings, and our experiences... All is valid and binding.

—Signatures

INTERFAITH KETUBAH
Interfaith ketubot serves the same purpose expressing love and commitment of the bride and groom, and it can be written without

---

[174] Information in this Section is based on:
Wikipedia: Ketubah.
Celebrating Interfaith Marriage by Rabbi Devon A. Lerner, An Owl Book, 1999.
The Everything Jewish Wedding Book by Helen Latner, 1998.
http://www.interfaithfamily.com/life_cycle/weddings/Choosing_an_Interfaith_Ketubah.shtml.
https://www.mpartworks.com/orthodox-ketubah-text.htm.

mentioning any specific religion and if desired even without mentioning the word "God."

On the ___ day of... between the groom, ___, and the bride, ___.

The groom... says to the bride: "I will honor each other's culture as we link customs to form a trusting relationship. I shall treasure you, nourish you, and respect you as those who have devoted themselves to their wives with love and integrity throughout the generations."

The bride... says to the groom: "I will honor each other's culture as we link customs to form a trusting relationship. I shall treasure you, nourish you, and respect you as those who have devoted themselves to their husbands with love and integrity throughout the generations."

And... pledged together: "We promise to be ever accepting of one another while treasuring each other's individuality; to comfort and support each other through life's disappointments and sorrows; to revel and share in each other's joys and accomplishments; to share our hopes and dreams; to strive for an intimacy that will allow us to accomplish this promise and permit us to become the persons we are yet to be. We vow to establish a home open to all of life's potential; a home filled with respect for all people; a home based on love and understanding. May we live each day as the first, the last, the only day we will have with each other. All of this we take upon ourselves as valid and binding."

—Signatures

Section 4.3: Parents Are Usually Left with No Options

Mahesh says:

Hindu-Jew Marriage situation: I found this Forum very interesting. In my opinion, observation or experience, we as parents, are usually left with no options, but to yield or concede to our children's choices. I feel as a parent, in such situations of Inter-Faith Marriages, the children are looking at today, aware of but not concerned about tomorrow, for example children after marriage. One faith or the parents, grand parents override the decisions, made by the children before the marriage. That's where the conflict begins and henceforth a very high percentage divorce rate. Knowing the figures and facts before will bring more happiness and prosperity later. —Mahesh

There cannot be friendship without equality.
—Swami Vivekananda

Chapter V: Muslim-Hindu Marriages

Couples in Muslim-Hindu relationship are requested to first read/view:
- Section 2.3: FAQ on Interfaith Marriages
- Section 2.8: Ten Points of Dating a Hindu
- Section 2.15: Interfaith Marriage and Divorce Laws
- Section 12.6: The Koran on Hindus?
- Watch these videos prepared by InterfaithShaadi:
  https://www.youtube.com/watch?v=gvZSqdmnxKM
  https://www.youtube.com/watch?v=RiWLGEKusIg

Section 5.1: Hindu-Muslim Marriages

Interfaith marriage is one of the most fundamental sinful actions in Islam after shirk, rebellion against parental authority and killing a person without any legal reason.[175] However, according to our research, 45% of Muslims marry outside their faith in America.[176] It is a common practice for this "interfaith" marriage problem to be solved by conversion of the non-Muslim fiancé(e) to Islam.

The Koran states "You shall not marry Mushrik women (idolatresses or who ascribe God's attributes to other than Allah) unless they embrace the Faith. A believing slave woman is better than a Mushrik woman although she may please you."[177,178]

Hinduism views marriage as a sacred union but Islamic nikaah (marriage) is a contract to obey Allah. A non-Muslim is expected to take shahadah oaths before the nikaah. Shahadah is the declaration that there is no god but Allah and Prophet Mohammad is the messenger of Allah. Associating partners (like Lord Shiva) with Allah, including worship of idols (murtis), offering prayers or supplications to anyone, living or dead, is the greatest of all sins. No imam will perform nikaah wedding without the shahadah religious conversion. A Hindu wedding is not a valid marriage as per Islamic laws. The union of a man and a woman without a valid nikaah is considered adultery punishable by stoning to death.[179] In short, for a Hindu, conversion to Islam before nikaah is a must.

Shahadah is an oath required to be taken by a non-Muslim to irreversibly convert to Islam. Muslim Caliphates invited all Muslim civilians to be involved in defending the Islamic state from attack by non-Muslims. Religious conversion from Islam was therefore conceptualized as a vital criminal violation that might be punishable by death[180] because a former Muslim would endanger the existence of all Muslims by allying with an enemy of Islam.[181]

---

[175] http://www.academia.edu/6606072/Inter-Religious_Marriage_from_Socio-Historical_Islamic_Perspectives.
[176] Section 2.5.
[177] Koran 2:221.
[178] Also read "The Koran on Hindus?" (Section 12.6).
[179] Bukhari 6:60:79 on adultory. (Bukhari was one of the compilers of Hadith.)
[180] Mohammad said, "Whoever changes his Islamic religion, then kill him." (Bukhari 9:84:57).
[181] http://www.academia.edu/6606072/Inter-Religious_Marriage_from_Socio-Historical_Islamic_Perspectives.

117

According to anecdotal evidence and our experience dealing with many youths in love relationships, most Hindu-Muslim marriages are performed by nikaah only and in a few cases by civil secular wedding. Nikaah is performed after conversion of the Hindu fiancé(e) to Islam and in the presence of a very few relatives from the former Hindu spouse's family. In a few cases, the Hindu marriage is also performed after the Islamic nikaah. However, after conversion, this Hindu marriage is a totally superfluous, because it is a Muslim-Muslim wedding performed by a Hindu priest in the presence of all Hindu Gods! Generally, Muslim relatives will not attend a Hindu ceremony because Gods other than Allah are being worshiped. At least as of now, there is no fusion of Hindu-Muslim marriage rituals.

A marriage is not just the union of two individuals but, believe it or not, a union of two families and two communities. Historically, Islam and Hinduism have been at odds for more than 1300 years in India. Much of this history records the Muslim invasions of India, repeated destruction of Hindu temples (e.g. Somanath in Gujarat), imposition of Jizya tax on Hindus and forced conversions to Islam. This history will inevitably have some impact on an interfaith couple's life. Hindu-Muslim interfaith marriage with equality is only possible if both spouses and their extended families are willing to share two religious beliefs and follow each other's practices without coercing each other.

Islam has very strict requirements for marriage. The requirements are stricter for a Dharmic (Sikh, Buddhist, Jain or Hindu) rather than for a Christian or Jew (People of the Book; Abrahamic). In most cases, a Dharmic in a relationship with a Muslim will learn some of these expectations just before the wedding. After years of being in a romantic relationship, reluctantly accepting the religious conversion may be the only way of averting a marital breakup.

If a proud Hindu wishes to avoid the religious conversion, choosing not to have the Islamic nikaah is the only option. However, issues will come up while raising children in two faiths. It is easy for young children to get confused with conflicting messages. For example, when they visit a Hindu or Jain temple, they are asked to believe in, respect and bow to several forms of God. But when they visit a mosque, they hear just the opposite messages. When confronted with such conflicting ideas, children may lose faith in God or religion. It is possible that later the Hindu spouse may be forbidden to practice his/her Dharmic religion so that the children will not be able to learn and follow it. Also, the Muslim spouse or his/her family may not like to be part of a Hindu religious activity while at Hindu parents' home. When the honeymoon stage ends and is transformed into a routine married life, these issues will become sore points in the married life.

Hindus do not proselytize and there is no requirement for a non-Hindu to convert to Hindu Dharma before getting married. In most cases, the Muslim may try to convince the Hindu intended spouse to convert to Islam (by shahadah) just because that is a requirement in Islam. The Muslim does not have to reciprocate however because that is not a requirement in Hinduism. Actually, formal religious conversion to Hinduism can be done and the Muslims should be given that option to be fair and allow both spouses to demonstrate interfaith relationships with equality!

Interfaith relationships should be based on mutual respect for both faiths, and marriage should be solemnized without imposing religious conversion on a spouse. After marriage, both spouse's faiths should get equal respect and consideration in home life and raising children. Eventually children will find their own solutions to the irreconcilable differences between the two religions.

(For additional information on Hindu-Muslim marriages, watch these videos[182] prepared by InterfaithShaadi.)

---

[182] https://www.youtube.com/watch?v=gvZSqdmnxKM and https://www.youtube.com/watch?v=RiWLGEKusIg.

FAQ for Hindu-Muslim Marriages

➢ Do I have to convert to Islam by taking a shahadah oath before Islamic nikaah?

➢ Do I (male) have to undergo Sunat (circumcision) before the nikaah?

➢ Do I have to adopt a Muslim name?

➢ Can we also have a Hindu marriage ceremony?

➢ After marriage, can I wear Hindu symbols, such as a Bindi (head dot)?

➢ Do I have to ever put on a veil?

➢ Can our children have non-Arabic names?

➢ Must our male children undergo religious circumcision (Sunat/Khatna)?

➢ Do we have to raise children in the Islamic faith only?

➢ Can I worship Hindu Gods at home and have a murti of Lord Ganesh in our living room?

➢ As per Pillars of Islam, do we have to give charity to Muslim causes up to 2.5% of our total assets every year? Can I also donate the same amount to Hindu causes every year?

➢ Are your parents aware of what you are promising me today? Can we discuss these issues with them face-to-face to get their acceptance and approval?

Section 5.2: Nikaah: The Muslim Marriage Contract

Islamic Law permits a Muslim man to marry up to four (non-Muslim) women[183] from the People of the Book (that is, Christians and Jews) but all of the children must be brought up as Muslims.[184] However, there cannot be an Islamic nikaah wedding between a Muslim and a Hindu (Sikh, Jain or Buddhist). For this reason, a Hindu will be asked to take shahadah oath. It takes merely 2 minutes for conversion to Islam. After that, the Muslim bride and Muslim groom can have the nikaah wedding.

Shahadah:

Shahadah[185] is the declaration that there is no god but Allah and Prophet Mohammad is the messenger of Allah (*La-ilaha-iLLaLLah-Mohammadur-Rasulullah*). Worship Allah and join no partner with Him. Associating partners with Allah is called Shirk. Shirk is not only the worship of idols, but also offering prayers or supplications to anyone, living or dead. Shirk is the greatest of all sins.

Nikaah Marriage Certificate:

Nikaah is a contract and not a sacred union. It can be terminated by the husband engaging in the *Talaq*[186] process or the wife seeking a *Khula.*[187] The marriage Nikaah-nama certificate is simple. It will have name, address and birth dates of bride and groom. The amount of dower (dowry) will be spelled in the contract. It will also include information if there is any delegation of power of divorce. If the bridegroom has any additional wives, it has to be spelled out here.

Considering this is a within-faith Islamic marriage, custody of a Muslim child will be difficult after divorce for the former Hindu spouse if he/she now wishes to raise the child in the Hindu faith.

---

[183] Koran 4:3.
[184] http://en.wikipedia.org/wiki/Interfaith_marriage_in_Islam.
[185] http://www.albalagh.net/kids/understanding_deen/Shahadah.shtml.
[186] http://en.wikipedia.org/wiki/Divorce_(Islamic).
[187] http://en.wikipedia.org/wiki/Khula.

Section 5.3: Islamic Perspective: Six Points of Hindu-Muslim Dating

Mac contributes at InterfaithShaadi.org as an Islamic expert. His mother is a former Brahmin-Hindu and he himself, at one point, was in an interfaith love relationship with a Brahmin-Hindu girl in his college. Here he conveys that Hindu-Muslim marriage with equality is not possible.

Mac says:

This message is for those Muslim and non-Muslim youths considering marriage. Since this website (InerfaithShaadi) promotes interfaith marriage with equality, so a Muslim girl or boy must know that in the name of equality, he or she might be out of Islam and become unofficially an apostate. In such marriages, couples from both sides are needed to make some compromises. If the compromise takes one completely out of Islam, then where is the equality in marriage?

1. Food habit: Muslims are generally non-vegetarian. It is because Islam tells Muslims that Allah has made both plants and animals for benefit of humans and the animals that are eatable, can be eaten. Now if anyone doesn`t like to eat meat, it's okay, it doesn't make him/her non-Muslim. One can be perfectly Muslim if he/she is vegetarian. But if he or she is forced to leave non-vegetarian food because of the other belief that animals are holy or sacred, then there is a problem. Allah has already told that except Him, no one is holy. So if you leave eating non-vegetarian for dogmatic belief of another religion, then certainly you are going against Islamic principles.

2. Wedding: A Muslim's marriage is only legal in front of Allah and only if it undergoes through the technical "nikaah." Involvement in other marriage ceremonies like Hindu rituals or Christian rituals (where oaths are taken in the name of other gods like Jesus or Krishna) is not allowed in Islam and considered as shirk. Shirk is the biggest sin in Islam. Any relationship without Islamic nikaah is considered as zina (fornication). Do you want to fornicate throughout your whole life in the eyes of Allah?

3. Circumcision: Circumcision is a religious requirement for Muslims as well as Jews. Jews circumcise on the 8th day of life whereas Muslims are free to circumcise at any age, but it is preferred at the 7th day of life because Mohammad circumcised his two grandsons al-Hasan and al-Hussein on 7th day of the birth.

4. Alcoholic beverages: It is sin for a Muslim to drink or serve wine or alcohol. So if any Muslim girl is married to a non-Muslim husband and her husband is a drinker, then he may ask her to serve alcohol. Even if she doesn't forbid him from drinking, there will be sin upon her.

5. Statue (murti) Worship: Worship of any form of statues, murtis, and pictures is sin in Islam and there is no pardon for that. It is the highest form of sin in Islam. Allah can forgive everything except shirk. So when your non-Muslim husband/wife is doing shirk in front of Ram or Krishna, it is the obligation of a Muslim spouse to stop him/her from doing this, else you will be part of shirk. Now if you stop them from doing puja to their pictures or statue of god, then there will be no equality.

6. Funeral: Is your body going to be cremated or be buried as per laws of Allah? According to Islam, no human being has the right to burn another human being whether alive or dead. Allah made Satan from fire; Allah doesn't want that fire to touch your body.

In reality, interfaith marriage with a Hindu is not possible for a Muslim partner. Either the Hindu has to convert to Islam or the Muslim partner has to compromise, that technically (as per Koran), takes him/her out of Islam. —Mac

---

For me, baptizing the child who doesn't even know what is happening is giving a label to the child. Religious labels are like names. They stick with one throughout life.
As one loves one's name and completely identifies with it, so does one accept religion? This makes our growth limited and we are unable to expand beyond the prevailing mind-set of the religion of our birth.
A wall of division always exists and it is difficult to break.
—Kalpesh Gajiwala
http://www.patheos.com/Resources/Additional-Resources/Bindis-and-Baptism.html

Section 5.4: I Salute a Muslim

Following is based on a letter By Seema (Ghufran) Maheshwari titled "Loyalty and the Indian Muslims" that appeared in INDIA ABROAD on November 27, 2009.

Seema believes that Major Nidal Hasan's[188] murderous rampage at Fort Hood, Texas, was due to his divided loyalties between being an American soldier and a Muslim. Major Nidal Hasan felt that the two positions were mutually exclusive. Same dilemma is faced by Indian Muslims, some of whom consider themselves Indians first. On the other side of the divide are homegrown Muslim terrorists who speak for themselves.

Seema's father's family faced the loyalty dilemma in 1947. Her father, Brigadier Mohammed Ghufran, and her elder uncle, Brigadier Mohammed Usman, were in the Indian Army during Partition.

The newly formed Pakistani government wanted Brigadier Usman to move to Pakistan to become the chief of Pakistan's army. Her uncle refused as her family considered themselves Indians first. He now had to fight his friends and fellow Muslims and a prize of Rs. 50,000 was put on his head. He was killed on July 3, 1948, while leading a battle in Naushera and is now known as Naushera Ka Sher (the tiger of Naushera) by many.

Even though her father and the rest of the family were devastated by Brigadier Usman's death, no one ever questioned his decision. The pride and loyalty instilled in Seema as a child, for being Indian, with roots which can be traced back hundreds of years, are as strong now as they were 38 years ago when she migrated to USA.

If her family had made the decision to move to Pakistan 62 years ago, she would not have written the letter to *INDIA ABROAD* about Indian pride and certainly would not be having the married surname of Maheshwari.

[Seema's Muslim family had made immense contributions to India's Independence and to Bollywood. Some of her relatives include Khwaja Gulam Abbas, who gave up his life in Panipat during 1857 independence movement, film director Padma Shri K. A. Abbas, Mahavir Chakra awardee Brigadier Mohammad Osman, father Brigadier Mohammed Ghufran, Neelima Azeem, and Shahid Kapoor]

---

[188] https://en.wikipedia.org/wiki/Nidal_Malik_Hasan.

Reply by author (Dilip Amin)

As appeared in INDIA ABROAD, December 4, 2009.

Salute, Seema

I am really moved by a letter about loyalty and the Indian Muslim (November 27) from a proud Indian Muslim, Seema Maheshwari.

The sacrifice by her family for India should be well recognized. She has wonderfully articulated some of the issues, saying, some Muslims consider themselves Indians first, whereas homegrown Muslim terrorists speak for themselves. She also pointed out that if her family had migrated to Pakistan, she would not bear the married surname of Maheshwari.

Now we, Muslims and Hindus, having moved to America, are facing a different challenge, this time not due to communal divisions but due to interfaith marriages within our next generation. Our research shows that 38 percent of Hindus and 45 percent of Muslims marry outside their faiths, and these include many Hindu-Muslim marriages. It remains to be seen how loyalties to their religion and to their spouses are sorted out. Are these loyalties mutually exclusive?

Taking Seema Maheshwari as a role model, rather than Major Nidal Hasan, I hope interfaith couples and their families keep intolerance to each other's faith and conversion practices out of their new relationships.
—Dilip Amin

Section 5.5: Hindu: Finally I Have to Unwillingly Revert to Islam

At InterfaithShaadi.org, the majority of posts (more than 700) and comments are related to non-Muslim-to-Muslim marriages. Considering this is a major subject of interest, the author has included real life experiences of 55 couples in such relationships in this book. Interfaith dating couples should read these real life experiences and decide their own path forward.

Ayesha (former Deepa) says:

I am married to a Muslim guy for last eight months and reverted[189] (converted) to Islam five months ago. I met my husband during college days almost seven years ago and spent some good time as a very great friend together. When college was over we separated. We were passively in contact until we met face to face two years ago. This time when we started to spend time together, we ended getting married through the Special Marriage Act 1954.

He never talked about Islam ever and religious conversion was far of the talk but there was good opposition from my family stating that it would be very difficult for me to settle in a Muslim family. I didn't pay heed to them and thought will manage some how but unfortunately my parents' family was true. When I entered my in-laws house, I faced hostility and non-cooperation and very much unfriendly environment. My mother-in-law wanted me to revert to Islam and my hubby's sister suggested me to do so to be accepted in the family. My husband was silent.

I asked my husband to move in separate apartment but he refused to move since he cannot leave his family and I cannot leave my husband. So after 3 months finally I had to give up and unwillingly revert to Islam. I was given a new name "AYESHA" and had a nikaah. After that my life changed completely. I was compelled to leave my job; I did that.

Now my in-laws are becoming friendlier and happier. My Mother-in-law taught me to offer salah (prayer) that I have to do compulsorily five times. There is no chance of missing any of those salah. In free time she teaches me Koran and hadiths. There are many restrictions applied to me. I have to wear black gown called abaya and hijab and if I don't, they get angry. Also whenever going outside or at home, I have to wear hijab and

---

[189] Muslims consider that everyone is born a Muslim. Thus they use the word "revert" instead of "convert" when a non-Muslim becomes a Muslim.

abaya, a new experience from jeans. They haven't asked me to wear a veil yet but I won't be able to escape from it for long.

Most of my documents like passport and voter-Id card have new identity of me. My name of Ayesha has been added in Ration card, and I have applied Adhar (Indian identity) card as same. My old identity has been almost erased, except from my mind.

I am also going away from Hindu identity to a Muslim one. There are occasion of unhappiness and often suffocation but I have to live with it. My parents are very sad about it but they haven't abandoned me yet completely but I am now hardly in any contact with them.

Only saving grace is my husband. There is no attitude change from his side. He still loves me same that was earlier although he sometimes advises me to go to some Islamic seminary to learn more about Islam, so that my life can be easier in a new shell but no force.

Anybody marrying a Muslim must keep in view that it's not easy to go with this kind of marriages and have to often sacrifice. Woman shares most of the portion of sacrifice. —Ayesha

Ayesha says (3 months later): I don't have any attachment for any faith... I am just practicing Islam casually. —Ayesha

Ayesha says (6 months later): Hi Admin, I was aware that it won't be easy to get accepted by the mother-in-law of mine. Anyways if I had not reverted our marriage would have not lasted long, may be a year or two. Now I hope it can go long as I wish. Now I don't have any complaints. It was favorable to me as I am now compatible to Islam and its tradition. I am happy. —Ayesha

Section 5.6: He (Muslim) Could Not Understand the Concept of Pluralism

The author found a major difference in the mindset of two types of new adults. A pluralist and inclusivist has no problem being a part of an intended spouse's belief system while in an exclusivist's mind being a part of other's faiths is not acceptable. Let's read Agnostic and Madhavi's experiences in the next two sections.

Agnostic says:

I am a Brahmin girl. I live in US, and was in Canada for a lot of my life. I did like a Pakistani guy for a bit. He was broad minded, undergrad in Computer Science, and had a good job. His family lives abroad too, and hence is a lot more tolerant.

There were a lot of things though which were uncomfortable:

1. I am a strict vegetarian. In fact after coming to America, I have adopted veganism. They can't live without meat even a single day. It was really hard for me to even see them cutting goat on Eid, etc. I was afraid that in the future, I would have to touch meat and cut it, etc.

2. In the later stage of our relationship, he disclosed that **his kids would have to be Muslim**. But I could be what I want. This was not reasonable to me. I think if your having an inter religious marriage you should be tolerant to your partners beliefs. I wanted my kids to be aware of both Hindu and Muslim traditions, grow up broad-minded. He/She has to be as much Hindu with my family and as much Muslim with his. He couldn't understand the concept of pluralism.

3. I didn't think he would be ok with me having a puja room in my home. For me, it's important. I'm fine with visiting a mosque, but I also want to visit a temple.

Anyway, my boyfriend was very honest. He didn't try to manipulate me. He told me the truth in black and white, and asked me to make a decision knowing all the facts. After thinking through it, we decided to split up.

Yes, the first few months were horrible. But I feel happy that we split. For the prolonged happiness of two people it's very important to retain your individuality and personality. You should not be ever stripped of your identity.

I am as opposed to Muslims converting to Hinduism for marriage as Hindus converting to Islam. **I think conversion is a social evil.**

Regarding your (Dimple) story…

1. If he is from a conservative family, leave him now. No matter how much he loves you, he will always love his family more. All of us love our family more. And this will influence him when he has to eventually choose your religion and culture over blocking you from following them. If he is from a broad minded, non-religious family, then maybe it's fine.

2. As a Brahmin, you probably are pure vegetarian. And even if not religious, want to go to the temple on your birthday, Diwali, Pongal, etc. This is the way we bond too. He might not support you in any of this. It's not his fault but the difference in culture. Your kids will hardly spend time with your parents, and eventually you will not either.

3. If you still want to be with this guy, do the following: a) Wait till you're professionally and financially stable. If things go wrong you will need a safety net. This way you will be a bit older and more mature. b) Don't do it till you are in late 20s. I don't think people are sufficiently unbiased and mature at 23. c) I know I shouldn't say this, but I will. PLEASE don't get tempted or encourage any physical relationship. In plain words, have no sexual relationship. Once this happens, all of a sudden the power and dominance is with the guy and not with the girl. This will emotionally and mentally condition you, and will make you want to be with him no matter what, without thinking of the repercussions.

Always better to be calm, and not too attached before making a decision. I really don't believe that love is enough to sustain a marriage. Once frustration crops in, love will go out of the window.

With this said, I am not averse to Muslims. Lot of my close circle of friends comprise of them. I just believe in accurately clarifying expectations before you decide to marry, and, being firm in your principles, and maintaining your self-respect.

Also, this BS that once you fall in love, everything else does not matter is false. You'll be surprised at how fast feelings change with time.

Just because I broke up, doesn't mean I'll be single forever. And, after all these years, we are still good friends. —Agnostic

Admin says:

Excellent thoughts! On pluralism, let's take example of the so-called open-minded Bollywood superstar Aamir Khan. Read his interview:

Question to Aamir Khan:[190] "Did you face any religious dilemma while you were married to a Hindu lady Reena Dutta and later on to Kiran Rao?" Aamir Khan replied: "No, none whatsoever. We never practiced each other's religion neither did we force each other to do so. But, of course, I had made it very clear that my kids will always follow only Islamic religion."

What does Aamir means by "my" kids? Are they not kids by "both" parents? Is giving sperm more important than carrying the baby for 9 months? **Is Aamir Khan a Male chauvinist or an intolerant Muslim?** We could not understand the mentality of Aamir Khan, who likes Hindu wives but could not tolerate Hindu children! —Admin

> *If nothing else, this author at least hopes to impress upon a couple entering a Hindu-Muslim relationship that they need to pay close attention to resolving religious differences. Tackle the inter-faith problems directly... don't sweep them under the rug. Don't assume that you will resolve differences sometime after you get married. Pre-marital problems generally grow into "Hindenburg class disasters" after marriage.*
> (Based on http://www.religioustolerance.org/ifm_divo1.htm)

[190] http://ssmusiq.blogspot.in/2010/08/my-wives-may-be-hindu-but-my-kids-will.html.

Section 5.7: About to Marry a Muslim Guy, but Now No More

Madhavi says:

First of all thank you so much for giving me this wonderful platform where I can express my emotions.

I am a Hindu Brahmin girl. I was in a relationship with a Muslim guy since last 1 year... and in due course of time; I came to know much about Islam and Muslim people. They are not bad at all but I condemn the teachings. I was so happy thinking my boyfriend is so supportive... then as time passed by and we actually began to think about the marriage... first he asked me to choose a name. I asked why? He said I need to have a Muslim name in order to get married to a Muslim guy. Initially I was so happy thinking my boyfriend is so supportive. Later I sternly refused to change my name, but he said that is indispensable. I somehow, out of love, or out of madness agreed to do so... please don't yell on me now.

After that, Ramadan came, he asked me to keep Roza. I asked my panditji (priest) if I can... he said all Gods are same. We, all human beings have same destinations, though the paths may be different. Panditji said our religion recognizes and respects all Gods and all other religions. He said you could believe in Ram ji, believe in Allah and believe in Jesus as well. So, I started keeping Rozas, with proper *sehri*, *iftaari*, and reciting *duas*.

It was his birthday, and I wanted to go to a (Hindu) temple and pray for his better future. When I asked him to come along with me, he refused and even asked me not to go. Why? He said, because I kept Roza, so I can't. He said now you cannot worship your gods. You just have to accept Allah and nobody else... I completely refused. I went to the temple, but continued with the Roza.

And yes, he celebrated Diwali with me last year and he accompanied me to Mahalaxmi temple, though he didn't know how to do puja but he bowed his head and at least stepped into the temple. However I won't be allowed doing so after marriage.

I love him, but the fact that his parents would never accept me as a Hindu, and I can't change myself to win his love. Love has no religion.
—Madhavi

Madhavi says:

I was about to marry a Muslim guy, but after reading this[191] I actually changed my decision. I was researching in Islam when I came across this blog… thank you so much for making me realize what horrible mistake I was going to commit.

Its not that I hate Islam, I kept all Rozas this year, but I fail to understand the following points… I would be highly obliged if someone can throw some light on them…

1. Why is Islam so sex oriented? I mean there is life beyond sex too… e.g. wife can be beaten if she protests against having sex?
2. Why women have to wear burka and hijab but not men?
3. Why men can be polygamist and not women?
4. Why Allah does not recognizes any other religion when Hinduism states that every God and every religion is equal?
5. Is *qurbaani* on Bakra Eid is justified? I know Hinduism has the same thing called *bali* but now its illegal and not practiced anymore… but is Allah so happy to see his men killing innocent animals and tear them and eat them? This is a height of cruelty! And to top it, the flesh is also given in charity… charity of cruelness, brutal, indecent, punishable behavior, that too with innocent animals?

Today I am so proud to be a Hindu, and I will be till my last breath… Om Namah Shivaye… —Madhavi

> *When you get married, romance and chemistry become secondary, if not tertiary.*
> —Shasha (Section 5.8)

---

[191] https://www.interfaithshaadi.org/blog/?p=1022.

Section 5.8: Failed Love or a Smart Move?

Religion and culture may not be important to youths in their early 20s but as they mature, people tend to go back to their roots. Let's read Sasha's life experiences.

Sasha says:

Aziza,

I would first like to say that you are a very young girl. Having nearly passed my twenties and approaching my thirties, I have learned many things about myself. Firstly, what you want at 21 is completely different than what you want when you are a little bit older and mature to get married. I'm not trying to say that your love is not true or that your feelings are not real. I am certain they are.

We often find ourselves in a struggle of love at the age you are for the following reasons. 1) It's the time we start becoming adults and our feelings are intensified as we start developing more meaningful relationships than what we did in our teenage years; 2) This is the age that we start thinking about marriage and our future so meeting someone wonderful during this time makes us believe we are more in love than we truly are.

I'm saying this from experience. The love you share with your boyfriend now will change over time. So you must really think deep and hard if this boy really has every single quality you are looking for in a man. I'm not talking about just romance and "chemistry." When you get married, romance and chemistry become secondary, if not tertiary.

I have been in love with a Hindu and now I am married to my Muslim husband. Few years back, I wanted to marry this Hindu. I felt like life could not go on without him and it was all over and there was no life without him. I don't feel any of that now. It's not that the love went away or it wasn't real, but marriage encompasses so many other aspects besides what you share at a young age. I had to really sit down and put my romantic feelings aside and determine if this person has the qualities that will SUSTAIN a marriage. My Hindu boyfriend at that time was wonderful, romantic, madly in love with me. However, when I thought about raising kids with him, our values clashed. I am practicing (moderately) Muslim. I wanted to make sure I had someone to fast with in Ramadan, someone to push me to read namaz and live by the values of Islam. All this nonsense of honor killing and community is problematic in some areas but really put that aside and think about you.

133

Marriage is holistic, Fatima. It doesn't become about you and him anymore. It becomes about family interactions. For example, pujas for Hindus and Ramadan for Muslims. Doing things together that bind you as a family. It takes INCREDIBLE strength to try to manage two cultures/religions and unhappy families. I've seen it with my own eyes. I've also seen it work in many instances, but I've always heard (especially from the woman) that it's a very big challenge. The only way the challenges are minimized is when you have two very modern families whose beliefs are more lax. It all depends on YOUR strength, your relationship with your parents and your deen.

If you are a religious person to some extent, then you will want someone to believe in Islam the way that you do when you are older. It won't matter anymore that he's funny or cute or romantic, or even a good human. That's not enough when it comes to marriage if you in fact want to incorporate religion in your life.

If you are open to practicing both and incorporating both then you both have to discuss this at a very mature level. Once you two have an understanding of how you can live together you must consider parents/extended family. While the shock does fade over time, I can tell you that the relationships change, especially daughters and mothers. I could not dare to hurt my mother so it was a big reason I left him, but later realized it's what I wanted inside because I truly wanted my children and myself to improve in my own faith. I wasn't ready to incorporate another faith that I didn't grow up with or believe in.

You need to think about all this. I was the same as you. I wanted to marry him, couldn't live without him. Again, I am able to and I love my husband and I love that my family is happy. I realized now that my feelings were so intensified due to our chemistry but if I had married him (Hindu) I would not have been content now.

Another thing is about him being settled. It adds much burden to one's relationship, so you also have that factor on your shoulders. However, I'm assuming he is also quite young. Darling, I know how emotional this situation can be. If you remove all the emotion and stick to the facts it becomes easier. If you truly cannot imagine your life without this guy and see your values, ideals, future plans, personalities, all in line then you must be prepared to fight and have A LOT of patience.

If I know Muslim parents, they are very strong-minded and you will face much resistance. Some races/religions are more open and some more closely knit. One is not better than the other. This nonsense someone posted about Muslim wives being tortured is so narrow. Maybe in small very desolate communities but in most cases especially in America no man keeps 4 wives. And even the ones that do, it's not out of disrespect but other familial reasons that we cannot judge. People are so easily jumping to conclude it's "torture." Even in Hindu communities there is much hypocrisy and unfairness against women. This is not Hindu/Muslim battle. Both and all cultures have their pros and cons. There are many great Muslim boys out there as well as Hindus. Let's look past at criticizing the other and focus on the real challenges within interfaith marriage.

Aziza, my duas are with you. —Sasha

> What you are is what you have been. What you'll be is what you do now.
> —Buddha

Section 5.9: Me Converting (from Hinduism), of course, Not Her!

Concerns with expectation of religious (even fake) conversion have been a major theme at InterfaithShaadi. For this reason, this topic is covered extensively in this book and in the next about 10 sections.

Sanjay says:

I was in a "semi-serious" relationship with a Muslim girl for several months. I say that in quotes because let's be honest, we all knew where it was headed. Initially of course it just started out as a mutual attraction, we loved spending time together, all that good stuff. Then as we grew more emotionally attached, she began bringing up conversion. It is me converting (from Hinduism), of course, not her. At first it was easy to laugh it off, but the same question kept coming up over and over again.

As we grew closer I discovered that she was not a very religious Muslim at all and had a much more open-minded and worldly view of God and faith than is usually taught by Islam—so really we weren't that incompatible after all—but at the same time I found it stunning the degree to which she had been brainwashed.

I was raised in a fairly religious Hindu household, but really I don't consider myself "Hindu" as much as a "Hindu/Buddhist/Agnostic/ Spiritual"—but that's beside the point. The problem lay with her family, who would surely never approve of me, not to speak of what they would think of her. She never told her family about me (nor did I tell mine), and I ended up moving away. So, gradually our relationship came to an end, but not without a good amount of stress and angst for both of us.

Thankfully we've both found new significant others from similar religious backgrounds and remain decent friends, but the moral of the story is still there—for anyone from a Dharmic background considering a serious relationship with a Muslim—just know what you're getting into. YOU'RE the one who's going to be asked to convert, to sacrifice who you are, to turn your back on your culture and heritage. Not them. This is not something to take lightly. —Sanjay

Section 5.10: He Expects Me to Convert to Islam

Kajol says:

I am in a bit of confusion right now. I have been seeing a Muslim Egyptian man for the past 5 years. He has been good to me and now says he wants to marry me. I have met his family and friends and he has met mine. However, I am Hindu and he is Muslim. I need some advice on whether or not I should marry him as he expects me to convert to Islam and also any children we have in the future will be Muslims. Please help. Many thanks. —Kajol

Admin says:

Hi Kajol,

There are all types of Muslims and it is difficult to generalize. However, find out if your Muslim boyfriend is tolerant or intolerant type.

Since he clearly told you that he wants you to be a Muslim (take shahadah oath), it tells that he is intolerant type. So are you looking forward to a life like Chitra's?[192] Like Chitra (not by her choice!), are you willing to leave your mom, dad, brother, sister, cousins, uncles, aunts, and all your Hindu friends? Are you willing to start your new Muslim life with your new Muslim relatives and potentially move back to Egypt?

The shahadah will be a turning point for your life. Though he will tell you that "I did not know this coming," "Do it to please my dad," "Do it for the heck of it" or whatever, shahadah will change everything for you. Apparently, converting you to Islam is more important for him than your love. If you say no to shahadah, will he walk away from your life without any hesitation? Are you in a love-trap by a love-jihadi?

The shahadah is a one-way street. Check the latest Egyptian laws of apostasy. Remember it is applicable even after your husband has 4 wives or after your talaak (divorce). Read what Alkaff[193] has to say, "Do not revert into a kufr and you will be killed if you are found out! You should not mix with your kufr (Hindu) family anymore." Are you ready for this?

Also check Egyptian laws for divorce initiated by a woman and a kafir Hindu's chance of winning their Muslim children's custody after divorce.

---

[192] Section 5.32.
[193] https://www.interfaithshaadi.org/blog/?p=855#comment-28739.

Tell him that you will never take the 2 minutes of shahadah oath, but instead you will be a better Muslim than most other Muslims by following all Islamic traditions: eat only Halal food, perform namaz five times a day, put on a vale for a mosque visit on Fridays and fast during Ramadan. Find out if the shahadah labeling or you practicing a good Muslim life (but without the label of shahadah) is important for him.

In the past, Hindus had a bad practice of caste system where the label counted more than what that person did or how much that person contributed to this world. Mahatma Gandhi worked hard and tried hard to eradicate this system. Why would one want to endorse a new type of caste system where one religion is superior over all others?

Muslims believe that if you take the shahadah oath and convert to Islam, Allah will send you to heaven. Alternatively, Christians believe if you take that dip in water and are baptized, Jesus will remove all your sins and you will be salvaged. Likewise, Jews will not rest till the interfaith child gets the bris and bar mitzvah label. Isn't it your karma, not a label that will decide your fate?

Why did he not ask for the religious conversion during the past 5 years of your romantic relationship? Ask your Muslim boyfriend to explain what religious conversion has to do with your love?

Let a carnation be a carnation, don't convert it to a rose! Tell him that you are a Hindu and will die as a Hindu. Ask him to show his true love for you and marry a "Hindu" Kajol. —Admin

Section 5.11: Muslim Will Marry Me Only If I Convert

Dr. Manu says:

I am in love with a girl for several years and she is a Muslim. She is not Indian. I went to her house to convince her parents two times but they never agreed and when I asked my girlfriend to marry me against her family's wish she refused. She told me that she would marry me only if I convert and stay with her in her country but I'm not ready for it. Also, she said if we have children she wants them all to follow Islam.

My family is against our marriage even then I told her that I will stay with her. For me she doesn't have to convert to Hinduism or do puja and all. I am ready to accept her as who she is but she is not ready to accept me as who I am. She said she would marry me only if I am Muslim.

I love her a lot for past 5 years. I do consider her as my wife. Do you think she loves me truly? Or I am stupid that I love her a lot and she just wants to take advantage of it to make me Muslim. I don't know what to do. Can you give me any advice? —Dr. Manu

Admin says:

Dr. Manu,

Considering that you are a doctor with a good education and many options to do that is right, let's analyze your situation critically.

We believe interfaith marriages will be successful and everlasting if it is I'm-We (Interfaith Marriage with Equality). You know it well that the "love" driven by your testosterone in your blood and altered 5HT levels in brain cells will be metabolized in a year or two. Considering the very high rate of divorce in interfaith marriages, you must make a rational decision.

She wants to make you something that you are not. She believes in converting a rose to a carnation. If she wants a carnation, why is she not looking for one; there are plenty around. If her goal is to please her parents and take you to her country, you had better be ready to be a true Muslim. However your comments do not lead us to think you are ready to be a Muslim, ready to leave your country and possibly start over in your profession.

First read the Koran. Then spend at least 6 months in a madrasa if possible and learn about Islam. When you think you are ready to dump the murtis of Lord Rama, Krishna and Goddess Laxmi into the garbage, only then should you think of becoming a Muslim.

She may even tell you that "I don't care about this conversion, but just do it for my father" (or whatever); don't believe her. She sounds like a love-proselytizer. She will not tolerate a shadow of your Hindu parents and your Hindu friends. Basically, you must be ready to abandon your parents who sacrificed their life savings to make you a doctor.

The most critical point she made is "children, she wants that they all be raised as Muslims." One day your Muslim children and great grandchildren may go and convert more Hindus to Islam. So... where will this saga end... until there are no more Hindus (or Sikhs and Christians) left to convert? Was this your childhood dream and life objective? It is time for a change and you should bring that change by taking a right step now.

Does this exclusivist and intolerant thinking have a place in I'm-We? You will never be able to please her, even if you (fake) convert just for marriage, because you will not be able to keep up with her demands unless you become a true Muslim.

Tell her up front your reservations about becoming a Muslim and that the children will not be Muslims only, but both. If necessary, take a trial separation for several months (no phone calls or text) to give you both time to reevaluate your feelings for each other. She sounds set in her opinions and religious beliefs and may not be the best choice for you in the long run, however, a trial separation may change her mind, if she has the potential for an interfaith marriage with equality. Give it a try! Best wishes. —Admin

You were not born with faith, but the faith was installed into you by your parents and surroundings.

Section 5.12: I Pray for His Conversion to Islam in Every Namaz

Eman says:

He's Brahmin and very religious. I too am very religious. I pray for his conversion to Islam, every time in namaz. He's a great guy, very good at heart, probably nicer than hundreds of Muslim guys. We love each other a lot and can't think of life without each other.

Having affair is prohibited in Islam but I believe pure love has to be acceptable in the eyes of Allah. But the problem is our parents' approval and how our life would be after marriage. I am thinking of having children and giving them both Islamic and Hindu teachings. Let them decide what religion to choose when they are old enough. I am sure if they get Islamic teachings they will surely follow Islam.

If as a *bahu* (wife) I may be asked to perform some rituals, I will do without heart. And I do have arguments on religious topics. What do I do to convince him that Islam is a true religion without straining our relationship? If I don't get him I may never marry in my life.

Also he belongs to a family who are very narrow-minded, consider Muslims impure and all that shit. He too was like that before I came, but still he has some flinch for other Muslims. He can accept my family and me but the fact that he doesn't respect my community drowns me.

I get over emotional over religious topics because I follow and believe in Islam, not just because I am born into it but I have actually understood it. Now I want him to understand, but preconceptions and ego will not allow him to see what I am trying to say.

Is there any way I can at least make him understand without ruining our relationship? —Eman

Admin says:

Hi Eman,

Allah knows everything and does everything. Perhaps Allah has made you fall in love with that Brahmin boy and sent you to us.

You said, "He's a great guy, probably nicer than hundreds of Muslim guys," why? You liked that Hindu for a reason. Why did you not like hundreds of other Muslim guys you came across in your life? Because the Muslim husband, as per Sharia (see Figure 2) laws, can have multiple wives, can lightly beat[194] you and can give you a talaak? Knowing this, why would you want that Brahmin to convert to Islam and give him all these new options? If you are smart and truly love him, marry him as is, as a Brahmin. Instead of "I pray for his conversion to Islam", you should thank Allah that he cannot legally follow all of these practices.

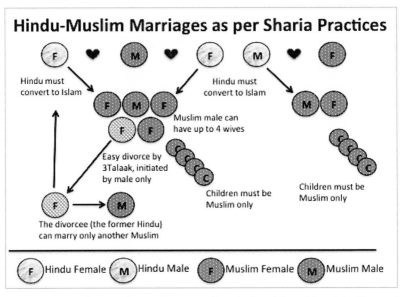

Figure 2: Sharia Practices: If you are in relationship with a Muslim and are asked for shahadah religious conversion, understand how such conversion will impact your life.[195]

You have presented beautiful, pluralistic views i.e. "I am thinking of having children, giving them both Islamic and Hindu teachings." That is the way it should be. Let the child decide his/her own faith when he/she is 21 years old.

You said, "Perform some rituals which I will do without heart," yes just do it for his sake. It is your faith that is important.

---

[194] Koran 4:34 and http://www.timesofisrael.com/egyptian-cleric-advises-men-beat-your-wife-so-she-will-mend-her-ways/.
[195] View this video for full explanation:
https://www.youtube.com/watch?v=RiWLGEKusIg.

You said, "He belongs to a family who is very narrow-minded." Then you will have to educate them. Likewise, you have also presented yourself as equally narrow-minded by wishing him to convert. We strongly advise you to give up this idea of conversion and learn to love and respect each other.

We question your statement "I have actually understood (Islam)." If you understood it, you would not have gotten into a relationship with a Hindu Brahmin to start with.

Love is not easy to come by. If you are truly in love, maintain it. Love him the way he is. Do not fake-convert him into what he is not. By showing your true love for him (instead of being a love-jihadi), you could change his thinking for other Muslims. Ultimately, it will be a win-win for both of you.

The bottom line is, you have two choices—accept him as is (that is as a Brahmin) or marry a true Muslim boy who prays five times a day and follows Mohammad's teachings. Make up your mind. Best wishes. — Admin

---

Interfaith Marriage is a game of "High Stakes Poker." You cannot see which cards are in the hands of in-laws, neighbors, acquaintances, church members etc.
—Ron (Section 3.16)

Section 5.13: I Fear Converting to Islam

Alpa says:

I need a suggestion. I am a Hindu Brahmin girl planning to marry a Muslim Guy. I read that without converting we can register as per Special Marriage Act. But is it practical in day-to-day life? I respect all religion and believe in God, only the way of worship is different. But still I have fear in converting as I feel it is a big sin. If at all I convert I cannot stop praying to Hindu God, as it's inborn in me. I am aware if I keep idols and pray I am not considered a Muslim. So there is no point in converting. However, his parents are ready to accept me only if I convert. I am ready to learn Islamic culture and follow but I cannot give up my religion nor can I leave him. —Alpa

Admin says:

Dear Alpa,

We feel your pain. It is unfortunate that their primary interest is to convert you to Islam. They do not see how good a person you are; their bottom line is to expand Islam. Be very clear that if you don't convert, most probably, your fiancé will leave you.

To have an Islamic nikaah (wedding), both couples must be Muslim. Not a single imam will perform nikaah of a "Hindu" to a Muslim. You must take 2 minutes of the shahadah oath and convert to Islam if you wish a nikaah. After conversion, the Islamic community will make sure you become a complete Muslim and remain 0% Hindu.

Why you said, "If I keep idols and pray?" You do not pray to idols, you pray to murtis.[196] You see God through an object, made of a marble. Muslims use the Kaaba black cube building as an object to pray to their Allah, Christians use a wooden cross and Jews go to the Jerusalem Stone Wall. There is no difference. All are either idols or Godly objects. Jesus and Mohammad are the most glorified human beings in this world's history. Tell your boyfriend to remove Muslim symbols from home before you remove your murtis out of your life.

You have good reason to be fearful of converting. Convert only if you wish to be a true Muslim. Remember the FAKE-conversion will ruin your life as well as your husband's. Do not plan to fool your future

---

[196] Section 2.11.

husband, his relatives, his imam, the Muslim community and God. Please do not fake-convert. Best wishes. —Admin

> Please don't get tempted or encouraged into any physical relationship. Once this happens, all of a sudden the power and dominance tends to be with the man and not the woman. This can emotionally and mentally condition you and will make you want to be with him no matter what, without thinking of the repercussions.
> —Agnostic (Section 5.6)

Section 5.14: I am Not Going to Change My Religion at Any Cost

Falguni says:

I am Hindu girl in a relationship with a Muslim boy for the last seven years. We both love each other a lot and his parents have even accepted me. But my parents are against this relationship and above all I am the only daughter of my parents. So I am in a big dilemma now. Neither can I leave my parents nor can I stay without my boyfriend. What should I do? Please help me to make a decision, please. —Falguni

Admin says:

Falguni,

You have left out the most critical information, does he or his family expect you to change your religion? It does not matter what excuse he uses; bottom line, do you have to convert?

If conversion is expected (in almost all cases), are you willing to live Muslim life proudly? Considering the risks are VERY high, is it worth putting your parents to shame? If you get the talaak after marrying him, what is your backup plan? We hope not your parents!

Tell him that you will never ever convert in this life; this is who you are and will remain that way. Take it or leave it. We are sure he will accept you as you are. If not, you are only 23 and have a long way to go for your life; you will have other options. Get back to us for more guidance. Don't jump into the well blindly! —Admin

Falguni says:

Ya, he did tell me that if I have to marry him then I'll surely have to convert since a Muslim guy can perform nikaah only with a Muslim girl. But he did add that I'll be allowed to visit temples and that I can keep idols of God along with me. But now am going to tell him that I am not going to change my religion at any cost. Let me see if he can accept me that way. Anyway, thanks for your valuable advice Sir! I'll surely get back to you for more guidance. —Falguni

Section 5.15: I Will Not Convert

Vijya says:

I was born into a practicing Hindu family and was raised in the West. I grew up spending massive amounts of time at the temple and found many parts of the religion beautiful. Today, I am not really a practicing Hindu but expect that I will become slightly more religious as I grow older. I have avoided dating outside of my religion my entire life due to respecting my parents' wishes as well as what you (Srinivas[197]) have outlined. However after dating many Hindu guys, I was not able to find someone suited for myself.

It has now been two years since I started seeing my best friend from High School who comes from a Muslim background. He himself is not religious and we share equal views (be a good person and good things shall follow). We both are kind, generous and charitable. His mother is the only practicing member of the household and his parents are very accepting of our relationship. However, I know that this news will break my father's heart. I truly believe I am making the right decision to marry my boyfriend and would love if they could partake in my life's decision.

I believe that my parents were raised around others who were taught everything you (Srinivas) have outlined and so I don't blame them for their opinion but wish that they would realize that one GOD has created each human being, and we should all coexist.

I am extremely against the Islamic definition of marriage (accepting Allah as the almighty). Marriage is a sacred union of hearts and minds. Nothing about this ceremony should be forced. I was willing to do a nikaah if his parents would like us to however Islam will not recognize it as a true marriage since I will not convert so I don't believe this will happen.

My boyfriend agrees to do the Hindu ceremony. In terms of our children, since neither he nor I attend the temple or mosque I don't believe this will be an issue. However I would like to make them aware of not just these two but ALL religions and practices as they wish. If I choose to go to the mandir later in life, I will also take them with me sometimes to give them the experience.

Please share any unbiased opinion and advice including topics of children, marriage ceremony, etc. —Vijya

---

[197] https://www.interfaithshaadi.org/blog/?p=4628&cpage=1#comment-40032.

Admin says:

Vijya,

You asked for unbiased advice; let's lay all of the information in front of you and you can make a decision that is right for you.

Many people like novelty and that is why they get attracted to people not from their background (read 10 points of dating[198]). The grass is always greener on the other side—this common saying might apply here. Love also tends to be blind from some of the negative realities. Muslim girls know the issues Islamic women have to face, but you don't. Please do your research on what is expected of a Muslim wife, even if you have assurances from your boyfriend that he is not a practicing Muslim. Likewise, your boyfriend should do his homework and learn as much about marrying a Hindu.[199]

How truly Muslim are they? No two Muslims are the same (read Azad[200]). Please read all 30 points[201] that a "true" Muslim may be expected to follow. Print the list out. Write down your expectations/agreement/disagreement on each point/issue. Ask him to do the same. You will both see how closely aligned or how far apart your true views are. This is called an "informed" decision. If you agree enough to continue with your plans, keep this written list and present it to both sets of parents. We also hope your father will come around to seeing your point of view after you have presented it this way. It might be painful, but we would rather see you take the pain now rather than after marriage (even worst, after childbirth). Marriages may be made in heaven, but about half[202] end in divorces in the West. In many cases, the divorce costs much more than the marriage!

Do not be afraid of this list of 30 points. If he is in America and if he is not religious, perhaps none will apply. Let us know how it goes. Best wishes. —Admin

---

[198] Section 2.2.
[199] Section 2.8.
[200] Section 6.1.
[201] https://www.interfaithshaadi.org/blog/?p=2402.
[202] 48% of first marriages end in divorce or separation in 20 years: http://www.avvo.com/legal-guides/ugc/marriage-divorce-statistics.

Section 5.16: Is It Possible that I Convert to Islam Just as a Formality?

Many youths decided to convert to the spouse's faith without truly understanding the faith. The next few sections give such examples.

Yogin says:

I am a Hindu man who has been in a relationship with a Muslim girl for the last 3 years. We are both over 30 and the reason we have been waiting this long is because we were hoping her parents would accept this relationship. But alas that doesn't seem to be happening.

We have discussed the problems most inter-faith marriages face many times and have come to the conclusion that one possible way of avoiding future problems would be to let go of the wish to have children, since we have seen, once children come into the picture of interfaith marriage, that really puts a strain on the relationship.

We have also agreed that the best way to keep the peace going would be to continue believing in what each of us believe and we have no expectations or wishes that either of us will convert. However, having said that, we do realize that the only way her parents can come on board is if I convert to Islam.

What I wanted to know from reliable and experienced people like you is if it is possible to convert to Islam just as a formality? Can I continue keeping my Hindu name even after I convert? Also once I convert, are there any religious implications or problems? If we both are comfortable, can I continue believing in Hinduism? We would obviously not lie to her parents and we would like to tell them that this conversion is ONLY for the marriage to happen? What I want to know is if it is possible? I would greatly appreciate some inputs. —Yogin

Admin says:

A very simple answer to your question—never ever "fake" convert. We are sorry, this is a blunt answer but it is true. Are you such a person who will go and lie to Allah, your parents, your Hindu community, her Muslim community, imam and most importantly, you yourself? This "fake" conversion will ruin the lives of both you and your girlfriend, and both sides' extended families. Once you are a Muslim, even in namesake, following Hindu practices is considered sin. Later, your conversion back to Hinduism is considered apostasy punishable by death in some areas of the world. Instead of a fake-conversion, spend time learning about Islam

149

and if you like it, consider converting with true faith. If, however, you disagree with Islam, be clear that you will never convert and continue to worship in your own faith (and she in hers) as you have already agreed upon. The parents' issues need to remain with the parents' and you will need to figure out how to distance yourself from their disapproval, if they in fact do not "come on board."

She may be using her parents as an excuse. It is possible that deep in her heart, she wishes to see you as a Muslim, so this is something to consider. Best wishes. —Admin

> *To ask for religious conversion for marriage after years of romantic relationship is an ugly form of proselytization.*

Section 5.17: Fake-conversion for Marriage?

Tarun says:

I come from a multi-religious family. My Dad is a Brahmin (we eat just about anything under the sun although his family was pure vegetarian). My Mum is half Christian (father is half Christian and half Hindu) and half Muslim (Mother is a Muslim). My mum's sister is married to a Muslim man and he is the only one who is venomous when it comes to hypocrisy. He never lets his daughters mingle with me even though earlier they were really close to me. But he encourages his son to mix and mingle with his non-Muslim cousin sisters. This is too much!

My own sister is in love with a Muslim man for years, although it's not working out in my opinion. My brother is married to a Muslim girl, and well he did not have to convert as she came from a secular and rich family.

I am married to Muslim girl and I had to temporarily convert to make her folks happy. Now I have come back to Hinduism. Although I haven't asked her to convert (to Hinduism), she has no issues at all to perform Hindu customs as long as I do not force her. Is that not amazing? She prays in her style and I never question her.

She is my wife for over a few months. Her family is happy, but she does everything like a Hindu and appreciates me going to my temple, doing just about anything Hindu under the sun. She has never been happier. — Tarun

Admin says:

Tarun,

Why did you make lies and deception a foundation of your married life? If you had no intention to be a Muslim, why did you take fake-shahadah oaths and a fake-conversion to Islam? Is this not an insult to her faith, her parents, her imams and to Islam?

Why would an honest person with high self-esteem lie to everyone just to get married, when there are many other good options available? What is wrong with having a civil marriage?

If you believe in God, why would you lie to Allah (or Krishna)? Alternatively, if you don't believe in God, why did you have to marry by religious ceremonies? Why couldn't you keep your marriage secular? Are you saying lies and fake-conversion are good, while the truth and honesty are anti-religious?

Tarun, we do not mean to be harsh on you. These are issues you and the rest of society need to come to terms with. You are not necessarily a liar, yet are compelled to lie. It is not your fault; you are a victim of the politicians and the priest class. At your young age, no one expects you to be a Gandhi out to change the world. Please love and take good care of your Muslim wife in a Brahmin home; this is really a Godly work. Let's hope others will learn from your example (except no fake-conversion!).
—Admin

Life is never like a rose garden; and even if it is, roses always have thorns. Learn to live and let others live.

Section 5.18: My Children Must Follow Islam

The most important question in any interfaith relationship is the religion of children. Here, Toral has no idea what Islam is all about but agreed to raise her children as Muslims.

Toral says:

I am a Hindu and my boyfriend is Muslim. I am going to run away to get married. I am not going to change my religion or name. My boyfriend has no problem with it. As far as it's about my conversion into Islam, my boyfriend doesn't want me to get converted seriously... and his mother too.

He is very co-operative. We will not do nikaah but we will get married under the Special Marriage Act. My children will follow Islam. I can't do anything in this regard, but Hinduism will also be a part of their lives as am going to do each and every ritual I am doing right now. Any suggestions? —Toral

Admin says:

Hi Toral,

We are glad that his mom agreed that you do not have to convert and that you will marry by the Special Marriage Act 1954. How about his dad and other close relatives? Have you talked to them personally about this or have you just heard that conversion is not necessary from your boyfriend? If his dad and close relatives have not agreed to this, your boyfriend may change his tune as you get closer to your wedding day.

Why do you wish to run away from your parents to get married? It is possible that you will be ending your relationship with your parents and relatives forever. Where will you go if there is a serious problem in your new married life (which is more likely in an interfaith marriage)? There is a saying, don't burn your bridges behind you. Tell your parents all the facts and face all the fights and shouting. Give them time to adjust and stand firmly in your belief and your parents may turn around to support you. Are you running away because you just want to avoid confrontation? This seems like a cowardly way out.

Why must you raise your children as Muslim only, especially if you are planning to get married by the Special Marriage Act of 1954, without nikaah? That should give you more leeway. You do not need to be so submissive then and give into male or Muslim dominance.

Why not raise children as both Muslim and Hindu? Why not have the first child's name Mohammad and the second Krishna? Why are you not expecting equality of faiths? Demand it from him and if he truly loves you, he will agree. If he is a religious fanatic, you had better know it now.

Why not let your children decide their faith when they reach 21? President Barack Obama had a Muslim father and Christian mother, and was raised as both. When he was in college, he decided to be baptized. What is wrong with such liberty given to a child? Don't agree to "label" your children Muslim now.

A legal point—if you marry with an agreement that your children will only be Muslim, then there is a legal consequence when asking for child custody after divorce. A judge may not give you (a Hindu) custody of Muslim children, especially because you agreed to raise them as Muslims. If you agreed to raise your children in both faiths, the judge may give the custody of the children to their mother.

Do you know what it means to raise Muslim children? Have you visited mosques and madrasas? If you have not visted them yet, please go there several times and spend hours there. Learn what is being taught there because one day you will have to teach it to your children. Have you read the Koran? Are you comfortable with your children reciting the Koran every day? Ask Muslims on the streets about what they think of Hindus and Hindu Gods.

Let us know what you will gain by raising Muslim children, rather than Hindu-Muslim children? Please explain it to us. —Admin

Toral added:

I don't have a problem raising my children as Muslims. His dad also doesn't have problem and he doesn't care about his relatives at all. Once in my home there was Satyanarayan puja, next day I went to their house and I gave some prasad and kheer to them to eat, and I am so glad that they didn't refuse. *Ulta unhone kaha ki next time puja hoga to phir se dena* (Actually they told to bring it again next time). I don't like Mohammad because I don't like the path he showed to the people.[203] — Toral

---

[203] Toral agreed to raise children in Islamic faith without realizing the important of Prophet Mohammad in Islam. The statement is slightly modified by the author.

Section 5.19: Hindu: I've Decided to Take Up Islam

Love is blind. It is easy to get proselytized when in love. However, when reality hits, one may want to go back to one's own roots. For this reason, it is good not to love-proselytize and not to fake-convert just for marriage. Let's read Sujan's interesting life experience.

Sujan says:

This site has been helping me a lot in finding useful reviews and information. My name is Sujan, a Hindu guy in love with a Muslim girl for past 4 years. Currently we both are financially independent. We both are professional.

In her home they're planning to get her married to her cousin. We both love each other truly and I promised her that I'll do anything to make it happen. I am only son to my parents. I've decided to take up Islam so as to make her parents accept me. Here I don't mean Fake Conversion.

I would like **to take up the religion truly from my heart**. She never asked me to convert to Islam. I hope things will ease up soon in both our houses. I'm ready to undergo the circumcision process and also name my kids in Arabic.

Any suggestions are welcome. Please guide me whether I'm doing things in a correct way. Thanks in Advance. —Sujan

Admin says:

Dear Sujan,

You have yourself read all that is said here by others on cases similar to yours.[204] We are confident that, in the end, you will make the right decision for yourself (even if that decision is to be a Muslim).

We have two major concerns for your decision to convert to Islam: 1) You are probably in early 20s and 2) your initial motive to convert to Islam is your love for a Muslim girl.

Our first comment: Can you wait to convert to Islam and to marry her after a few more years? Your viewpoints for life may change in a few years.

Our second comment: Be sure you understand and agree with all of the beliefs and requirements of Islam, beyond the love for your girlfriend.

---

[204] https://www.interfaithshaadi.org/blog/?cat=9.

Yes, Islam is a great religion for many and it has a lot to offer to them. However, do not make a decision to change your birth religion based on your lover. If she was a Sikh, would you convert to Sikhism?... And if she was a Christian would you get baptized? Be sure you are converting to Islam because of Islam, and not just to "whatever my fiancée's religion is." You are converting "to make her parents accept me," is that correct? If you had never met this girl, would you still have considered becoming a Muslim?

If you went to buy a car, would you go to your car dealer uncle and buy an expensive car from him because he was insisting on it? Would you not at least check the prices with other dealers? How many other religions have you explored? Have you ever read the Koran, Bible, Geeta and material on Buddhism? These are all superb scriptures; how did you come to a decision that Islam is the best religion among all others, beyond that it is your girlfriend's religion and would make your life easier if you converted?

Tell us 5 main points that you liked about Koranic teachings or about Islam (other than your girl!) that you did not see in Hinduism? In addition, tell us—do you believe that God made this world in 2+4 days and Darwin's theory of evolution was wrong? Do you believe Mohammad is God's last messenger? Do you believe that Islam is the only true religion while Christianity, Jainism, Judaism, Hinduism and the rest are not? Do you believe in the Judgment Day that One God Allah will decide everyone's fate in an hour and that Hindu Mahatma Gandhiji and your parents may get Hell Fire because they are/were kafir and not Muslims? Do you believe that God can be and should be prayed to only in the direction of Saudi Arabia? Someday, will you let all your children and great grandchildren date Hindus and convert them to Islam (until there are no more Hindus left to convert)?

You asked, "Whether I'm doing things in a correct way." The answer is it depends. Only if you are converting for you and your true belief in Islam, is conversion the correct way. Separate your love issue from your decision to change your religion. Best wishes. —Admin

Sujan says:

Hey guys,

Sorry for troubling you and thanks to all of you who've been constantly trying to help me. But I guess our relationship is over. I heard from her friend that she was kind of forcefully and secretly married to her cousin. Seems like there will never be peace of mind in our hearts.

156

I have decided to forget all this stuff and move abroad to pursue my further degree.

And conversion is no more an option. I guess **I had no other specific reason for conversion except her**.

And to be true, Hinduism is far better as the girl's parents never seem to do all this marriage stuff forcefully. It happens with the willingness of the girl.

Thanks once again for helping me guys. Hope to have everyone's well wishes for my career. Really big THANKS. —Sujan

---

An exclusivist will say, "I don't want our children to get confused between two religions." Basically, he/she is saying, "There is one God and that is MINE!"

Section 5.20: Will Do Nikaah as well as a Hindu Marriage

Many times youths in love are totally naïve about their intended spouse's faith and community's expectations. Next, let's read Nisha and Dimple's experiences.

Nisha says:

Even I have the same problem... my boyfriend is Muslim and I am Hindu... I will not undergo any conversion to marry him. We will do nikaah as well as a Hindu marriage. I am a Hindu and I will remain as a Hindu for the rest of my life. —Nisha

Admin says:

Dear Nisha,

Please prove us wrong.

Please go and talk to 10 imams and ask if nikaah is possible without shahadah religious conversion.

Our experience has been: "There is no imam in this world who will perform an Islamic nikaah of a 'Hindu' to a Muslim. Hindus MUST convert."

We feel your boyfriend is simply fooling you, nothing more. Best wishes. —Admin

Satyen says:

Nisha,

Let me tell you the reality of the love of your boyfriend for you. It's just to convert you to Islam. There is a trick to convert without letting you know that you are being converted. You will hear the following or something similar:

1. You don't need to convert. Just repeat the shahadah (conversion oath) and sign the papers, this is just for formality so that nikaah could be administered.

2. I love you so much and cannot live without you. In Islam, it's required to go through shahadah to get married. Without shahadah, you cannot get married. Later we will live separately in another house and you can profess Hinduism.

3. I am fine with your religion but just to convince my parents/family/friends, you need to verbally go through shahadah.

The above innocuous looking suggestions are part of many Muslim boys' game plan called **Taqiyya** in Islam. It means they can adopt even seemingly non-Islamic practices to convert non-Muslims! They can even go to the temple and eat prasad!

If they cannot convert you fully due to your determination, they will definitely make your children Muslims. When you are married by nikaah (even though you keep your Hindu traditions after shahadah); Sharia laws will be applicable to you. So, they will raise your children as a Muslim as you cannot do anything else among their family members. Even you cannot divorce your Muslim hubby as easily as Sharia law will govern your marital status and women have limited say in these cases. Moreover, you will not want to leave your children with them after you have known their true colors.

Your present family members will become kafirs for you. Your Muslim family may not allow you to visit your Hindu parents/brothers/sisters in their homes. Forget about celebrating Hindu festivals such as Deevali, Holi, Navaratri etc. Be prepared to see the beef and halal styled meat in your home and the Koranic, Sunat (circumcision) practices! In fact, all these may happen even if you marry by the Special Marriage Act!

To summarize, you will be opening a Pandora's Box by undergoing nikaah. Many of the problems will exist even if you marry with the Special Marriage Act!

The choice is yours and the future is in your hands. But once married, many of life's options will be closed to you. So, think thrice before marrying a Muslim. —Satyen

---

Shahadah Conversion to Islam:

La-ilaha-iLLaLLah- Mohammadur-Rasulullah

لا إله إلا الله محمد رسول الله

There is no god but God
and Mohammad is the messenger of God.

159

Section 5.21: We Will Marry by Hindu Then Muslim Ceremonies

Many youths in love have a misconception that a Hindu and a Muslim can marry by two respective marriage ceremonies. Here, a Muslim woman Farah helped a Hindu girl realize the truth.

Dimple says:

I am a Hindu girl and in love with a Muslim boy. Now we have decided to get married. The boy has decided we get married in Hindu ceremony and then in Muslim ceremony. As per the boy's imam, the boy can perform all rituals except the saath phere (7 circles) round the fire. But I am telling the boy he needs to do that because it is necessary in the wedding. Please advise. —Dimple

Admin says:

Hi Dimple,

The boy has to decide if he wants a "Hindu" ceremony or wants to please the imam; he cannot have both. If you ask an imam, what else can you expect other than that answer? The imam is just doing his job. Further, be very clear that the Muslim wedding—Islamic nikaah—cannot be between a "Hindu" and a Muslim; both MUST be Muslims only. That means you MUST CONVERT to Islam before your nikaah.

Now you have to decide if Islam is the right religion for you. If you decide to convert to Islam, make sure you mean it and are willing to be an obedient Muslim wife and ready to raise Muslim children. Unless you are 100% sure of it, do not "fake" convert just to please your lover. This "fake" conversion, just to please the imam, will bring hell in THIS life, not only for you, but also for your boyfriend and both extended families.

Ask your boyfriend what conversion has to do with your love? If you are not sure about changing your faith, get married by the Special Marriage Act 1954. Best wishes. —Admin

Farah says:

Please be aware in nikaah, your Hindu parents are not allowed to attend. Your guy wouldn't be a true Muslim if he allows them to attend. As you said you are not going to convert, please leave the Muslim guy. Please don't spoil the Muslim boy; our religion does not permit marriage to you a kafir. You are haram and you kids will be harami, if you marry him.

I wonder how our Muslim boys are marrying you Hindus. As your parents have no love for you, so they tolerate you getting our Muslim guy. You Hindu girls are cheapest. I hope you see the truth and become Muslim and leave you stupid faltu (fake) religion. I will never allow my daughter to marry a Hindu. —Farah

Dimple (to Farah) **says:**

Ok, now I am realizing. Thanks a lot. —Dimple

> *The lady, who is obedient and follows all rules of the husband, will go to heaven in the AFTER life.*
> *Contrary to that, the lady who believes in living a life with pride and dignity will have heaven in THIS life!*

Section 5.22: I Told Him I Will Not Change My Religion

Youths have to learn to read in between lines. Here Admin is trying to help Urvi to interpret some statements.

Urvi says:

I am in love with a Muslim guy since 2 years but I knew him for 6 years. He is my best friend who turned as my lover now. So I know him very well, who has promised me not to change my religion if we get married. He came from a poor family but he got educated by doing part time work and now he is earning enough. He is family kind, funny, softhearted person. He knows more about Hinduism than me. To be frank I am not a religious kind. I don't believe in idol worship since my 7th standard, but just to check him I told him I will not change my religion and he agreed easily.

I have not decided about our kids. I have no problem if they follow Islamic culture. **I don't want them to get confused between two religions** in their young age. But I want them to respect both religions.

Now my love is working out of India. Before going there he asked my hand with my mom and my mom refused. My mom likes him very much but she is scared of the society and prestige. She feels that if I marry him, it will bring shame to our family because no guy will marry my sister. Now proposals are coming for her.

I can't think of a life without him. I feel like running away from home but it will affect my sister's future and even my boyfriend doesn't like this. He is coming back to India in few months and again going to ask my hand. I am scared. Please every one does pray for us.

Love someone and marry some other is not correct. I know my love. He will never ever ditch me, but I don't know what to do. I am stuck between my mom and my love. I am in my mid 20's and still don't have a right to decide about my future. Please pray for us and do give your opinion. —Urvi

Admin says:

Dear Urvi,

We are very sorry to hear of your situation. We agree that it is very difficult to let your lover go just for society and prestige. Sometimes you have to make a tough decision and do the right thing. Luckily you have a few months to explore some facts and make an informed decision. There are plenty of girls who married a Muslim and got "burned" but we hope your lover is different.

Before you decide how to handle your own family's wishes, do your "homework" as we advise everyone on this site. Seriously consider the following issues that will impact your long term happiness if you marry a Muslim. If you decide to marry your Muslim boyfriend, the issue of your mother's wishes and your sister's welfare can at least be approached with more knowledge.

First ask him for a Hindu-Muslim marriage with EQUALITY. Tell him that you will never change you religion (it is good that he agreed to it; it is critical that his parents also agree). Tell him you will not have Islamic nikaah (that needs conversion; there is no way around this) and most importantly, tell him children will not be only Muslim but Hindu and Muslim and they will learn *Ishvara Allah tero nam*. Please meet his family soon and make sure they agree to all these requests. If you see any discrepencies between what he is saying and his parents' and society's expectations, then know that a major disaster is waiting for you.

Some of your statements are of concern to us. It creates some doubts as to whether he is a love-proselytizer. You have stated that "he knows more about Hinduism than me," "I don't believe in idol worship" and "(kids) get confused between two religions." All of these are linked and need some elaboration.

Is his interest in Hinduism in order to find holes in your current beliefs, to try to confuse you and ultimately make you a Muslim? Please find out his intentions for learning about Hinduism.

The idea that "idol worship" and "kids will get confused between two religions" are an Abrahamic thought process and the result of their scripture's intolerant teachings.[205] Is he trying to brainwash you to be an exclusivist Muslim? As a Hindu, you know there are many ways to worship God and your children can be taught to value all of these ways and eventually make their own decisions as to what to believe.

First, Hindus don't pray to idols, but use murtis or deities in ritual worship or as a means to develop a personal connection with God. Christians and Muslims are also equally idol-worshippers. Jesus and Mohammad are the most glorified human beings in this world's history. Is there any other human as glorified? Christians have wood and gold

---

[205] Chapter XII and Section 2.11.

163

crosses, statues (idols?) of baby Jesus, Jesus, Mary, John, Paul, Peter, and Santa and so on; are not these idols? Muslim idols include Kaaba, Koran, Mohammad, Mecca, Dargah of Saints, Ayatollah, Persian writings, the Apostle's act of kissing the stone, going to a grave and praying the dead, etc. Why do Muslims bow down in the direction of Saudi Arabia but refuse to bow to our own *matru-bhumi* (Mother India)?

Why can't a child be raised in two (or no) faiths? When a Jain and a Hindu marry, there is no major confusion in raising a child. Hindu-Jain parents can teach both religions and take their children to derasars and temples. The problem comes when Christians and Muslims want to teach messages of their jealous One God theory. Barack Obama's mother taught him about ALL faiths. Obama turned out to be a fine human being even though he was not given a religious "label" in his childhood. In his adulthood he chose his religious faith. In the same way, tell your boyfriend that your children will NOT be Hindu or Muslim (no circumcision or sunat), but BOTH. Tell him that you will make sure your children will not get confused, but instead will be more open-minded.

Do you want your children to be Muslim and read Koran every day? Have you read the Koran? Are you comfortable with your children reciting those verses every day? All scriptures have their own limitations (including Hinduism). There are dogmas and there is the reality of living one's life. We suggest not making children Muslims or Hindus, but both. Take them to a mosque and a temple every week. Celebrate Diwali and Eid. Take the best from both and give the rest to religious fanatics. We hope your lover will agree to this.

In summary, please have a serious conversation with your Muslim boyfriend: 1) Tell him that you will raise children in BOTH faiths, but will not put a religious label on them. 2) Meet his parents and discuss your plans to get married in a court, that you are not converting and that your children will decide their religion at age 21+, 3) If they agree to that, go marry that guy in a court. Your sister will have to manage her life on her own. 4) However, if he or his parents don't agree (especially for the children's formal religion), then you have to get alarmed. Do not risk your life, your sister's life and your family for someone less reliable. Best wishes. —Admin

Section 5.23: My Girlfriend Is a Pure Muslim

Interfaith marriages are complex and it takes full maturity to understand all issues. Next three chaptes cover youths in their early 20s. Here, Agnostic is recommending Shiv to set priorities in life.

Shiv says:

I have a girlfriend. She is pure Muslim. We are best friends for the last one-year. I love her very much. But she is not accepting me because I am a Hindu boy. Her thought is little bit same about my thought, but her family is pure Muslim. We both are good and intelligent students. I know that India is a secular country and also I am not saying about any region. I believe in Allah as well as Hindu God. I am not discriminating against any religion. What can I do?

And I also want to crack IIT so that in future I will become a good engineer. Can her parents accept me after am successful? —Shiv

Agnostic says:

Firstly:

1. You mention you're trying to crack IIT. I assume you are 17-18. Forget about love. What do you know about how you will think 4 years ahead? And IIT is no cakewalk. When I was doing it, this was ALL I believed in, ate, slept, and worked on. IIT was like my religion (was much harder being a girl—no peer group). Either ways, You CANNOT have a relationship like this and hope to crack the IIT. Forget everything and go study—listen to me.

2. Again, you are VERY young. At this age, your thoughts will change super quickly. Your future plans might be totally different from hers 4-5 years down the road. Do you want to be in a relationship at the prime of your life at 21, just because you jumped into it without thinking? And another thing: you will change a lot during your undergrad, we all do. You will have grown as a person, and will definitely want different things later.

3. If she is not accepting you, it's possibly because she is not ready to go through with the challenges involved. Respect her choice. You should think before you step in to this. It's NOT an easy road. Unless BOTH of you accept each other and discuss the major points on religion, you should not take even one step ahead. Also your parents will not even take you seriously at this age. Most Hindu parents place a HIGH emphasis on education. Meet those expectations first.

4. There is a chance that you might have drifted apart during your undergrad from this girl due to rapidly changing personalities and experiences. Give that a chance to happen. Her life may be totally different from yours. It's a BAD idea to get into a relationship at your stage.

Also, if it's destined you'll make it together anyway and will be more convinced and mature to deal with such complicated things later on. — Agnostic

> It is easy to get married but divorces are painful and long drawn. In many cases, the divorce costs a lot more than the marriage!

Section 5.24: LOVE versus ARRANGED Marriage

Aziza says:

I'm a 21-year-old Muslim girl from India. I am in love with a Hindu guy. He loves me truly but my parents will never accept this relation. They are now in a hurry to look a perfect man for me. The guy I love has not got a good job yet. I am having a pretty good job now and waiting for him to settle in life. I can't tell my parents. Please help me with solution. — Aziza

Admin says:

Aziza,

It is fashionable to say LOVE marriage is better over ARRANGED marriage. Further, today's youths think why not go though interfaith marriage if your love is true. However, interfaith marriage is not for everyone. You are educated and smart, and thus should think through all possibilities before making a final decision for your life.

Jameela[206] had her own ways of interpreting Islamic scriptures ("if you quote say it's prohibited in Islam, it WAS prohibited. That rule was only valid within a context. I don't need anyone's interpretation to explain it"). In her case, she did not like Omar and was being forced by her parents to marry Omar against her wishes. Ultimately she married Vijay. We hope your parents are more considerate and not like Jameela's parents.

You mentioned that your parents are trying to find a "perfect" boy/man for you. Give them some time. Go talk to all the men they propose. If you come across a man that you start liking and he is comparable to your current Hindu boyfriend, go for him. If after meeting these men, you come to a decision that your Hindu boyfriend is much better over all the Muslim men proposed by your parents, go for the Hindu guy.

You know that it is absolutely no-no for a Muslim girl to marry a Hindu. Are you ready to go against your parents, brothers, sisters, relatives, imams and what the Koran says about Hindus?[207] Are all of these issues worth facing, to marry a Hindu lover?

If you are the one who is hoping that your boyfriend will convert to Islam by shahadah before your Islamic nikaah, you are nothing but a

---

[206] Section 5.29.
[207] Section 12.6.

love-jihadi. Do not ask a Hindu to fake-convert to Islam. Do not try now to love-proselytize him to make him a Muslim. Marriages involving religious conversion under lies, deceptions and love-pressure are not going to be happy in the long run. In this day and age, don't even dream of it.

Are you a true pluralist? Are you really ready to marry a Hindu and be a part of a Hindu family? Are you going to be comfortable being a part of Hindu wedding ceremony where multiple deities are being worshipped? Some day, your new Hindu family will have a Satya Narayan Katha or Diwali puja. Are you going to keep your distance during those family activities? If you don't take part in such pujas and sit in a different room, how will you expect your Hindu relatives to respect you?

Some day you will have to take your children to a Hindu mandir to pray to multiple forms of Supreme God. Are you going to be comfortable with it? Alternatively, are you going to decline all these deity puja and keep insisting that God's name is only Allah (not Ishvara as in Sanskrit) and further, all Hindus (and Christians) are going to get Hell Fire on the Judgment Day? If you believe that all Hindus are sinners (not following Koranic teachings), why will you want to associate with them? So first make up your mind—what do you wish to do?

We are not pro- or against- interfaith marriages or trying to discourage your love marriage, but wish to help you make a fully informed decision. You are only 21. Unless your parents are forcing you now to marry someone you don't like, please give some time to think through all these issues. Later, your Hindu boyfriend will also be working and thus will be in a strong financial position that will help if you wish to go against your parents and community. Best wishes. —Admin

---

Why was it necessary to convert and become Christian? Does God accept this that you fall in love and later don't agree to marry if the girl doesn't change religion! This is just not justified.
—Neena (Section 3.10)

Section 5.25: Gujarati UK Muslim in Love with a Hindu

In most interfaith relationships, there are issues relating to different faiths and cultures. Here, Noreen and her boyfriend have the same culture but different religions. Let's see what she has to say.

Noreen says:

I am an Indian Muslim living in the UK, and I am in love with a Hindu boy. He is also from the UK. I have known him for about 5 years. Everything is perfect between him and me, the language (Gujarati) is the same, our families are very similar and we make each other very happy. I have not found this type of relationship with a Muslim boy, and I truly am deeply in love with this Hindu boy. We both do want a future together. We both respect our own religions, and we both want to keep our own. I would not expect him to convert, nor will I convert either.

My family found out about him last year (we were seen together), and they are not happy and they are not allowing me to see him ever again. My mother was unhappy with me that I was seen with a guy from a different religion. This may have been because I am still young and so they do not want me making any mistakes. Behind their back I have been seeing this Hindu boy, and recently, his family found out (we were seen together, again). They are not happy with him at all, and he thinks they (Hindus) will never accept me because of this religion barrier.

I don't know what to do, because we are both deeply in love with each other and can see a future. It is just that our families will not accept. I know that it is more important that his family accepts me because I will be going into his family and living with them (as much as I would want my family to accept), how can I get them to accept me?

I am thinking of trying to meet them and maybe let them get to know me? I am unsure of what to do, because I do not want this relationship to end. He is a big part of my life now. I really can't live without him!

I would appreciate any advice and help on this. Thank you. —Noreen

Admin says:

Noreen,

You and your boyfriend's families have the same common ancestors, speak the same Gujarati language, eat the same delicious Gujarati food (with extra sugar!), drink water from the same river, go to the same schools and colleges, breathe the same dusty air, get baked in the same hot sun, and what not. Then why there should be any differences between you two? Well, the difference is religion.

Do not go to his parents yet and try to convince them of anything, because you yourself don't know who you are. Have you read the Koran? What does Islam means to you? If you say you are a proud Muslim believing in Mohammad, then are you going to have Islamic nikaah and ask your Hindu boyfriend to fake-convert to Islam by shahadah? If not, it is anti-Islamic to marry or to tolerate a Hindu as a husband.

If you feel strongly that you want to practice Islam, with its religious ceremonies and customs, give your Muslim parents time to find a potential husband who is educated and can provide a good future for you. Date him and see if he will treat you with dignity and respect for life. If you do find a Muslim man like that, strongly consider him; it may be better for you in the long run to remain within your religion. If your parents can't find a suitable match for you, then resume your relationship to your Hindu boyfriend (assuming he accepts this brief exploration).

If you are in UK, then wait till you are financially independent. If you do decide to get married, rent a flat and plan to live there separate from parents. Keep in touch with both sets of parents and love them. It may take several years of married life to win their trust, but it will happen.

The bottom line is, educate yourself, decide who you are, decide what is the rational thing to do, be financially independent, get married without conversion, triple love both sets of parents, have patience and ultimately you will win. You will feel joyous to see two former enemy families are now hugging each other and loving each other; that is a Godly work! — Admin

Noreen says:

Hi Admin,

Thank you for your reply!

I know for sure I really want to spend the rest of my life with him. I am aware I am young, however, his family now knows about me and so I need to act fast. They are not happy that I am Muslim. I haven't yet told him that I would like to meet his parents. I feel I should as this can give them a chance to get to know me and see that I am very serious about him, and that I would like to spend my future with him.

Marriage wise, I am not sure how it would take place, me being Muslim and him still being Hindu. As you were saying he couldn't be part of the nikaah if he is still Hindu, so I am not sure how a marriage ritual can take place between us. This would be in years to come once he and I are financially stable, but I do wonder how the marriage can take place in the UK.

He does feel his parents may not accept, and that is why I feel I should introduce myself to them because he is getting a very hard time at home from them too. I know my parents may not accept either, and that I would risk losing my whole family, which is a very huge step for me. I really want to be happy, and that is with him, but I know there would need to be big sacrifices for that to happen. —Noreen

Like salad in a bowl, where tomato stays tomato and celery stays celery; merge and respect each other's faith. There is no need for anyone to convert. Enjoy the interfaith marriage with equality of both faiths.

Section 5.26: How to Convince My Muslim Parents?

"How to convince my parents" is a common question asked at InterfaithShaadi. Before convincing parents, youths have to convince themselves for what they are getting into. Next three sections cover such cases.

Jameel says:

Well, I (Muslim) also have a query. I'm in a relationship with a Brahmin gal for around 4 years. I'm still pursuing my education. We both are comfortable with each other's religion, but the main problem is convincing the parents. I don't want to convert my partner to Islam for the heck of it, if she doesn't believe truly. I don't give a damn to what the society would say. But I don't want to hurt my parents. How could I convince them? —Jameel

Admin:

Are you typical of Muslim youth that we found on this web site? During your dating period, will you keep convincing the Hindu (or Christian) that you don't have to convert, that you respect their religion, and that there is only one God so why to fight over it, and that you don't give a damn what society will say, blah…blah…blah… After years of romantic relationship however, will you change your tune i.e. "please convert for my parents," "I didn't know this coming," "please convert for the heck of it," "it (shahadah) doesn't not mean anything" and so and so.

You have mentioned, "I don't want my partner to convert to Islam for the heck of it, if she doesn't believes truly," so will you change your mind and love-proselytize to convince her that Islam is the only true religion? In the end, if she doesn't convert for nikaah, are you going to dump her for the sake of Islam and your parents?

We apologize if we stereotyped you. Let's hope you are a different, like Jameela,[208] Azad,[209] Seema[210] and Shah Rukh Khan.[211] We admire your thoughts of not trying to convert her. The fake conversion of a Hindu just to please your imam and parents will not be any good for anyone. In the

---

[208] Section 5.29.
[209] Section 6.1.
[210] Section 5.4.
[211] http://www.youtube.com/watch?v=Py7sFkIGi-k.

end, she will curse you for being coerced into an Islamic life that she had no intention of being in. Please continue to think of other options.

Tell your parents that this world is for everyone, be that Muslims, Hindus, Christians, Jews, Jains or atheists. Every religious leader tries to prove that they have the true religion and others are wrong. Religious institutions have a vested interest that religious divisions should continue among people; otherwise they will not have money to pay their utility bills. Do not get trapped into religious leaders' problems. Do what is the humane thing to do.

The religious labeling (BBS) has no place in an interfaith marriage with equality. It is time to respect fellow humans the way they are. Remind your parents that neither you nor they are true Muslims unless you are praying five times a day/every day and conducting your lives 100% as written in Islamic books. What was written thousands of years may have been relevant in it's own historical context, but many suggestions may not be relevant today.

Ask them how they would feel if your girlfriend asked you to convert to Hinduism?

By making your Brahmin girlfriend take 2 minutes of shahadah oath for conversion, you would please your parents and the imam, but perhaps not God. God is no fool. He knows what you are up to! Your girlfriend will also not be fooled for long. One day she may curse you for making her change her birth religion. Instead, respect her the way she is and she will double her respect for who you are. Your parents may not like this interfaith marriage in the beginning, but we hope that ultimately they will realize the truth—that she is good human being who respects your faith. Best wishes convincing your parents. —Admin

> *Pujas for Hindus and Ramadan for Muslims.*
> *Doing things together that bind you as a family. It takes*
> *INCREDIBLE strength to try to manage two cultures/religions*
> *and unhappy families.*
> *—Shasha (Section 5.8)*

Section 5.27: I Am a Brahmin Girl Dating a Shia Muslim

Gita says:

I am a Brahmin girl and I am dating a boy who is Shia Muslim. I love him a lot and want to spend my whole life with him. But neither my parents nor his parents want us to marry. Now please tell me what should I do? —Gita

Admin says:

You may marry by the Indian Special Marriage Act 1954. There are many advantages, like no easy talaak, he can't have multiple wives, there is no need to convert as you would for nikaah, it will assure your parents that he is not a love-jihadi, etc. If many Bollywood celebrities have done it, why you can't? Don't convert to Islam just for nikaah (marriage), unless you truly believe in Koranic teachings. Why don't you propose it to your boyfriend?

We believe it is best to discover the facts now. You both need to collect the courage and present your plan to both parents. Let it be a big *hungama* (agitation) but you may find a good way out of it.

It is important for you (a Brahmin) and him (a Muslim) to make an "informed" decision. Please have you and your boyfriend review, come to an agreement and then sign this Q&A form. Present it to your parents.

Ten Questions:

Q1) How will you get married? Hindu wedding? Islamic nikaah? Court only marriage? All three?

Q2) Do you or do you not have to have a religious conversion to Islam by shahadah?

Q3) Do you have to accept a new Muslim first name?

Q4) Are you allowed to bring a few Hindu Gods/Murtis in your/their Muslim home and will you be allowed to have a daily puja? (and also have a photo of the Kaaba in your altar?)

Q5) Are the Muslim boyfriend and his parents planning to join you at your Hindu temple and be a part of Satyanarayan Katha while at your parents' home (and your parents reciprocate by attending a mosque)?

Q6) Do you have to eat meat during Muslim festivals like Bakra-Eid?

Q7) Can your first child have a Hindu name like Arjun and your second child have a Muslim name like Mohammad?

Q8) Do your male children have to have a sunat circumcision?

Q9) Can you teach your children from the Geeta as well from the Koran? Will your (future) husband also do the same to educate them?

Q10) What will you teach your children about who is God(s)? Who are Allah, Jesus, Krishna-Radha, Rama and Laxmi?

Do not assume anything; instead find the facts now. It will be good for BOTH of you to know what you are getting into.

The main reason for any divorce is the complaint that the other party "changed" after the marriage. Actually no one changes, but when in love, one may fail to recognize the totality of the other person. We know you will make a better decision when it is a fully "informed" decision. We wish you to have a happy and long lasting Brahmin-Muslim married life with equality. Best wishes. —Admin

Refugees and immigrant Muslims in Christian majority nations demand religious equality but most Muslim majority nations (e.g., Malaysia, read Section 2.15) have created laws to marginalize Christians and non-Muslim minorities.

Section 5.28: How Can I Convince My Muslim Parents That This Is Not Going against Islam?

Naazli says:

I want to marry my Hindu boyfriend but how can I convince my parents that this is not going against Islam? I have done research on the internet and all I see is that Koran does not allow a Muslim to marry a non-Muslim.

Azad and Tejpreet,[212] if you guys can read this, please let me know your opinions about this. My parents are very supportive but they are worried that I will go against Allah. Please help. Thank you. —Naazli

Admin says:

Dear Naazli,

Before convincing your parents, first you have to be convinced for yourself. You have made very contrasting statements. On one side you said "I want to marry my Hindu boyfriend" and on the other side "this is not going against Islam" and "worried that I will go against Allah."

If your primary objective is to please Allah and follow the Koran, DO NOT EVER marry an idol-worshipper kafir Hindu; do not even dream. Instead find a true Muslim who performs namaz five times a day. This is the way to make Allah happy. If not in THIS life, you will certainly have a good AFTER life, according to Islam.

We believe the worst you could do is to ask the Hindu to "fake" convert to Islam. This "fake" conversion will ruin the lives of both of you and both sides' extended families.

Interfaith marriages are for people who believe in interpreting scriptures in their own way, not literally. For example, Jameela[213] has stated, "it WAS prohibited, that rule was only valid within a context." Are you open for interpretation of the Koran in your own way that makes sense in today's world?

We recommend you to sit down with both sets of parents and be transparent with each other's expectations. Do not rush into marriage for at least a year or two and make a fully "informed" decision. —Admin

---

[212] Section 6.1.
[213] Section 5.29.

Section 5.29: A Muslim Girl: My Boyfriend Is a Hindu - Vijay or Omar?

At InterfaithShaadi, we came across a very few Muslims (out of more than 700) who were truly pluralist. The next two sections cover such examples.

Jameela says:

Salam,

Jameela here I'm in a difficult situation. My boyfriend is a Hindu. My parents don't like him talking to me. Actually it's high time and they are forcing me to marry a guy in my area, Omar. I'm crying day and night. I just want to marry Vijay and spend my life with him. But no one from my family is supporting me for marriage with him, due to his religion; I don't want him to change (his religion).

My dad has given me warning to stop seeing Vijay. I'm educated. I love my parents, but I can't stand their torture anymore for marriage to Omar. I will run away or die one day, I don't know. Vijay is earning. His family is nice and he will take care of me. What should I do? I have very less time; I don't want to leave him. —Jameela

Jameela says:

Salam,

Muslim brother Abdul. I don't agree with you. I believe in Allah, and I also believe in the existence of other Gods as well. Just because I love a guy who is non-Muslim, do you think I have no faith? I am sorry to say you have same thinking as my father. Tell me a concrete reason why I should not marry Vijay. Have you met him? What do you mean by this site (InterfaithShaadi) being anti-Muslim? When I saw the case of Punita,[214] she is Jain-Hindu and loves a Muslim boy; you did not say anything? This narrow-minded mentality that my father has is what I don't like. I love Vijay, because he will keep me happy and let me practice my religion. I will be working too. My Allah has no problem but you half-Muslim half-narrow minded Muslim have. —Jameela

---

[214] Section 7.1.

177

Jameela says:

Hi Srinivas,

I dont think Muslims attack Hindus for marrying Muslim girls. It's only those Muslim who feel inferiority complex. I am educated Muslim girl and I know about Allah and humanity. Why can't Muslim girls fall in love with Hindu boys? **If you say it's prohibited in Islam, it WAS prohibited**. That rule was only valid within a context. I don't need anyone's interpretation to explain it. Why only girls suffer from all the rules? Muslim boys have Hindu girlfriend. That is banned too in Islam but no one preaches Koranic lessons then, but only when we Muslim girls love a human being all the hell breaks loose.

I hate people like Abdul who only misrepresent Islam, he wants everyone to convert to Islam else you are a fool. He is narrow-minded person. I don't want to get married to a driver or an electrician. I love Vijay. He loves me so much. He accepts me as a Muslim. I have made it clear that I would not convert to Hinduism, even though I respect it just like Islam and that's all I want. For Vijay I will do everything. If my family hurts him, I will be with Vijay and seek police help. —Jameela

Jameela says (two months later):

By grace of Allah I am married to Vijay now. I cannot tell how happy I am. There is nothing that comes in between our love. I pray and Vijay prays with me. I see so many discussions on this site (InterfaithShaadi) on Hindu and Muslim marriage, I just want to say that some fundamentalists want everyone to convert to Islam, but they don't know Islam can't be forced. It's in Koran. I have seen my parents' biased opinions on Muslim women marriage versus Muslim boys (Muslim boys are given much freedom, which is against Islam). What I see is lack of love for different religions and culture in their circle, which is usually like being with only Muslims, no diversity. I hope that changes and peace comes to all of us. —Jameela

Jameela says (five months later):

Hi everybody,

Ever since I am married with Vijay, fortune appears to be changing dramatically for good. Both of us have got a good job in a MNC and soon shall be going to Singapore. Another most exciting event of my life is that I am pregnant now. Wow! What a pleasant surprise. My parents have agreed, no problem now, reality has been accepted. —Jameela

Section 5.30: I Fell in Love with a Hindu Boy

Muslimah says:

I have been living my whole life in a Western country, but my parents are from an Asian Muslim country. Growing up with strict parents in a secular country was really hard for me. I was not allowed to do much without their permission. Going to school and college was my way out for freedom. My parents never had a problem with me studying, though they did always want me to marry as soon as possible. I managed to decline all the marriage proposals and continued studying and travelling around the world.

During my stay in India 3 years back I fell in love with a wonderful Hindu boy. To me he is everything and today we are still together despite the differences of religion and culture. We had our ups and downs but we love each other so much that nothing can stop us. We both live in two separate countries from each other but we have maintained our relationship very well and I am just really proud of us because of that.

My mom totally disapproves it and my dad will never accept it since he is a very strict religious Muslim. They will for sure disown me for a while and try to do anything to make me not be with my Hindu boyfriend. I really feel sad about the fact that my family is like this. I wish I could just be with him without causing much trouble in the family. I also feel very guilty about me being with someone who is not a Muslim just for the sake of my parents.

I respect Islam and also my parents believe in Islam, but I would like them to respect and accept my choice of being with a Hindu man for the rest of my life.

I believe in God, but I don't practice religion since I just don't think I need it personally. I am not against any religion and I just want my children to learn about all religions and they can choose any religion if they want.

I am planning to tell my parents about me wanting to marry him in a few months from now. At the moment I am busy with my M.Sc. and my boyfriend is focusing on his business in India. I am already financially independent and know how to manage things on my own.

I hope that everything works out for my boyfriend and me in the future. I also hope the same for other Muslim girls in the same situation. I know how hard it is but please don't give up if the man you are with is really

179

good to you and is making you happy. Because finding a good man is hard these days, regardless of any religion.

Once again I am not against Islam or any other religion. I highly respect all religions and the people who don't believe in the existence of god. I am not planning to convert to Hinduism and I am certainly not expecting my boyfriend to convert to Islam. Thanks. —Muslimah

Toleration means that I think that you are wrong and I am just allowing you to live. Is it not blasphemy to think that you and I are allowing others to live?
I accept all the religions that were in the past and worship with them all; I worship God with every one of them, in whatever form they worship Him.
—Swami Vivekananda (Pasadena, California, Jan 28, 1900)

Section 5.31: My Wife Calls Me Kafir… I Wish I Die

Sometimes, interfaith marriage takes an ugly turn and life becomes hell. The next four sections cover such cases.

Shyam says:

I am in a relationship with a Muslim for almost 18 years. I am a Hindu and she is a Muslim. We have 3 children. Initially when we fell in love, there were no religious boundaries but only love. Her family disowned her until we had our first child. She has brought up the kids as Muslims. More and more she is moving into the world of Islam and more and more am I moving away from her. Recently she has started wearing a veil. This is hard for me to accept. I am respected by her family but always treated as an outcast due to my religion and language. I love her but she has chosen her religion over me. She calls me and my family kafirs. She does not believe in birthdays or Hindu weddings. I am hurt so much.

Almost half my life has been spent with her and the kids. I used to love her but it is now turning into hatred of the Muslim religion for turning her into what she is. Today my children told me that they are Muslims and don't believe in Hinduism. What am I to do? I am a Hindu. I feel like I want to die. The pain is so great in my chest. I wish I had married a Hindu.

My life is a big lie. I lie to my parents about the kids being Hindus and not eating meat. I feel I am sinking and there is no one to pull me out. Every time the word Hindu is mentioned, I am called a kafir. Is this what I am at the age of forty? What have I done? I feel worthless and feel I should die before my mum and dad do. My sons or wife will not attend the funeral. I don't know what to do. I feel so sad. —Shyam

Shyam added (a month later):

I feel really bad. My days and nights are so long. My partner views Islam higher than me. After all I am a Hindu and a kafir in her eye. I live to support her and my 3 kids. I wish I die. I cannot be happy with my immediate family or hers. What is there in life to live for? I suffer from asthma and each day I hope I will have a big attack and die. I ask myself am I a kafir? Was I so low? My mother says no. She tells me that I am a Brahmin.

I see my pain and urge all Muslims and Hindus to never get involved in a relationship as it only ends up in pain. May be not right away, but eventually.

I feel like taking my life but find it hard because of my children. Why is life so hard? All communication has broken down. What is there to look for in life apart from death? I can't wait.

I would like to die before my mom and dad so they can cremate me. I can be free then. What a life of lies and misery, don't put yourself through this.

Should I leave her? I feel I can't due to the kids.

Should I die? This is easier.

Please help me. —Shyam

A Message to Parents about Interfaith Marriages

- *Assume your children could potentially marry interfaith and be prepared for it.*
- *Teach your children to follow interfaith equality in marriage.*
- *Ask them how the BBS religious labeling of offspring makes sense (or does not) in an interfaith marriage with equality.*
- *The "fake" religious conversion for marriage will bring only disaster later in life for the couple and two sets of families.*

Section 5.32: Life Has Been Sooo Difficult...

Chitra says:

I heard mixed opinions from so many people before I married my Muslim husband. In the end I went with my emotions that said, "as long as we two are happy that is enough, doesn't matter about the difference in religion." That was 10 years ago.

I can truly say that once the period of "marriage bliss" wore off, life has been sooo difficult... 10-fold after the children came. I've realized I cannot be a true mother to them. I had to give them Islamic names, go through Islamic traditions at their birth.

Now that they are older, I have to observe them praying and learning the Koran. I can't give them the experiences that I had in my childhood—certain dishes, clothing, Holi and Diwali. Birthday parties and photographs are forbidden in my home.

My (parents) family don't try to intervene, nor do they want their children to start thinking that it's ok for them to have an inter-religious marriage, so they (my family) avoid us. We (my family) don't quite fit into my husband's family so we avoid them. My husband wants our children to be strong Muslims so wants to create this atmosphere at home. So he doesn't allow the children to play in the street where they might mix with neighborhood non-Muslim children.

I feel isolated now and wish that things could be different. I hope this message gets to you (Gita) in time, before you make a decision that would change your life. Remember it's not just your lives that would be changing but also the lives of your parents, siblings and extended family. My family doesn't EVER say anything negative to me but I see it on their faces and their behavior. —Chitra

Chitra Added (five months later):

Anita,

My willingness to be cooperative with my husband's teachings is coming to an end. By my husband's behavior, I know he too realizes this. He now intentionally separates the children from me and teaches them that the people who try to question Islam are filled with evil and that they should hate and feel superior to all Non-Muslims; including their Non-Muslim mother.

I see the difference in their behavior: When a child hurts himself or feels hungry, won't he instinctively run to his mother who is in the home with him? Of late, the children phone my husband at work for their daily needs rather than come to me. They are also afraid to show affection to me in front of him—startle in the middle of a smile or a hug if they hear my husband's voice.

I hurt deeply when I ask myself—who are emotionally affected by all this manipulation? My husband believes he is one of many crusaders responsible to spread the belief of Islam and will continue to pivot his life around that for the rest of his life… with the intent of propagating the same to his children.

Anita, if I stay, amn't I harming my children? This is why I say that my days of tolerance are ending. —Chitra

> The Vedanta recognizes no sin; it only recognizes error. And the greatest error, says the Vedanta, is to say that you are weak, that you are a sinner, a miserable creature, and that you have no power and you cannot do this and that.
> —Swami Vivekananda

Section 5.33: He Would Beat Me Now and Then

Chetna says:

I am a Brahmin girl living with my mother.

My maternal grandparents, a hard-core Brahmin, brought me up. I began my Sanskrit education at home and was then sent to a Gurukul. I studied the Vedas, Upanishads and the Shastra. I always followed a satvik life and stayed at bay from non-veg, drinks, smoking, onions, garlic and other tamsic food. As a kid, I learnt to respect every animal, insect and plant and the panch tatva. My family never bought anything made of leather! We follow SHAIVISM and I am immensely in love with Lord Shiva, He is every thing to me!

Few years back I met a Muslim guy and we fell in love. He was always religious but in the beginning he was tolerant and we both used to share things about our religion. He use to take me to temples and eventually after 1 year we got married as per Hindu rights in the presence of a pandit, my mother and his friends. From here began our story of physical involvement (he is the only man who I ever have been physically involved with and that too after marrying him before Lord Shiva).

Soon I realized that this marriage meant nothing to him and may be it **was just a way to get me into his bed**. After 2-3 months of marriage he began to force me to convert to Islam. This was forbidden for me!!! The first shock that came my way was when he began taking me to marriages and parties. I could not eat anything. It was just beef, meat etc. (oh my God!) I had never seen all of this. Second shock that struck me was that he wanted me to cover my head 24×7.

I soon became dependent on him for every little thing and did whatever he said. I began reading the Koran, covered my head and used no make up, etc. But I refused to eat meat and leave my satvik life style. My son (dog) is the most important thing to me… more important than myself. I love him the way any mother would love his child. I realized soon he and his family wanted me to separate my son (the dog) from me. I objected because I could never understand their objections despite reading the Koran.

We began having fights over religion. He would insult my religion and idols etc., even wearing a teeka (head dot) would create issues. He began making faces every time I would even use a little bit of Sanskrit. I thought of giving in and decided to convert… for me my heart matters and that will always be ruled by Lord Shiva. I converted and tried every

185

bit to make him happy but not sacrificing on my basics of sattva guna, mother and goofy (my dog). I have always been a Hindu at heart. I am very tolerant and sensitive.

He knew my love for Lord Shiva and knew that I would die but will surely fast on Shivratri. After conversion this was my first Shivratri. True to what he thought, I fasted. He followed me on that day and the moment he saw me at a temple he thrashed me to death. From here began his beating. Now he would beat me every now and then.

I soon began feeling suffocated and one fine day, I told him that I can't act anymore and that I'm happy in my own religion. We had a huge fight. Finally after a month he got back. But for two years my life became a living hell. He would talk nothing but Islam and tell me how people who do not follow the book (the Koran) will be punished etc. Later, we had a huge fight as he came over to my house… and got mad at the puja that my mom and I were performing.

We broke up for 3 months, and we got back later, and again broke up. — Chetna

Chetna added (two months later):

Dear Admin, Satyen and all others,

Today I am leading a very happy and stable life. I am lucky; later things moved fast and in my favor. However, this would not have been possible without the support of InterfaithShaadi and all of you. Especially without Satyen Bhai, who has always been there and Admin who has been truly kind. LOVE. —Chetna

---

Innocent and emotional girls sometimes get trapped by whosoever appears to respect them, though this "respect" is false. There are so many anti social elements in the society who are disguised as gentlemen but are conspirator inside.
—Abida
(www.interfaithshaadi.org/blog/?p=2529&cpage=1#comment-31103)

Section 5.34: I Am a Hindu Now: A Former Muslim's Life Story

Madiha says:

I was born into a very staunch Muslim family in the US, learning to read the Koran the moment I could read. I was under the misconception that if I did not do as Allah told me to do, I would be punished severely. I was also told that if I didn't wear modest clothes I was being immoral. Right from a little girl I wore the headscarf. My friends would ask me why, and I would tell them "because God said so."

As I grew, strictness of my family started to go out of hand as they started disciplining me in just about everything. Pointing out to me things that I should do and forced me to do whatever they wanted. I was allowed no freedom outside as well as within the house for the most stupid reasons. My father also restrained me from going out. I was not allowed to speak to the opposite sex but being stubborn, I did just that. When my father found out, about me talking to a guy, when I was 14, my grandmother scolded me and even called me a prostitute. I cried for hours, her words cutting me deep.

Once my grandfather and grandmother went to meet our relative, that day I wore jeans and T-shirt and went out with the consent of my mother. I enjoyed with my school friends. When I came home I saw my grandmother was at home and she was abusing and beating my mother for allowing me to go out without hijab. My grandmother called me prostitute again and again.

I remember during Bakra Eid (sheep slaughtering festival), my mother and myself used to confine into room and used to cry while my family used to celebrate and rejoice in killing innocent animals. My mother and I were nothing but prisoner in our own house. I grew up seeing beating and abusing of my mother by my father and his family.

Majority of my school friends were non-Muslims. I was very much comfortable with Hindus, Sikhs and Christians. When my grandmother got to know about this, my grandmother scolded my mom and me and told me that we are not allowed to be friends with kafirs. When I asked her why, She said Hindus are filthy, Jews and Christians are apes and pigs and they are not Humans, they follow Satan. I was shocked.

Around the age of 14, I realized how much of life I was missing out on. How my father commanded that I do my prayers 5 times a day and never play any sports because they would only lead me to the devil. One night I

187

was talking to my parents about college and my father said that I would never go to college because he had chosen a boy for me and I was about to get married to him as soon as I turned 18. I was shocked... my mother ran out of the room crying. I began to plead with my father to let me go to college. But he said no. When I asked him why, he told me that Muslim women are not supposed to be educated or go to work. They are supposed to be good wives, who never disagree with their husbands and be good honorable women. I couldn't believe my ears. This man was still living in the dark-ages.

The next day after school I went to the mosque to talk with our Maulvi Sahab. When I told him about my father's irrational behavior, he agreed with him. He told me that if all the Muslim men in our community thought like my father, we would be in a really good place right now.

I was stuck and didn't know what to do. I kept thinking about it till late that night. At around 2 am my mom came to check up on me and found me crying. She told me that she had been a well-educated (Doctor) Hindu woman who had fallen in love with my father in India. During their courtship my father had told her that he was very broad-minded and did not want her to convert when they got married. Against my grandparents' wishes she married him and did the nikaah just so her mother-in-law would like her. That's where her nightmare began. Her in-laws would not let her go out of the house. No one could come and visit her. She was confined in a home where everyone would spit on her for being a "kafir." They made her read the Koran and do namaz. If she didn't they would beat her. My father would come home and force himself on her. When she would ask him not to, he would tell her that it was written in the Koran, and she was nothing more than a slave to him. After about a year of their marriage, they left for the US. My mom was already pregnant with me.

When I was born he was not too happy with my Mom. He said that if he had married someone of his own faith he would have had a boy for sure. Giving him a girl was the way Allah was punishing him for marrying a Hindu.

When I heard all this I began to hate my father and Islam. I promised to get my mom out of this situation and also never ever end up like her. When I turned 18, along with the help of a lawyer, I managed to get my mom and dad divorced. My mom actually went back to school and has a flourishing practice now.

As for me, you might say that I reverted. I am a practicing and loving Hindu now. I have changed my name (real name is not given with the fear of punishment of death for apostasy). I live a life full of love and adoration for a God who does not preach hate, who encourages me to think and gain knowledge, who shows me the way without fear and who loves everyone no matter who they are.

At the age of 23, I got married to my Hindu boyfriend and now we have one beautiful daughter. My loving hubby is a great guy. He gave me complete freedom and my rights that my father and his family never gave me. My hubby's families treat me like their own daughter; and even treat my mom as a part of our family. I thank God for all these. —Madiha

> *The main reason for any divorce is the complaint that the other party "changed" after the marriage. Actually no one changes, but in love, one fails to recognize the other person.*

Chapter VI: Sikh-Muslim Marriages

Couples in Sikh-Muslim relationship are requested to first read/view:
- Section 2.2: Ten Points of Interfaith Dating
- Section 2.3: FAQ on Interfaith Marriages
- Section 2.15: Interfaith Marriage and Divorce Laws
- Section 12.6: The Koran on Hindus?
- Watch these videos prepared by InterfaithShaadi:
  https://www.youtube.com/watch?v=gvZSqdmnxKM.
  https://www.youtube.com/watch?v=RiWLGEKusIg.

Section 6.1: Sikh-Muslim Marriage with Equality

The author believes this is a case of true interfaith marriage with equality.

Azad says:

My wife (Tejpreet) is Sikh and I am a Muslim. When we got married, she never said the shahadah (conversion) because in Islam that is a form of accepting Islam (which is the mainstream view) so she did not say it. We had a simple ceremony in the court, because we belonged to different religions. We had a reception after, just to celebrate and it was fine. No one in our families had a problem with that, and we are happy. But I think it depends on the spouse in question. These kinds of things should be discussed before the wedding ceremony so that both parties know where they stand.

My thinking is more open minded and liberal, so I will never ask my wife to do something that I know I could not do. If I cannot change my faith, who am I to ask her to do the same? That's hypocrisy. She is Sikh and will remain Sikh and I am still Muslim. We are happy and I don't think someone should say it just to "please" their spouse's family. I think your faith is a part of who you are, and even though I am a Muslim, whatever you are raised as, Hindu, Sikh, Jain, etc., you should stay within your faith because it is your identity.

My wife and I will teach our children the main tenets of both our faiths. We have even decided on names that are found in both religions. I was always raised liberal and my wife is also tolerant, so we don't see anything wrong in celebrating holidays and customs from both faiths. The more the merrier is what I always say, who wouldn't mind having more excuses to celebrate? Before we got married, my wife actually asked me the same and I told her nothing she believes contradicts my own beliefs. We both believe in One God, and we share the same language and homeland, and giving to charity. Being a good human being is the foundation of all great religions.

My parents accepted my wife for who she was. My own father, despite reading Koran everyday and praying 5 times, sits with my wife whom he loves as a daughter and even takes her to the Gurdwara so that she does not feel like she is married somewhere where she is not accepted. Instead of saying Allah hafiz or something in Urdu, he says things like Rab rakha because they accept my wife. At times I am still surprised to this day how much my parents adore her. She's the daughter they never had, and

193

my parents are quite religious. I don't think that Islam has taught them to be cruel. In fact my father is the most religious person and he gets along the most with my wife.

I think I did get lucky because I get to learn new things from her side of the family everyday. But if I'm honest, religion isn't really what comes across my mind when I'm with her. I just see her as the woman I fell in love with. I don't really care at that point what faith she belongs to or what faith I belong to. She completes me and I thank God everyday for her. —Azad

Tejpreet says:

I am not here trying to say go and marry out of religion. All I'm trying to say is that it's wrong to assume that anyone who does interfaith marriage is a shame on his or her culture. I always thought that above all God was love, and in my own belief I only believe in one God and that God is everyone's, not just God of a select few.

Why are others so concerned about my children? My husband and I are happy raising them, and contrary to your narrow-minded beliefs we do speak the same language and are from the same area back home. My family accepted my husband and vice versa because they knew him from the time we were young, and know he is hardworking and a kind individual. Why do you only look at a person's faith and nothing else?

I did not hide anything from my family and neither did he, nor did we get married against anyone's wishes. I don't think anyone has any right to wish ill upon my children or say that they will grow up confused because they are not. They know their culture, we celebrate holidays, they know their language, and I don't need to justify to anyone that my children are happy.

Interfaith marriages have been happening since the times of the Mughal empire, it's not something new, but people nowadays have two sides… either they are accepting or are very radical and intolerant. Whether you like it or not, the world is changing and the youth is taking steps to wipe out the barriers that communities have built. I'm not saying convert and disregard your culture and traditions, but to say that whoever falls in love with someone from a different faith is stupid if he/she doesn't know about their culture is ignorance. I don't think it works that way. Love is different. It doesn't matter what faith you belong to. I'm simply saying that we should refrain from saying ill about another's faith.

My husband and I are from different religions and we are very happy. I love him a lot and our families support us and we are both learned in our own cultures and traditions. Neither one of us converted into the other's faith nor do we fall into the traps of society and what people think. No one has ever won the world and they never will. —Tejpreet

---

People's opinions and people words are stronger than weapons and can completely ruin true love, something so beautiful and pure.
—David (Section 8.4)

Section 6.2: A Sikh Girl with a Muslim for 10 Years

Surinder says:

I am recently going under huge stress. I am in love with a Muslim guy. I am a Punjabi Sikh. We have been in love with each other for nearly ten years now… and now the time has come when my family has started to pressurize me to get married. My family is very nice. But in our culture it's going to be a big issue if I marry a non-Sikh and non-Indian guy.

I have not told my family that I am in love with a Muslim guy as that might cause chaos. But now the pressure is unbearable and I don't want to marry anyone else at any cost. I don't know how I should tell my family without hurting them. The guy I am with; he briefly got permission to marry me but he is unable to take it further as I am just terrified to tell my family about it. Has anyone experienced or going through similar situation I would like to hear, thanks. —Surinder

Admin says:

Hi Surinder,

Your parents will be hurt with your news but ultimately they will have to get over it. It is most critical to decide what is good for you in a long run. You need to make fully informed decision, so collect the facts without being emotional. For an ever-lasting happy married life (and to please your parents half way), it is important to have a Sikh-Muslim marriage with equality.

You have stated, "He briefly got permission (from Muslim parents) to marry" you. Is that permission with or without the shahadah religious conversion of a Sikh to Islam? Ideally, you should have asked this simple question much earlier in the course of your relationship, not after 10 years!

From your Muslim boyfriend and his family, find answers to these questions:
Q1) How will you get married? Sikh wedding? Islamic nikaah after shahadah? Court only marriage? All three?
Q2) What happens if you adamantly say NO to religious conversion to Islam?
Q3) Do you have to accept a new Muslim first name?
Q4) Are you allowed to bring Guru Granth Sahib and display Guru Nanak's photo in your living room (along with a photo of Kaaba)?

Q5) Are the Muslim boyfriend and his parents planning to join you to a Gurdwara and be a part of Sikh religious ceremonies while at your parents' home (and you attend his mosque)?

Q6) Can your first child have a Sikh name (and the second child have an Arabic name)?

Q7) Do your male children have to have a sunat circumcision?

Q8) Can you teach your children from Guru Granth Sahib as well from the Koran? Will your (future) husband also do the same to educate your children?

Q9) What will you teach your children about... Who is God? Are Sikh gurus and Mohammad the same; that is, messengers of same God?

Q10) Do you ever have to go under the burka or hijab cover?

After collecting all the facts, go to your parents with open mind. Do not lie to them or hide the facts. Do not get into irrational arguments; try to remain objective. Listen carefully to all their concerns and think it over for a few days. Then resume your discussion with your parents with your decision. Try to convince them that your boyfriend is the right person for you and explain why, without drama and without severing your relationship with your parents—one day you may need them again!

Convince your parents that your boyfriend is not a love-jihadi, but more like Azad,[215] Seema[216] and Shah Rukh khan,[217] who truly respect their spouses' religion and believe in interfaith marriage with equality. Best wishes. —Admin

---

[215] Section 6.1.

[216] Section 5.4.

[217] http://www.youtube.com/watch?v=Py7sFkIGi-k.

Section 6.3: I Couldn't Ask My Love to Embrace Islam

Tasneem says:

I think it's disgusting how people want to degrade each other's religions. I'm a Muslim woman in love with a Sikh man and although I feared what would happen and worried how we are going to be together, I have now come to the conclusion that I don't care what the world says. The Koran says a Muslim may marry whomever he or she wants to marry provided they are Muslim. I could not ask my love to embrace Islam because I don't want him to do it for me. If he learns about my religion it will help him understand. If during this learning he decides to be a Muslim then I will thank Allah for giving me this blessing. In turn I am willing to learn and understand his religion too.

If we can't get married and it isn't in our *kismet* (fortune) then we won't marry and may Allah give us the strength to live our lives righteously with each other. We will never marry anyone else.

I just pray people stop spreading hate and show respect to each other and their religion. —Tasneem

> *Interfaith lovers must realize that you are not only marrying a person but also his/her family and community.*

Chapter VII: Jain-Muslim Marriages

Couples in Jain-Muslim relationship are requested to first read/view:
- Section 2.3: FAQ on Interfaith Marriages
- Section 2.8: Ten Points of Dating a Hindu
- Chapter V: Muslim-Hindu Marraiges
- Section 12.6: The Koran on Hindus?
- Watch these videos prepared by InterfaithShaadi:
  https://www.youtube.com/watch?v=gvZSqdmnxKM.
  https://www.youtube.com/watch?v=RiWLGEKusIg.

Section 7.1: I'm Jain-Hindu girl in Love with a Muslim

Punita says:

I am a Jain-Hindu girl in love with a Bihari Muslim guy. We love each other and his family is very easygoing and broad-minded. His sister has married a Hindu too. I love him and we want to marry each other but my mum is not agreeing at all and we can't tell my dad as of now. His family loves us together. They are supportive, but my side people will not accept. Please help me! —Punita

Seema says:

You are only 22 and unless your boyfriend is wealthy, you may need your parents' financial support.

If you lived in the U.S, I would have said that go ahead and get married and wait for your parents to either come around or break contact with you. But you live in India. It's very hard if not impossible to break away from one's family. I got back from India two weeks ago and on any given day I would see 10-20 relatives and talk to at least ten more on the phone.

I met a couple a few weeks ago. They are both Hindus but from different parts of India. They had been dating for years. The girl's parents, while not thrilled, had given their blessings but the boy's parents were adamant that he would marry within his own caste. They told the boy that he had to choose between them and the girl. He chose her and they walked out. The couple went to a temple the same day and got married. Now, they have no place to live and no contact with the boy's family. Not only did the boy lose his parents but he also lost his Chachas, Chachis, Mamas, Maamis, cousins etc? Was it worth it? —Seema

Section 7.2: A Muslim Girl in Love with a Jain in Canada

Tabassum says:

I am a Muslim girl and in love with a Jain boy. We have been together for about 2 years and plan on getting married soon. He is a good kind hearted and understanding boy who is well established. I am still in college finishing my degree.

I am not too worried about what others have to say about my relationship as we live in Canada. However my parents may not fully agree to my marriage, his parents are pretty open minded and simple people who live in India.

My only worry is his family. I have not met them yet and do not know the extent of how they will react to a Muslim bride. My boyfriend's parents mean a lot to him and he means a lot to me.

I would like to know what it means to marry into a Jain family? We had spoken about religion and neither of us is too religious. Sometimes I feel that it may change as I am only 21 and I may adopt Islam at a heavier capacity. I know we love each other and that will not change, so I don't see the need of waiting. —Tabassum

Tabassum added:

Thank you very much for your (Admin's) response. We plan on living here in Canada as he has a well-established job here and I will soon have one after I am done college. We plan on doing a court marriage with a small party for our friends and few family members.

A few years down the road we plan on visiting India to meet his family. He plans on doing a Jain wedding in a temple for his family. I do respect his family and religion and don't mind doing that for him, however keep in mind I have no intention of converting.

In that case I have lived here in Canada with my mom for a few years. I believe that she won't be too reluctant of our relationship as she has known about us for a while and done nothing to stop us. As for my dads' family they are a bit more religious, and I am not sure how they will take the news. He is living in a Middle Eastern country. I hope that he will eventually come around. He is my father and means the world to me. I want to have his blessing as well.

On the matter of our children I would obviously like them to follow my religion but they will also be their father's children. He says it wouldn't matter as much as they will be born in a Western country and have their values. However, I would like to think that I would give my children more than just Western values. We plan on letting them decide what they feel is right in their heart when the time comes.

As for the rest we both plan on practicing our own religions. He says love is a universal language and that it does not matter what region we come from. I really hope that religion does not become an issue down the road for us, as we are very happy together! —Tabassum

Is this male chauvinism or religious fanaticism?

"My children will be Muslim only."
—Aamir Khan (Bollywood star)
http://ssmusiq.blogspot.in/2010/08/my-wives-may-be-hindu-but-my-kids-will.html

Section 7.3: Jain: Planning to Marry a Muslim Guy

Tanvi says:

I am a Jain and planning to marry a Muslim guy. We have been in a relationship since 3 years and planning to be in a relationship for the next 4 years. He has not asked me to convert to his religion, nor will he convert to mine. On the contrary, he is adamant that I should never change my religion. Moreover I have decided not to change my surname after marriage and he is perfectly fine with it.

Regarding upbringing of children, we have decided that our children surname will be having his and my surnames and they won't have Arabic or Muslim names. He is well educated and me too. He has never forced me to do any thing of his religion. On the contrary, he is willing to marry unbiased under the Special Marriage Act 1954.

Short and simple... love is above all religion. Never take decisions blindly, be practical too. And take time to take that decision. —Tanvi

Admin says:

Hi Tanvi,

A marriage is not just between two people but also between two families and two communities. That is where most problems will start. Most problems will appear only 6 months before the planned marriage. We recommend that you meet his parents ASAP and tell them your full plan. Likewise, take him to your parents. Let your two sets of parents meet as well. If you have not done this yet, you may be only dreaming. These parents' meetings might bring you back to earth. We wish you the best. —Admin

Section 7.4: A Muslim Boy in Love with a Jain

Nadeem says:

I am a Muslim guy in love with a Jain girl. I really love her and want to marry her. My parents are ready for all this but her parents are against our decision. In fact now they are not even allowing her to be out of house. Her uncle is a politician (minister and Member of Parliament). I don't want her to change her religion. I really love her and want to spend my whole life with her only. Please suggest me something—how can we live happy together forever.

Guys please suggest me whatever you can. I really need your help and most importantly she is ready to live with me going against her family but his uncle is a major problem. Please help me. —Nadeem

Admin says:

Hi Nadeem,

You mentioned that, "don't want her to change her religion." This is a very honorable thought. But, do you know what does that mean? Are you okay with not having an Islamic nikaah (including conversion)? If you marry a Jain without conversion, your marriage is not valid as per the Koran and all Islamic teachings. Are you ready to go against Islamic beliefs? Have you talked to your family and Islamic community about your plan?

What will you do after marrying a Jain (murti) idol-worshipper? Please read more from Tanvi.[218] This Muslim will marry in a court, not by nikaah and conversion. He is ready to give up meat when she is around. He is already going to Jain temples, bowing to her (Jain) Gods and taking part in *Parjyshan*. This Muslim will have children with non-Arabic names, will raise Jain (and Muslim) children and teach them from both scriptures. You have to wonder, is he really a Muslim? How far are you willing to go to please your new Jain family?

We are not here to tell you what you should and should not do. You must decide what the right thing is for you to do.

It is easy to talk of a secular life at age 20 something, but as a Muslim, it will be very difficult for you later on to raise a Jain-Muslim family. Again, we are not here to discourage you from being secular (or

---

[218] Section 7.3.

religious). Jameela,[219] Seema,[220] Azad[221] and Shah Rukh Khan[222] decided to run their life as secular/pluralists and apparently are happy, so why not you?

The most important advice we can give today is to get good education and then find a high paying job. Once you are financially independent and settled in a different city, the rest will be a lot easier for you two. Best wishes. —Admin

---

> Mahatma Gandhi worked hard to eradicate Caste system in Hinduism. Why would one want to endorse a different type of caste system where one religion is superior over all others?

---

[219] Section 5.29.
[220] Section 5.4.
[221] Section 6.1.
[222] http://www.youtube.com/watch?v=Py7sFkIGi-k.

Section 7.5: I Am a Jain Girl and Love a Muslim

Sweta says:

I am a Jain girl and I love a Muslim boy from the past 8 years. He also loves me a lot and can do anything for me. We have decided to tell my parents about our relationship after one or two years. He always says that he is with me, whatever be the situation.

At present, the biggest issue for me is "non-veg." I am not able to even think about that but he says that his family and even he never will force me to do this and he promises me that non-veg will never enter in our home.

I have complete trust in him. I know, in my future life with him, he will never put any boundaries on me as he always encourages me to achieve my goals and to do the things that I like. I feel so comfortable with him and hope things will be the same in future also.

I know it is a bit difficult to adjust in a Muslim family for us but do you think that if you marry a Hindu boy and he doesn't love you then it will be easy for you? There is no guarantee about future. I strongly believe a line "whatever is written in our destiny, we have to face it."

Eight years is not a short period. You will never be able to give his place in your heart to anyone. Even if you marry someone when you are in love with someone else, it really spoils three lives and it is totally unfair with new guy who thinks that you are his wife but you only love your boyfriend in your heart.

According to me "nothing is greater than love." Definitely one has to adjust a lot but if you both try to understand each other then everything will become easy and then religion doesn't matter. —Sweta

Section 7.6: Muslim: I Want to Convert to Jain

Wasim says:

Muslims are not treated with the same respect as people of other religion because they are like that. Being from the same religion, I am making a bold statement saying this and I might have to face consequences.

Here's my story. My girlfriend is a Jain and she has also read these posts (at InterfaithShaadi) and got so badly influenced that she almost had a nervous breakdown. But, I am not as you guys have been stereotyping other Muslim boys here. For the sake of my love and commitment to my relationship, I want to do something that no one does. I want to convert to Jainism. Our children will be given Jain names. I am a vegetarian by choice since last 4 years. It is even before meeting the love of my life.

As far as my parents are concerned, they know about her and me. They respect our relationship too. I know I will hurt them by converting into Jainism, but I am sure that they will understand. I don't want my love to face any sort of problem. As far as my relatives are concerned—to hell with them. We are better off without the relatives from my side. Those who respect my love will be with us, those who don't; won't have my respect either.

Before you so called Islamic centered guys start hitting me with bullshit, I am not interested in answering you. I don't have a fight with religion; I have a fight against orthodox enemies of love. Because of the influential people who misinterpret our holy books, innocent people like us have to suffer. But, for love, I will do the right thing. Bye closed minded rigid people.

I believe in one God, and will continue paying my gratitude in my own way, unbound by the rituals. Thanks! —Wasim

Chapter VIII: Christian-Muslim Marriages

Couples in Christian-Muslim relationship are requested to first read/view:
- Section 2.3: FAQ on Interfatih Marriages
- Section 2.5: 45% of Muslims Marry Outside their Faith in America
- Section 2.10: Can Allah be the Father God?
- Section 2.15: Interfaith Marriage and Divorce Laws
- Section 12.7: The Koran on Christians and Jews?
- Watch this video prepared by InterfaithShaadi: https://www.youtube.com/watch?v=RiWLGEKusIg.

Section 8.1: I'm in a Christian-Muslim Relationship in the States

Jennifer says:

I am in a Christian-Muslim relationship here in the United States of America. I care so much about him. I'm giving it my all to learn about Islam, and try to understand why he feels certain ways about things. Thank you Azad[223] for that story it meant so much to me! It gives me hope! —Jennifer

Admin says:

Hi Jennifer,

First find out who you are. Are you a "proud" Christian or just a "born" Christian? How much do your childhood Christian teachings mean to you? How much do you care for your Christian heritage?

The Azad example gave you "hope!" Does it mean you are looking for an interfaith relationship with equality?

Instead of assuming anything, why don't you two sit down and answer a few questions? Islam has very strict requirements for marriage. Most Muslims will expect an intended spouse to:

1) Convert to Islam by taking shahadah oaths before marriage (nikaah)
- are you okay with having an irreversible conversion from Christianity to Islam?
2) Be given a Muslim name.
- are you okay if you are given a new Arabic name?
3) Give the children Arabic names only.
- is that okay?
4) Have the children submit to sunat/khanna (religious circumcision) and raised in the Islamic faith. This means no Jesus (as the Son of Allah), no baptism, no praying to Virgin Mary and no Sunday church visits.
- is that okay?
5) Not display a picture of the Lord Jesus or a cross in your living room.
- is that okay?
6) Only marry via nikaah, without performing another Christian marriage ceremony.
- do you want a church wedding?

---

[223] Section 6.1.

If you both have true "love" instead of "love for man-made rituals," we propose a civil wedding (like Azad did). Let's hope you and your intended spouse are open-minded enough to follow through on your interfaith marriage and all that entails.

Now let's look at a deeper issue...

WHOSE GOD WINS?

Christians generally believe Lord Jesus is the Son of God and that faith in Jesus is the only way to achieve salvation. Contrary to that, the Koran teaches to have faith in Allah (God) and that Jesus, son of Mary, was no more than God's apostle.[224] Allah forbids that He Himself should beget a son![225] Further, those who say: "the Lord of Mercy has begotten a son" preach a monstrous falsehood.[226] Unbelievers are those that say: "God is the Messiah, the son of Mary"[227] and "God is one of three."[228] Unbelievers will get Hell Fire. Further, Allah said "Believers, take neither Jews nor the Christians for your friends."[229]

Which God will rule in your intended married life?
1) Will you be glorifying for most times Jesus or Mohammad? Would Lord Jesus Christ be the Son of God or just an apostle?
2) Will your children have sunat/khatna or baptism?
3) Are Allah, Jesus, God the Father, or all three, going to come on the Judgment Day?

You must decide on only one of two options in these questions above. There is nothing like "both" or a middle ground that includes sunat & baptism! If you decide "none" for these questions, on the Day of Judgment both Gods will be unhappy and you and your spouse will "not achieve salvation" from Jesus and on top of that will get "Hell of Fire" from Allah.

Tackle the inter-faith problems directly; don't sweep them under the rug. Don't assume that you will resolve differences sometime after you get married. Pre-marital problems generally grow into "Hindenburg class disasters" after marriage.

Does all of this make any sense? —Admin

---

[224] Koran 4:171.
[225] Koran 19:34.
[226] Koran 19:88.
[227] Koran 5:70.
[228] Koran 5:72.
[229] Koran 5:51.

Jennifer Replied:

Thank you for this. This is what I was looking for. I wanted more and a direction to follow things. I'm religious, I believe in God and Jesus, but I'm lacking in strong conviction. My boyfriend is pushing me to learn more, and he is there when I have questions. He was thrilled when I took upon myself to learn more. We haven't gotten to the bigger issues yet, but we will.

My mother is a devout Christian and my father was a Wiccan. So yes, I grew up in a household of two religions and I'm very open-minded. If and when the time comes for these decisions to be made, they will be made. If it means that much to him I have no problem for our children to be raised that way.

We are both divorced. I have a child already, he does not. So this is a new learning experience for the both of us. My only thing is, right now I have no feeling to convert and he understands and has never asked me of this. I don't think he ever will, but we will see.

Thank you (Admin) for this above. It means a great deal to me. — Jennifer

> *We remain a young nation, but in the words of Scripture, the time has come to set aside childish things. The time has come to reaffirm our enduring spirit; to choose our better history; to carry forward that precious gift, that noble idea, passed on from generation to generation: the God-given promise that all are equal, all are free and all deserve a chance to pursue their full measure of happiness... For we know, that our patchwork heritage is a strength, not a weakness. We are a nation of Christians and Muslims, Jews and Hindus, and nonbelievers.*
> —Barack Hussein Obama (Jan 20, 2009)

Section 8.2: I Am an American Christian and My Girlfriend Is Muslim

John says:

My girlfriend, who is a Muslim, is currently going through a dilemma. I am an American, a conservative Christian. My girlfriend is from the Middle East. She is a practicing Muslim. We both love our religion and love each other! My parents are okay with the whole situation but her parents would have none of it! Her mom said she would rather kill her than let her be with anyone who is not a Middle Eastern Muslim.

I want to go down to my girlfriend's house and meet her parents but I know that would only exacerbate the situation. Every time we are together she always tells me she doesn't want to go home. Just recently, her mom proposed two men to her for marriage but she refused both.

Now she is not allowed out of the house without a companion. Her father drives her to work and picks her up from work. We have both contemplated running away! But currently I can't because I am in medical school. I am a poor medical student!

This is what I have always told my girlfriend, that I love her, and that everything will be okay. I tell her that if God wants us to be together, we will be together. I tell her that we both need to work together to convince her parents. I tell her to engage her mom in friendly educated conversation. She should ask her mom how she got married, how did she feel about the way she got married, how does she now feel about her husband? According to my girlfriend, at first her mom was reluctant to talk about her past, but recently, that has changed! They both now do have few amicable conversations. I am hoping that eventually her mom (who got married when she was 15) would understand.

We are both young and I told her we can be patient, giving her parents time. Running away should be the last resort! Hopefully these traditional parents will understand that we are in a different era! Religion ought to be the substances that keep us together and (not) a poison that destroys our lives. —John

Admin says:

Hi John,

Please have patience. If your love is true (on both sides) and none of you is a religious fanatic, it should work out well in the end. However, be mindful of the honor killing practice.

You mentioned that you are a "conservative" Christian and she is a "practicing" Muslim. Wow! You are mixing milk and yogurt. Instead of not tolerating each other's faith and culture, tell your priest or pastor and her imam that "Like salad in a bowl, where tomato stays tomato and celery stays celery; we will merge and respect each other's faith. No one will convert. We will pray to Allah and Jesus, both." Unfortunately, this does not seem possible for a conservative and practicing Abrahamic.

So a question for you both: are you pluralists (salvation is possible through all faiths, including for atheists) or exclusivists (there is only One God, and that is MINE!)?

If you both are exclusivists, then who's God will win?

First, let's hope you are a realist. Please answer these questions that will help you realize some important issues:

1) Are you going to get married in a church? Is she willing to go through your church's prenuptial[230] agreement that children by this marriage will be baptized and raised as Christians only?
2) Are you going to marry by an Islamic nikaah? Are you ready to convert to Islam by shahadah for your Islamic wedding?
3) Are you both going to celebrate Christmas and Easter and fast during Ramadan? Will your extended families join you?
4) Are your children going to have Christian or Muslim names?
5) Will there be a baptism or sunat/khitan/khafd/khatna label on the child? Or both, baptism and Sunat! Are your children going to be called Christians, Muslims, both or none?
6) Are you going to take your children to a mosque on Friday and to a church on Sunday? Will your church welcome a Muslim son with a name Mohammad? Will her mosque welcome your baptized daughter named Mary?
7) What will you teach to your children about Jesus? Who is the father of Jesus, is that Joseph or God the Father?
8) On the Judgment Day, who is going to save you? Will that be Jesus with Lord God or Allah? If you believe in the Trinity, you are an

---

[230] Section 3.4.

unbeliever as per the Koran and will get Hell Fire. Is the Bible or Koran God's true word?

You have said eloquently, "Hopefully these traditional parents will understand that we are in a different era! Religion ought to be the substance that keeps us together and (not) a poison that destroys our lives." Before asking traditional parents to change, first find out who really you are.

There's dogma and there's life. Let's hope you will settle for life. — Admin

John added:

True be told, she doesn't really care about whether I convert or not! Even though she speaks and writes Arabic, she said the Koran doesn't seem consistent to her. Like the majority of Muslim kids, she said she grew up listening to her parents tell her that "Allah" was the only God and Mohamed his prophet. She said all she knows is what was taught to her, by her parents. But, according to her, as she matures, and begins reading the Koran on her own, she sees lot of things that aren't consistent with the nature of God!

She acknowledged that even though God is omnipotent, God is also compassionate and loving, but according to her, her faith focuses exclusively on the omnipotence of God while alienating his compassionate and loving nature. She is Western in her thoughts… she says lot of things, which I discourage her from saying to other Muslim folks, as they might hurt her. She has been begging me to take her to church sometime but I am not willing to risk her life, because I know what might happen to her if her parents found out that she went to a church.

Even though we have not seriously talked about marriage at this point, she told me she would not want any of her children to be raised as Muslim. She said and I quote, "I would not want any of my children, if I ever have any, to experience the hell I have and continue to live through, especially, my girl children."

I took her to a friend's wedding once, at a church and she loved it! My friend is from Middle East. His parents used to be Muslim but then converted… at the reception both Middle Eastern rituals and Western rituals were done! It was a blast!

If married, we are going to celebrate X-mas, Easter, Ramadan, etc.! Ramadan is a way to appreciate the food God has blessed us with…

Easter is to thank God for the harvest (corrections below[231]), and X-mas is to celebrate the birth of Christ. But as you might know, X-mas is commercialized now and it means nothing other than a time for people to buy expensive gifts for each other. About names, I am not going to change my name, and my children, if we have any, could be named anything except Jesus or Mohammad! We talked about the naming thing! I love names with meaning and majority of the Middle Eastern/Greek/Hebrew names are great!

I do not know what the future holds. We hope our children would choose a religion that is consistent with their beliefs. I am not going to take my kids to the mosque but if she thinks it is okay to do so, I would not have any problem with that. My philosophy is I do not have the power to save anyone. I can tell you all about God but it is only God who saves! I cannot do anything to influence my salvation in any shape or form. It is only by God's grace that I am who I am and have what I have. I love my girlfriend, and will do whatever necessary to keep her safe! I am very aware of the honor killing! Just told, some parents in England were found guilty of killing their daughter who according to them "was too westernized!"

It is not our duty as human beings to force people to accept God! God himself does not force people to come to Him. He gives us the liberty to choose! You can only force someone to obey you by doing certain things or acting in certain manner, but you cannot force a person to love you!
—John

---

[231] This is John' personal view that Ramadan is to appreciate food and Easter is for the harvest. Actually Easter is to celebrate Jesus' resurrection from the dead. The word Ramadan derived from "Ramad" means burn, the real meaning is burning of sins. If one fasts in the way that Allah (SWT) likes and wants, then He (SWT) will forgive all of one's sins just as fire burns the garbage. (based on http://www.muslimummah.org/articles/articles.php?itemno=247&&category=Ramadan)

Section 8.3: A Catholic Muslim Marriage

The most important question in any interfaith relationship is what will be the "formal" religion of your children. This point should be discussed sooner than later. Let's read Stacey's experience.

Stacey says:

This is a very interesting website and thank you for your articles. I am a Catholic Christian girl and I have been dating a Muslim for one and a half years and we have wanted to get married for a long time now. During the relationship he has always said that its okay for the kids to go to church with me and when they are older about 18 they can choose which religion they want—Christianity or Islam. I always thought this to mean that he accepted they would be Christians. How wrong I was. Now he insists that the kids have to be Muslim and that is his religion and he is not willing to compromise on that.

I feel so hurt. Initially I said I wanted them to be Catholic, but now I'm willing to compromise that they should learn about both religions. He is absolutely refusing this and thinks I will change my mind if I love him. I have said that we need to compromise as we have different religions and the kids will be half of me and half of him.

I cannot see myself changing my mind and the thought of them being Muslims does not sit well with me. Firstly I don't know so much about Islam apart from them praying 5 times a day, Ramadan, women covering their head, the big division between men and women (e.g. cannot pray next to each other in the mosque), and the men appearing very controlling. Also as a Christian, I would feel left out and don't see how I can fulfill my mothering duties without understanding Islam. Also, it's not even a case that I can go to the mosque and pray next to my Muslim male boys.

I know how very involved I need to be as a Mother. I am also concerned about the extreme rules and pressure from the wider community. To me it seems all too contrived. I am Catholic but I am very liberal and like my kids to be liberal too. I don't want the girls to cover their heads and bodies (neither do I want them to walk outside in too revealing clothes). I want them to believe there is one God.

I just can't see any future in this relationship. Also, my main concern is how strongly he holds on to his faith and he is not willing to compromise on this issue. I feel I have wasted my precious life time. What advice can you give me please? Thanks. —Stacey

Admin says:

Hi Stacey,

Can milk and yogurt mix and maintain their identity? Before a proud Catholic and a practicing Muslim decide to date, they should come to conclusion on the question whether Jesus is a Son of God or just an apostle? If you both are not practicing your own faith and willing to explain your scriptures in today's practical pluralistic sense, yes, happy and long lasting interfaith marriage is possible.

Christians believe that Jesus is the only Son of God and that faith in Jesus is the only way to achieve salvation and to enter heaven. Jesus said: "I am the way, the truth, and the life. No one comes to the Father except through me." However, quite contrary to that belief, Koran tells us that those who say: "the Lord of Mercy has begotten a son" preach a monstrous falsehood.[232] So, what will your children believe in... Koran or Bible?

Christianity and Islam are both exclusivist religions and, to some extent, believers are taught not to tolerate each other.[233] Further, both of you are also exclusivists. Your boyfriend said "he has insisted that the kids have to be Muslim" and you said "the thought of them being Muslims does not sit well with me." So, plan to get married but make sure not to have a child.

Actually he has proposed an excellent solution, "he has always said that it's okay for the kids to go to church." So take the kids to a mosque on Fridays and a church on Sundays, but do not label the children as Muslims by sunat or Christians by baptism (no BBS). At their adult age, like Barack Obama, let them decide their own faith. Is not this fair?

You want others to "believe there is One God" but which one... Jewish LORD God, Christian God the Father, Muslim's Allah or One God Ishvara as prayed by Hindus? Basically, you are saying there is only One God, and that is MINE only! There is only one true Barbie doll and that is mine! Grow up Stacey.

You have many fundamental problems, thus both of you will be better off marrying someone from your own religion. Best wishes. —Admin

---

[232] Koran 19:88.
[233] Based on past 1500 years of history and Section 12.7.

Section 8.4: I Have Dated a Muslim Girl but Had to End It

David says:

I was in a similar situation (Aafroze) and it is a very difficult one so I'm sorry that you have to go through this. I have dated a Muslim girl for 3 years and we had to end it. We were in college together so while away from our families, it worked but once we both went back to our respective states, problems occurred.

Unfortunately religiously there is nothing you (Aafroze) can do unless you were able to introduce him to Islam and he was able to embrace it and converted by his own will. I respect Islam and I have read parts of the Koran but I'm from a Middle Eastern Christian family which means converting isn't an option.

If he (Aafroze's boyfriend) isn't very religious and willing to accept Islam, that's one of your options. Other than that you have the option of following your heart, which is a sin but doesn't mean it won't work.

When I was in relationship I didn't keep pork in my house, I fasted with her. We celebrated Eid and at the same time she colored Easter eggs with me and decorated the Christmas tree so we embraced both religions.

If your family won't disown you and you are willing to go against the rules of the majority opinion, you can find a happy medium but you would be living in sin according to majority opinion of imams. It is a very hard decision. My ex-girlfriend couldn't go against her religion and family so it's ultimately up to how far you are willing to go for love and how far you are willing to go for God. Good luck, Inshallah. It will work out for you. —David

Admin says:

Hi David,

Is this conversion business for marriage justified? When will Christians and Muslims change their old intolerant practices and learn to live a pluralistic life? Will not this world be a better place to live if people start respecting each other's faith?

Was it not a beautiful feeling when "…we celebrated Eid and at the same time she colored Easter eggs with me and decorated the Christmas tree so we embraced both religions?" —Admin

David says:

I completely agree with you. I wish that people were more forward thinking because the world would be a much better place. I probably could have had a very happy marriage and nobody had to change at all. A person's faith has a part in creating the person you love so nobody should ever have to change who they are. Just living in unity with respecting one another and their faith should be enough. Unfortunately, in my experience its societal pressure which leads to the destruction of these kinds of relationships.

My family told me no matter what, they want me to be happy above all. They said if I want to be with her then be with her. But her family told her if she was a good Muslim, she would have never put herself in that situation and if she was a good Muslim I would have converted. Later, she had the family guilt and worried about what her society would think of her. This unfortunately happens too often. She had friends that had the same thing and the same outcome.

I have had this argument way too many times that an interfaith marriage is very feasible. It comes down to love and respect. It also comes down to letting go of what others think. But people's opinions and people words are stronger than weapons and can completely ruin something so beautiful and pure.

I do like your (Admin's) philosophy and train of thought. I hope others can come across this page and feel a comfort that what they feel isn't wrong and can learn to live for themselves following their hearts. — David

Section 8.5: My Family Would Die Rather than Allow Me to Marry a Non-Muslim

Sadia says:

Hi all of you.

I am in the worst phase of life currently. I'm not too happy with my career. I am educated but not working as one as I have come to my parents in the Middle East after completing my studies in India. There is zero scope in my field here. Anyway, that's the secondary issue.

The main thing is that I have been in a relationship with a guy back in India. He's a wonderful guy and my parents know him and his family and really like them too. I belong to a very religious Muslim family whereas my guy is a firm Christian. I have been with him for 8 years now. His family loves me and I love them all too.

My family wants me to get married and is looking for good proposals now. I have confessed about my relationship to my sisters and my mom. They have clearly told me that this has no future as our faiths are different and that I must get over him. I love him and also my parents, too dearly to break anyone's heart.

My man has been very supportive and never gets upset when I don't get to call him for days together because of problems at my place. He has changed all his career plans just for me and my problems at home. There is no looking back at this stage when I have spent almost a decade with him. I am very close to his family and they are open heartedly accepting me with the faith that I follow and do not expect me to convert to Christianity. However, my family is not so open-minded and would die rather than allow me to marry a non-Muslim.

I love my parents dearly. They have sacrificed a lot for me. My dad's health isn't all that great but still he's working at his old age so that he can provide me with all the luxuries and let me have a huge wedding. I am so upset. I cannot elope with my boyfriend. That's the last thing I want to do to my parents. I want to convince them, which deep down I know is impossible.

I feel suicidal and always pray to God that if things cannot be the way I want them to, please let me die. I can never choose between my parents and him. I feel very guilty to have my parents and my boyfriend in a situation like this. When we began dating we were just 15 and immature but by God's grace I found just the right guy for me even at that level of immaturity. He's the best anyone could ever get and I totally believe God is not upset with me for choosing a Christian instead of a Muslim because what I share with him is something so pure.

I don't know guys what to do. I am a firm believer in Allah and pray to him 24/7 to help us out. Please if any of you could help me with suggestions, whatsoever. Please do. Desperately waiting for comments and suggestions. —Sadia

Admin says:

Dear Sadia,

While suicide seems like the only way out of your torment right now, it is not truly an option. You are stronger than this as evidenced by your reaching out for help.

You have several options:

1) Tell your boyfriend that you are sorry that your Bollywood dream is over. Find a Muslim man who prays five times a day, follows Mohammad's teachings and life style, believes in all that is said in the Koran and Hadith, believes in Sharia law, and more. Your parents will be most proud of you. If you experience hell in THIS life after marriage, just ignore it because Allah has planned a heaven for you in the AFTER life.

2) Marry your love. Your parents will feel terrible for a few years, but may ultimately come to terms with your decision (possibly after you have a child). It will be an opportunity to teach your parents pluralism that you learned from Hindu majority India during your stay there.

3) Continue to do your self-study and consider the following points. Allah has made you beautiful and intelligent, now Allah has to take care of many other needy people. Do not expect Allah to spoon feed you; even your mother will not do that for you! Now it is up to you to take control of your life. You will have to do your own karma in THIS life. Instead of bothering Allah 24/7, start educating yourself about what we have written and ultimately Allah will inspire you to make a right decision.

Since you mentioned that "I am a firm believer in Allah," do you believe in Allah, meaning God, Ishvara, God the Father and LORD God, or the Allah whose apostle is Mohammad? You seem to be educated, please read all that is said about God on this web site.[234] Define for yourself what "Allah" means to you. When you come to that answer, you will have the answer to your problem.

Considering he is a Christian, you will have to address "Is Jesus a Son of Allah or just an apostle." This may be a heavy duty question for you. Another practical question you will have to answer is—are your children going to have baptism or Sunat and are they going to have Christian or Arabic names? Do not ignore thousands of years of Christian-Muslim religious conflicts. Both Christianity and Islam are absolutely exclusivist religions and believe in the superiority of their faith over each other and others. You will have to come to terms with whose God will win?

Rome was not built in a day. You are only 23. Give yourself a few more years to explore your beliefs and in that way, you will make fully "informed" decision.

In the mean time, tell your parents ASAP that you will marry only that Christian boy (even you are not sure). Let them fume over it; chances are it will die down in 6 months. Read the material on InterfaithShaadi and you will realize that you must give up your (and your parents') exclusivist thinking and be a pluralist if you wish to pursue an interfaith marriage. If you cannot resolve your religious differences in this time span, option #1 above is your choice.

Please come back with more specific thoughts/questions. —Admin

Sadia says:

Dear Admin,

Thanks for your advice and thoughts that you shared. I am thinking if my parents don't agree to marry me to him, I don't mind staying unmarried for life. I cannot marry anyone else. Nothing still remains in my favor though because my parents will die each day seeing me unmarried and that poor guy is paying a price for nothing. I just wish I can make my parents realize that he's amongst Abrahamics and consider us seriously. I don't know. Thanks a ton anyway. —Sadia

---

[234] https://www.interfaithshaadi.org/blog/?cat=10.

Shehnaz says:

Dear Sadia,

I read your life story and felt deeply touched. Don't be coward. If you do not marry any one, it is very difficult to survive blissfully in Muslim community. All evil eyes will be on you from ill motivated persons. At the old age, you will be in deep trouble, nobody will take care of you and you will be in depression throughout life.

Have courage and make up your mind. You are owner of your life. Parents will not be with you forever. In my opinion, if you are so determined, be in touch with your boyfriend. Finalize all modalities for future relations. Be tactful, have good relations with parents for the time being, don't show them that you are in touch with your boyfriend. Plan to visit India after 6 months or so and then get married with him under Special Marriage Act. God bless you. —Shehnaz

Section 8.6: Religion versus Culture

Rasid says:

I am a revert (to Islam) from Catholicism, and married to divorced Asian woman. I had no problem with her not being a virgin, as I was not either. I had a relationship before too.

I have grown to the life of a Muslim over the past 8 years, and am accepted in my community and mosque where I live. I believe that when children are sent to mixed schools, and then go on to college and university, each culture, both East and West, mix freely. However the community culture is different.

The elders of the Asian communities in the UK for example, not all of them, but the majority, think that to be a Muslim is all about culture. The elders can go around freely living the Western lifestyle but they want their women to be all cultural. Their young sons are to be married as soon as they are 17+, to a girl from Pakistan because they believe they will be more cultural than the girls in this country. But this is not always the case, as young men meet English girls and then are promised a girl from Pakistan. It is not the fault of the boy. He doesn't want to upset his family as it will shame them in the so called community. That is culture.

Asian girls in the UK, have it hard. They get married to someone they don't even know, sometimes from Pakistan who can't speak English and treats them badly. Then they feel trapped as they don't want to shame the family or let them down... culture again.

I have seen and heard a lot of stories similar to the women on this site. It's a shame that the family didn't let them chose their own partner.

Culture should stay in Pakistan, not in the West... then everyone would be happier. MasAllah. —Rasid

Section 8.7: Ahmadi Muslim Girl with Catholic Christian

Sara says:

Hi Admin,

I have got myself in a confusing situation. I'm an Ahmadi girl living in Pakistan. Not sure if you're familiar with the Ahmadi sect, but in Pakistan we are not considered Muslims, although Ahmadis believe that only their version of Islam is the true Islam and when it comes to marriage, we are ONLY allowed to marry within the Ahmadi Community. Even marriage to other mainstream Muslims is not permissible. If a girl is to marry outside the community, then even her parents are kicked out of the community. The other members of this faith are supposed to boycott them socially. So if I choose to marry outside the community, even my parents will have to face the consequences.

Now coming to the real problem, I have been dating a Catholic Christian boy for a year. I am still a student, pursuing a degree in Computer Science from a well reputed university, whereas he is working, but earning enough to only support himself. I have been visiting his house regularly, and I am on good terms with his family and relatives. As far as marriage is concerned, his family will not have a problem, but mine will. I'm afraid both my parents will go into depression and consider this the worst kind of betrayal by their daughter. My plan was to graduate next year, get a decent job and then tell my parents honestly that this is what I want. But I am afraid that this will create a great deal of distress and agony to them, and living in a conservative country like Pakistan, I think it will make matters even worse. What should I do? —Sara

Admin says:

Dear Sara,

We feel your pain. You are an innocent victim of this society. You are trapped into a silo created by religious leaders for their benefits.

We understand if you don't have the strength to fight against society or go against religious leaders. Your easiest solution would be to find and marry a well-educated and decent Ahmadi guy. However, if you cannot find a good match in your own community, then consider your other options.

For the next year, can you please focus on your education? Then get a decent paying job which will help you make the decisions for your future that are right for you. Eventually plan to find a job or continuing education outside of Pakistan. Without good education and financial independence, you will be at the mercy of others.

Now let's talk of the most critical issue, the interfaith marriage. You said, "I am on good terms with his family and relatives." What does that mean? Are they willing to accept you as a "Muslim" and is he willing to marry you without converting you to Christianity? How will you get married, by nikaah, a church wedding, both or a civil wedding? Which imam and/or Christian priest/pastor will be willing to perform your dual marriages? What will be the names of your children, Muslim or Christian? Will your children have baptism to announce them as Christians or will they be Muslims in a Christian home? What will you teach your children—who is the Father of Jesus? If you want to learn the truth, tell his parents that your children will never be baptized, and see their reaction. Best wishes. —Admin

Sara says:

Dear Admin,

Thank you for bringing that to my knowledge. I wanted to tell you that although it was difficult, I did have a talk with my boyfriend about baptism of our children and church wedding.

Thank you for taking time out to reply, even the fact that someone out there is taking time out to help me brings joy to my heart. —Sara

Section 8.8: Malaysian Muslim: I Follow Christianity

Interfaith love with a Malay is one of the most popular themes at InterfaithShaadi.[235] Readers are advised to read unfair interfaith marriage laws in Malaysia (Section 2.15).

Syed says:

I'm a Malay (Malaysian Muslim) man married to a Catholic girl. She had a Muslim name after (Islamic marriage) registration but she remains Catholic. So are my children, they are all raised Catholic. I too don't practice Muslim faith and follow my wife's faith. I live in an area that is mostly non-Muslim to avoid problem. —Syed

Admin says:

Hi Syed,

We are sympathetic to your situation. Ideally, one should have freedom of religion. Unfortunately this is not possible in Muslim majority countries like Malaysia. Lets us explain issues that you will face.[236]

Your wife converted to Islam for your nikaah and was given a new Muslim name for your marriage registration. That name is (probably) in her Malaysian MyKad ID card and passport. Further, her ID card (probably) says her faith as "Islam."

Your children will also have Muslim names and their ID will ultimately have "Islam" on it. This will go on for your grand children and great grandchildren; even if none of you wish to follow Islam. Now any time any one of you tries to change the Muslim name to a Catholic name, Malay government will not allow and will punish you.

Any time your children and great grand children marry to any one other than a Muslim, the non-Muslim party will have to convert to Islam. When any of you die, the Malay Sharia police may come and take away the dead body from your Catholic family and give a Muslim final rite. So, in your after life, you may wish to meet Jesus but you will go with Mohammad.

Any time if any one reports to the Sharia police that you (or your great grandchildren) are practicing a non-Muslim faith, you will be in deep trouble for apostasy.

---

[235] https://www.interfaithshaadi.org/blog/?cat=112.
[236] For all supportive evidence and laws in Malaysia, read Subsection 2.15.3.

Bottom line, you think you are fooling the Malay government but in reality you and your all future generations are in a trap, you can't escape (unless you move out of Malaysia). You can run, but not hide. It is only a matter of time. As far we are concerned, people should not follow your footsteps.

It is notable that refugees and immigrant Muslims in Christian majority nations demand religious equality but most Muslim majority nations[237] have created laws to marginalize Christians and non-Muslim minorities.

Syed, it is certainly sad that your liberty to express your faith is taken away by the government. This is not fair. We wish you the best. —Admin

---

[237] Hiddush (marriage.hiddush.org) conducted Freedom of Marriage survey and found severe marriage restrictions in 62% Muslim, 7% Christian but not in Hindu/Buddhist (0%) majority nations. Also read laws in Malaysia (Subsection 2.15.3).

Chapter IX: Inter-racial Inter-faith Marriages

Couples in inter-racial relationship are requested to first read/view:
- Section 2.2: Ten Points of Interfaith Dating
- Section 2.14: Meera versus Margaret: Discrimination of Own Type
- Section 2.15: Interfaith Marriage and Divorce Laws
- Chapter XII: Scriptures and Interfaith Marriages
- Watch this video prepared by InterfaithShaadi: https://www.youtube.com/watch?v=hlAuY85RlcE.

Section 9.1: I Am Jain and Love a Black American

Jigisha says:

I am a Jain Girl. I'm so confused how to tell my parents about my situation? Should I tell them or not? Should I go ahead or not? I'm working in the Middle East and my parents are staying back home in India. They are seeking proposals for me. I am in love with a Black American, who is my colleague. We share good chemistry. I like him. He believes in vegetarian food habit and eats 90% vegetarian food. He has expressed his feeling many times. He respects my religion and my family values.

He is a very decent guy. He has told me many times that he will take care of me like anything. He asks me to talk to my parents also but I haven't shown seriousness. I'm afraid how would they behave with him? As far as I know, my parents are so strict. I have only one thing in my mind that I want to marry him. Can someone help me? Please. —Jigisha

Admin says:

Dear Jigisha,

This is certainly a difficult decision. Married life itself is complex, on top of that you add inter-faith issues, inter-cultural issues and interracial issues, and all of a sudden you have so much more to chew and digest.

You said, "I have only one thing in my mind that I want to marry him," but in the West, about half of marriages ultimately end in divorce.[238] In many cases, the divorce costs more than the marriage. We believe most marriages fail because it seems one's spouse has changed after marriage. No one in fact has changed, but there was a failure to realize who he or she truly was while dating. Take the time to know him without emotions or love.

You are probably in your mid 20's and probably want to settle down. As might be expected, your parents want to preserve their heritage and culture and wish you to settle for an arranged marriage with someone Jain. It is important for you to help them realize that you are now a different person from the little girl you were at age 6. You are not going to settle for someone just because your parents are telling you to, unless the boy recommended by them is fully competent and you feel a connection with him. You are not doing anything wrong so please do not

---

[238] http://www.avvo.com/legal-guides/ugc/marriage-divorce-statistics.

carry any feelings of guilt. This world is changing and parents have to come to terms with this new reality of life.

Considering you have the power to make a decision that is right for you, this freedom comes with a heavy price to pay. You need to make sure your decision is the right one, otherwise you will likely lose the support of your parents and there will not be any shoulder to cry on!

You cannot make a rational decision when you are holding hands with your lover and when high levels of sex hormones are streaming through your blood. Somehow you will have to find a way to see through this "blinding" love.

You are in the the Middle East and thus you do not have your familial support system nearby to guide you. Don't worry; we are here to assist.

How well do you know him? We are not talking about his "face-value," but his culture, family and his childhood? Are his parents divorced? Have you met his parents at the place where they live? Can you live his life, AS IS, if you have to? Was his father respecting his mother? Was his father an alcoholic? Remember, what goes around, comes around!

If he is from America, it is unlikely that you are his first girlfriend. Find out how many girls he has slept with and decide whether you are comfortable with such a situation. Do not have any physical relationship if you are searching for the truth.

A major problem with East-West relationships is that the Westerners have plenty of experience dating while in many cases, for the Eastern girl, it is the first guy who has ever touched her. How much prior dating experience do you have? If you are a naive dater, be careful. In Cricket terms, it is comparable to the first time ever bowler versus a century batsman! You are prone to make mistakes. We feel Eastern parents should let their children, who are living and working outside their native country, have dating experiences, considering many of them end up marrying outside their faith anyways.

What is wrong in checking out what kinds of Jain (or Hindu) men your parents have to offer? Without bias, go and check them out. Generally, in Jain communities, women are treated with dignity and respect. If you did come across a reasonably good Jain man (including in the Middle East), why settle for so much uncertainly with your American boyfriend?

If he is a Christian, ask if you have to be baptized for their church wedding. Most importantly, check to see if your children have to be baptized and raised as Christians. If he is a Muslim, he will ask you for religious conversion before an Islamic nikaah.

Are you comfortable being part of a black community? Are you going to be proud raising mixed race children? Are you ready to defend your decision to your parents and friends and win their hearts?

We should also tell you not to get stuck on these black-brown-white differences. It is only a temporary thing. Once you are part of it, the difference will fade. President Barack Obama was a black President to start with, but now people see him only as President Obama. Now his performance is judged not by his color but his deeds.

You will have to learn to live with color discrimination when you are in your Jain community. Instead of fighting to remove people's prejudice, just learn to smile with your relatives if they make insulting comments about your boyfriend/husband. Eventually others will get used to him and start seeing his inner beauty.

Sometimes, being with an African American could be an advantage to you. He may truly accept you with love and respect. He has seen discrimination all his life and thus may treat you with double respect for who you are.

Jigisha, there are so many factors at play here that there is no easy guidance one can give you. Now all the responsibility lies on your shoulders (and without any prior experience). Please keep us posted. Best wishes. —Admin

Chapter X: Parsi-Hindu Interfaith Marriages

Couples in Parsi-Hindu relationship are requested to first read:
- Section 2.2: Ten Points of Interfaith Dating
- Section 2.3: FAQ on Interfaith Marriages
- Section 2.8: Ten Points on Dating a Hindu
- Section 2.15: Interfaith Marriage and Divorce Laws
- Section 12.2: The Geeta on Abrahamics?

Section 10.1: Hindu: I Am in Relationship with a Parsi

Sujata says:

I am in a relationship with a Parsi guy. I want to ask something. Is it ok to marry a Parsi? I mean I don't know the religion much. Please explain me about his religion and what's the difference between Parsi and Farsi? — Sujata

Admin says:

Hello Sujata,

Obviously yes, it is okay to marry anyone. However considering there are only a very few Parsis left in India, they are very protective of their culture (Parsi) and religion (Zoroastrian).

If a Parsi marries a Hindu, he/she may ask for:
1) A marriage without Hindu rituals (a marriage in front of fire is not allowed in their religion), and
2) The children by this marriage must have Parsi names and be raised as Parsis only.

In these respects, for Hindus, Parsis are not any different than Muslims, Christians and Jews. However, unlike Christians and Muslims, Parsis and Jews do not believe in proselytism.

Please note that Farsi is a language of ancient Persians, while Parsi refers to a group of people. Here is the information that you requested from stated relevant sources:

Who is a Parsi?[239]   "A Parsi or Parsee is an ethnic Persian member of Zoroastrian communities in India. They descended from Greater Iran who immigrated to Gujarat in western India during the 8th or 10th century to avoid persecution by Muslim invaders who were in the process of conquering Iran."

Why only a few Parsis left? [240]   "Perhaps 61,000 Parsis are left in India today, three-quarters of them in Mumbai. Parsis often marry late or not at all and therefore have a low birth rate. Many migrate to the West. The group's closed nature poses more problems. The children of women who marry outside do not count as Parsis, despite an otherwise progressive

---

[239] http://en.wikipedia.org/wiki/Parsi.
[240] http://www.economist.com/node/21561946.

attitude to women. Some Zoroastrian priests do not admit converts." —
Admin

> The moment you fear, you are no body. It is the fear that is
> the greatest cause of miseries in the World. It is fear that is
> the greatest of all superstitions. It is fear that is the cause of
> our woes, and it is fearlessness that brings heaven in a
> moment.
> —Swami Vivekananda

Section 10.2: Zoroastrian in Love with a Hindu

Aspi says:

I am a Zoroastrian and love a Hindu girl. Her family wants the wedding to happen according to Hindu rituals and that mean the 7 pheras around a fire.

I am not really bothered doing all this. However some members in my family have been telling me not to do the pheras as it would mean conversion to Hinduism and denouncing Zoroastrianism.

I don't really follow religious practices or faith. I do however visit the fire temple when I feel like which is usually once or twice a year to attend my father's baj or something like that.

Now my fiancée and I have decided that we will have our freedom to do whatever we choose to do and kids at this point are a no-no.

I want to know in detail what are the legal implications of going through with a traditional Hindu wedding? —Aspi

Admin says:

Why you said, "Kids at this point are a no-no"? It is possible that after a few years of marriage, you may feel like having children. Is it because of religious conflicts or just your choice?

We wish somehow you manage to keep traditions from both faiths. Take best from both faiths and leave the rest for others. Be a pluralist and tolerant of each other's religious beliefs and teach the same to both sets of in-laws. Respect and honor both sets of parents but don't submit to parents' irrational request to give up the other faith.

We are not legal experts but please read Indian Marriage Laws[241] and cross-references into it. As far as we understand, it is the first marriage that counts. For this reason, go to have a Civil marriage first. After that you could have a Hindu as well as Zoroastrian marriages (and Jain, Christian, Sikh... as many marriages you wish to have). This way, you have no choice but to be neutral and will not be questioned if you got converted from one to other and the same for her. If any Hindu priest says you must convert, find a new one!

Your parents said that being in a Hindu wedding ceremony means you converted to Hinduism. We believe a pandit sprinkling water and

---

[241] Section 2.15.

chanting Sanskrit slokas does not fulfill "legal" definition of conversion. For example, being in Islamic nikaah does not make one a Muslim, but before marriage the imam will ask one to take shahadah oath of conversion to Islam and that is a legal conversion. Further, going to a church every Sunday does not make one a legal Christian but one has to be baptized to be a Christian. A Hindu could be a believer in Jesus' teachings and a Christian could love yoga and messages in Geeta. These are choices, beliefs and faiths but do not constitute a legal conversion. — Admin

Aspi **says:**

Thanks Admin. Really appreciate it. —Aspi

It doesn't matter if he/she is from different faith; all you need is to have faith in each other.
—Suketu (Hindu-Jain marriage experience; Section 11.1)

Chapter XI: Jain-Hindu Interfaith Marriages

Couples in Jain-Hindu relationship are requested to first read:
- Section 2.4: 38% of Hindus Marry Abrahamics in America
- Section 2.14: Meera versus Margaret: Discrimination of Own Type
- Chapter VII: Jain-Muslim Marriages
- Section 12.1: Scriptures and Interfaith Marriages

Section 11.1: Jain-Hindu Marriages

Hinduism and Jainism are two distinct religions but with many common Dharmic value systems. In the West, there are many Hindu-Jain temples under one roof and devotees praying side-by-side. Historically, there is no reported war or killing in the name of religion between these two faiths. In spite of these, Hindu-Jain marriages are not going to be without their own set of problems; however, generally, there is no expectation of religious conversion by any one side. We have seen most married Jain-Hindu couples following both practices, may be more of one and less of the other.

Here, the author has listed 11 representative cases out of some 40 Jain-non-Jain relationship experiences at InterfaithShaadi.[242]

Suketu says:

I am a Hindu guy (non-veg) married to a Jain girl (pure-veg). We are together for 5 years. We do have cultural differences. Neither do I completely understand Jainism nor does she understand my faith. Irrespective of our differences, we still are happy. We are together because we both respect each other's beliefs and cultural values. We help each other out even if we have to do some rituals belonging to each other's faiths. So what I am saying is—it doesn't matter if he/she is from different faith, all you need is to have faith in each other. —Suketu

Kavita says:

I am a Jain girl and my boyfriend is Sindhi (non vegetarian; Hindu). We are together for last 5 years. We have the same issues as discussed above about our beliefs. He doesn't eat non-vegitarian for me but his family does. I don't know how to tackle this thing. I love him a lot and can't be without him. —Kavita

Sital says:

I am Jain and my boyfriend is Hindu. In December I am going to marry him but my question is that I don't want to change my surname. Can I do that? I want to follow Jainism (my boyfriend and his family don't mind, they allow me) so can I write Hindu-Jain as caste after marriage? I don't want to write Hindu as a caste. Will I be able to do this? —Sital

---

[242] https://www.interfaithshaadi.org/blog/?cat=38.

Parag says:

I am a Hindu and I loved a Jain girl. You don't know how much I suffered. I have been crying for last 1 year. She left me now because of the religious feeling of her parents. —Parag

Tulsi says:

I am in love with a Jain boy and I am a Brahmin girl. We are in relation for last 2 years but I am really scared of telling my parents about our relationship. I am depressed. —Tulsi

Neil says:

I love a Jain girl. My parents agreed for the marriage but her parents have not. Her parents told her if she will marry me then they will not be allowed to follow their religion. Not because of the society but because this inter-caste marriage will destroy their family religion. I wanted to know, is this only an excuse they gave her or there is some truth in this? —Neil

Preya says:

My boyfriend (Jain) has been unable to talk to his parents about me (Hindu). If we are blessed by a priest, can we overrule his parents' consent? This is only to say because there are underlying threats of him being disowned by his parents… (*more than 2 years later*) Thank you for your advice. Now my boyfriend and I are married since a year, with consent from his parents. He follows Jainism while I follow Hinduism. Of course, there is still bitterness of the past but generally we all behave ourselves. I am writing this as a thank you, and best wishes to all others who may face a situation similar to ours. —Preya

Parlin says:

I was born as a Hindu Brahmin girl. But my parents were very open, educated and never tried to tie me into any religious boundaries. When I was finishing my graduation, I fell in love with a Jain guy. Everything started with flirting but we became serious for each other and we dated for 3.5 years. My Jain-ex never introduced me to his parents but me being stupid introduced him to everyone in my family. Though he promised that he will marry me, he never did. So after 3 years I asked for his decision and he told me very clearly many a times that he doesn't want to go against his parents' will. His parents are old and they may die if he marries me because he is a Jain and I am a Hindu. I was feeling like an idiot and shed tears for almost one year. He married a girl of his community.

I had no choice but to move on in my life. Later, I shifted my base to Canada for doctorate, married to a French Canadian Christian Pentecostal guy. —Parlin

Anand says:

I am a Hindu boy and I am non-vegetarian. I fell in love with a Jain (marwadi) girl 3 years back. She too is in love with me but she is damn afraid of her family because her parents are strict. I am ready to convince and talk to her parents and ready to get converted (to Jainism) too. Will it be easy to convince them and will it work out? —Anand

Shanti says:

I am a Jain girl and I want to marry a Brahmin guy. His parents want me to perform all rituals and worship Hindu Gods. I feel bit hesitating in doing so. On the other hand my parents can't see me doing all these things, so they are against it. His family wants me to accept Brahminism completely and forget about Jainism. I am just afraid if this condition prevails we can't marry each other. Our families are highly religious at their ends, but we love each other and want to marry. Please help. — Shanti

Section 11.2: Jain-Hindu Wonderful Married Life

Bina says:

About 30+ years back, we (Bride: Hindu and Groom: Jain) were engaged in India via a suggestion but ultimately, love marriage. We came to the West and had a non-denominational court wedding.

As a couple, we visit both, Jain and Hindu temples and participate in religious customs of both. No special ceremony was performed to declare our children Jain or Hindu. Over the years, we have celebrated both holidays: Paryushan, Janmashtami, and Diwali. And life has been wonderful!

I attribute to our successful marriage to the minimal cultural differences between Jains and Hindus, our parents' consent, and respect for both religious beliefs. —Bina

Admin says:

Hello Bina,

Thank you for sharing your wonderful life story. This is what we call—Interfaith Marriage with Equality.

We hear in news every day of bombing and killing due to religious intolerance. On our web site, many youths in interfaith love come crying because of religious conflicts. You and your two faiths have done something that all should know and learn. This is very commendable. You are a role model for all interfaith lovers.

Jainism and Hinduism are two distinct religions[243] with different scriptures. It is impressive that Hindus and Jains have lived side by side for over 2000 years but, to the best of our knowledge, there has not been a single case of killing in the name of God. Compared to that, people carrying exclusivist and supremacist beliefs have killed millions.

How wonderful it is to visit both faith temples, to give children freedom to follow both faiths and to enjoy both sets of holidays equally. Probably yours is a dream come true type interfaith marriage for most of today's interfaith dating youths. Unfortunately, a religious fanatic would counter by saying: 1) you are going against your God/faith, 2) your children will get confused between two faiths and 3) you will get Hell Fire in the after-life because you mixed two faiths. Silly, is it not?

---

[243] http://www.jaina.org/page/Myths.

You said your successful marriage is attributed to "the minimal cultural differences." We believe there is more to it. There is also minimal cultural difference between Shia and Sunni Muslims but today the Middle East is burning. Even they may have the same culture and religion; a Mormon has to re-baptize to marry a Catholic and has to agree to raise children only in one of two faiths. We believe the marriages of Seema,[244] Jameela,[245] Azad,[246] Shah Rukh Khan,[247] and yours worked because of pluralistic and tolerant beliefs. Peace will come on this earth when exclusivists will learn to be pluralists. —Admin

---

[244] Section 5.4.
[245] Section 5.29.
[246] Section 6.1.
[247] http://www.youtube.com/watch?v=Py7sFkIGi-k.

Chapter XII: Scriptures

Section 12.1: Scriptures and Interfaith Marriages

Religions and scriptures are the guiding principles of life for many. Dharmic and Abrahamic religious chornology is shown in Figure 3. Most of the time, scriptures teach us to live in peace and harmony with others. There are many pluralistic themes in different scriptures like Lord Jesus guiding us to "Love thy neighbors," [248] Allah stating, "To you We have given the scriptures, just as We have given the scriptures to people before you (Jews, Christians, Hindus, Buddhists, etc.[249])" and Lord Krishna's message, "Who is friendly to every living being—he certainly comes to Me."[250] In spite of God's many inclusivist and loving messages, millions have been killed in His/Her name. Is this due to conflicting messages given by God or is it human's inability to comprehend God's true message? Assuming the latter, the author recommends all interfaith couples not to get stuck on scriptures and instead learn to enjoy Interfaith Marriage with Equality.

	Krishna (3228 BC)
Abraham (1943 BC) -LORD God	**Vedas written (1000-6000 BC)**
Isaac	
Jacob-Israel	
Moses (1593 BC)	**Buddha (563 BC)**
David	**Mahavir (527 BC)**
Solomon	
Jesus (0 CE) –Son of Father God	
Mohammad (570 CE) –Allah	
	Guru Nanak (1469 CE)
Estimated dates as found in the Wikipedia	

Figure 3: Religious Chronology

Considering many unifying themes in different scriptures will not hurt interfaith dating couples if they were not aware of them, the author has focused in this book on quotes which may be potentially interpreted as objectionable from an inclusivist viewpoint. Select verses/ayat/stanza from different scriptures are listed in the following sections that the interfaith dating couples should know.

---

[248] Matthew 22:39.
[249] Koran 5:48 and https://www.interfaithshaadi.org/blog/?p=8038.
[250] Geeta 11:55.

- The Geeta on Abrahamic? (Section 12.2)
- The Torah on Hindus?[251] (Section 12.3)
- Bat Mitzvah on Hindus? (Section 12.4)
- The Bible on Hindus? (Section 12.5)
- The Koran on Hindus? (Section 12.6)
- The Koran on Christians and Jews? (Section 12.7)

It is possible that some Hindus as well as Abrahamics may find that listing these verses without detailed explanations for each in this book is not appropriate.[252] The author recommends an interfaith dating couple to read respective scriptures for full context and discuss together how these select verses may impact their planned married life.

While consulting with more than 900 interfaith dating youths over the past 9 years, the author has learned that—initially, the majority of interfaith dating youths don't have interest in religious scriptures. However, this changes later when the relationship gets serious. Sometimes, increased interest in one's religion/scripture by the intended spouse could be a warning sign of trouble on the way; for example, the reason for initiating discussion on "Who is God?" and comparison of two scriptures may be to ultimately prove superiority of one's faith over the other. The proposition to agree on "We will not idol-worship" is to convince the other that "Your idols are idols, while my idols are Godly."[253] The talk of "Children may get confused in two religions"[254] is meant to say, "Children should follow my faith and not yours." The objective of "ONE God" talk could be to express religious exclusivity that "There is ONE God and that is MINE!" Love proselytism precedes disclosure of the need of religious conversion for marriage. It is hoped that the following sections will help dating people be better prepared against a potential religious fanatic.

The author believes happy and successful interfaith marriage is possible provided the couple has true respect for each other's beliefs and has learned to interpret scriptures in their historical context.

---

[251] The author has used Hindu as a representative Dharmic (including Jain, Buddhist and Sikh) faith.
[252] The author apologizes if listing of these verses hurt sentimental feelings of some but felt paramount to educate interfaith dating youths about potential sources of trouble in their planned married life later.
[253] Section 2.11.
[254] Section 5.22.

Section 12.2: The Geeta on Abrahamics?

In general Hindus are pluralists (*Ishvara Allah tero nam*; meaning one God having different names[255]). The author has not found many verses in the Holy Geeta that portrayed Hinduism as an exclusivist and supremacist religion. Further, there is no mention of interfaith marriages and no criticism of other religions, probably because most other religions came into existence after the Hindu scriptures were written. In spite of all these, the author found few verses that could be objectionable to an Abrahamic dating person. The Hindu-Abrahamic couple should read these together and decide what it means to their planned married life.

Below are translations of verses from Geeta[256] given by God (Lord Krishna[257]) to Arjuna on the battlefield of Kuruksetra. Reflections on potentially how to interpret these scriptures are provided in italics.

- •3:32 But those who cavil at My teaching and do not follow it, know them to be absolutely ignorant, devoid of all knowledge and lost. [*Can one achieve perfection by following the Holy Bible, Torah or Koran?*]
- •4:11 As all surrender unto Me, I reward them accordingly. Everyone follows My path in all respects, O son of Pritha. [*Does "Everyone" include Christians, Jews, Muslims and atheists?*]
- •6:14 Serene-minded, fearless, firm in the vow of Brahmacharya, having controlled the mind, thinking on Me and balanced, let him sit, having Me as the Supreme Goal.
- •6:47 And among all Yogis, he who, full of faith, with his inner-self merged in Me, worships Me, is, accoding to Me, the most devout.
- •7:7 There is nothing else higher than Me, O' Arjuna. Everything is strung on Me, like the clusters of gems on a string. [*In seemingly contrast to Krishna's message, Jesus said, "No one comes to the Father (God) except through Me" (John 14:6) and Allah said, "Those*

---

[255] The author conducted a small survey amongst proud Hindu devotes in one California Hindu temple asking, "Are Jesus, Mahavir, Allah, Buddha, Ganesh ... Gods (or Godly)?" and found 86% believed that ALL are God (Godly) including Allah and Jesus.

[256] The Holy Geeta by Prabha Duneja, Govindram Hasanand Publishing, Delhi, India, The Holy Geeta by Swami Chinmayananda, Central Chinmaya Mission Trust, 2006 or Bhagavad-Gita, As It Is, by His Divine Grace A. C. Bhaktivedanta Swami Prabhupada, second edition.

[257] Here Lord Krishna should not be interpreted as a person but the Ultimate Being, God or Brahman. (Geeta 9:11)

*that embrace Islam pursue the right path." (Koran 3:19 and 72:13)
Interfaith couple needs to discuss—are all messengers telling us the
same thing or are these different messages?*]

- •7:15 The evil-doers, deluded and the lowest among men do not seek
refuge in Me; being deluded by the illusive nature (Maya), they lack
proper knowledge and follow the ways of the demons.

- •7:23 Verily the "fruit" that accures to those men of little-intelligence is
finite. The worshippers of the Devas go to the Devas but My devotees
come to Me.

- •9:11 The fools disregard Me, dwelling in human form. They do not
know My transcendental nature. [*Some Jews and Muslims may have
problem accepting the concept of God in a human form.*]

- •9:23 Those who are devotees of other gods and who worship them with
faith actually worship only Me, O son of Kunti, but they do so in a
wrong way. [*As discussed later for the Torah (Subsection 12.3.3),
Bible (Subsection 12.5.2) and Koran (Section 12.6), similar verses
raise questions for who is "God" and who are "other gods." It may
confuse interfaith couples for which one of these scriptures to follow
or which one of these Gods to believe in. It should be noted that Lord
Krishna does not instruct devotees to conduct violence against those
who do not believe in Him, believe in other Gods or are atheist.*]

- •10:20 I am the Supersoul, O Arjuna, seated in the hearts of all living
entities. I am the beginning, the middle and the end of all beings.

- •11:55 My dear Arjuna, he who engages in My pure devotional service,
free from the contaminations of fruitive activities and mental
speculation, he who works for Me, who makes Me the supreme goal
of his life, and who is friendly to every living being—he certainly
comes to Me. [*Two people may interpret a single verse/ayat/stanza in
different ways. For example, here "friendly to every living being" is
certainly a pluralistic inclusivist message, but someone else may find
Lord Krishna's message "makes Me the supreme goal" as an
exclusivist message. Likewise, Lord Jesus also gave seemingly
conflicting messages in the Bible. Jesus said, "Love thy
neighbors,"[258] "He who is not with Me is against Me"[259] and "Do not
suppose that I have come to bring peace to the earth. I did not come
to bring peace, but a sword."[260] Further, if one interprets "Me" in
these scriptures as the Supreme Being (The Creator, LORD God,*]

---

[258] Matthew 22:39.
[259] Matthews 12:30.
[260] Matthew 10:34; also Luke 12:51.

Allah or Father the God) then there would be not a conflict in interpreting different scriptures but it would be wrong to interpret "Me" as a person or a personal God.]

- 12:6-7 But those who worship Me, giving up all their activities unto Me and being devoted to Me without deviation, engaged in devotional service and always meditating upon Me, having fixed their minds upon Me, O son of Pritha—for them I am the swift deliverer from the ocean of birth and death. [*An Abrahamic may not believe in reincarnation*]

- 12:8 Settle your mind in Me alone, let your intellect dwell in Me, then you will live in Me alone, there is no doubt about this.

- 18:65 Always think of Me, become My devotee, worship Me and offer your homage unto Me. Thus you will come to Me without fail. I promise you this because you are very dear friend.

- 18:66 Abandon all varieties of religion[261] and just surrender unto Me. I shall deliver you from all sinful reactions. Do not fear. [*Is Lord Krishna asking abandoning Abrahamic faiths?*]

---

[261] Actual word is dharma and not religion (in Sanskrit: *Sarva dharman parityajya*, ...). See Glossary (Appedix A) for explanation of dharma.

Section 12.3: The Torah on Hindus?

The Torah, the first five chapters of the Bible, is the holiest scripture of the Jews. The Torah covers revelations from God to different apostles up to Moses. It is part of Old Testament and as such forms the core of Christian belief. The apostles described in the Torah are also recognized by Bible and Koran.

Though Jews, Christians and Muslims believe in the same God, they are at odds while practicing their faith. First, they call God by different but not inter-changeable names, like LORD God (or God of Israel), God the Father (Jesus as the Son) and Allah (God in Arabic), respectively. Though the Bible and Koran do recognize God's messages in the Torah, the Koran recommends Muslims not to be friends of Christians and Jews.[262] On the other hand, Jews may not recognize Jesus as the "Son" of God or Mohammad as the "last" messenger of LORD God.

Jews, Christians and Muslim are collectively referred to as Abrahamic and "People of the Book." In general, Abrahamics are monotheist and exclusivist and believe in the superiority of their faith over each other and others. Some of them may consider Hindus to be polytheists and idol-worshippers.

It is not the intention of this author to criticize any scripture. This section is written to help Abrahamic-Dharmic interfaith couples make knowledgeable decisions for their planned married life.

Ideally, it would be easy if one believes that scriptures were written (but inspired by God) by apostles/sages ages ago and should be interpreted in the context of their time. If a Jew believes that the Torah is literally a direct message from God and is to be followed literally, the Hindu partner has to wonder why the LORD God of Israel did not consult Ishvara before giving some conflicting statements.

For an interfaith couple, it is not what is stated in an individual's scripture that is important but what an individual has learned from it. Here, select quotations from the Torah[263] are listed that a Hindu-Jew couple must read together to answer how these verses will impact their marriage.

---

[262] Koran 5:51.
[263] Quotations are from multiple sources including The Torah: The Five Books of Moses (The Jewish Publication Society), Holy Bible (The Gideons International), New Heart English Bible and others.

12.3.1 The Second Commandment

God gave the Ten Commandments to Moses on Mount Sinai (circa 1593 BC). The Second Commandment should be of major concern to any interfaith couple. Here, an angry and jealous God gives a message of absolute intolerance towards other belief systems. Any form or ways of worshipping God other than that described in the Torah is prohibited.

The Second Commandment: "You shall have no other gods before Me. You shall not make for yourself a carved image - any likeness of anything that is in heaven above, or that is in the earth beneath, or that is in the water under the earth; you shall not bow down to them nor serve them. For I, the LORD your God, am a jealous God, visiting the iniquity of the fathers upon the children to the third and fourth generations of those who reject Me." (Exodus 20:3-5)

Compared to the above, Jesus stated the Second Commandment as, "And the Second is like it: You shall love your neighbor as yourself."[264] Further, Jesus added, "There is no commandment greater than these (love thy neighbors)."[265] Unfortunately, Jesus' followers continued to highlight and repeat God's seemingly exclusivist messages while writing the Bible. Koran prescribes even more severe punishments for unbelievers.

If a Dharmic is considering a lifelong relationship with an Abrahamic, it would be wise to know what kind of interpretation your intended spouse has learned during his/her lifetime. To make an "informed" decision, the Dharmic should ask the Abrahamic: 1) Does Lord Krishna qualify as God?; 2) During a Hindu wedding ceremony, the Hindu priest will invoke many Gods from heaven and earth. Are you going to accept being a part of such a wedding?; and 3) Are you going to fear your Jealous God if you enter a Hindu, Jain or Sikh temple, take prasad (offerings from God), or are invited to be a part of other Hindu rituals at my parents' home?

For a Jew-Hindu couple, it is important to make sure that the intended spouse does not believe in this Second Commandment literally and is not intolerant to the Hindu belief that the Almighty may be worshipped in one or more different forms. If any person holds an exclusivist vision of God or religion—that only their religion is the true path—an interfaith relationship is not for them. If someone in a Jewish-Hindu couple finds some irreconsilable differences, they need to explore them fully before getting married.

---

[264] Matthew 22:39.
[265] Mark 12:31.

12.3.2 Angry and Jealous God

The Torah has described God as a "Jealous God" 10 times, as an "Angry God" 40 times and the word "fear" is used 60 times; many of these statements are made by God Himself.

If a potential Jewish spouse is fearful of a jealous LORD God's stern messages for other faiths, it could create problems in your married life while practicing the Hindu belief system of seeing the Almighty in any and all possible forms, including females, animals, plants, rivers, mountains, the sun and moon.

12.3.3 Torah on the "Other" Gods

Hindu Dharma believes in one Ultimate Reality (Brahman), but Hindus have liberty to express the All Mighty God by different names and forms (*Ekam sat vipra bahudha vadanti*[266]). Likewise, the Torah teaches that there is absolutely only one God or ultimate reality. However, the Torah has stern warnings for those who believe in "other gods" or express God with names or in any form and shape. If so, are Gods as described in the Hindu scriptures "other" gods?

The reference to the "other" gods in the Torah is in reference to the Pagan practices at that time and probably not to Hindu ways of believing in God. Likewise, Lord Krishna also said, "Those who are devotees of 'other' gods and who worship them with faith actually worship only Me, but they do so in a wrong way."[267] This Krishna's message is not directed to the Abrahamic concept of God. As it is said all along in this book, an interfaith couple must learn to interpret scriptures in its context for happier outcomes.

Below is a list of citations[268] from the Torah about warnings against praying to "other" gods or idol worshipping:

• Anyone you find your gods with shall not live. (Genesis 31:32)

• You shall not have the gods of others in My presence. (Exodus 20:3)

• You shall not make [images of anything that is] with Me. Gods of silver or gods of gold you shall not make for yourselves. (Exodus 20:4)

---

[266] Rigveda 1:164:46.
[267] Geeta 9:23 (also read Section 12.2).
[268] Taken from http://www.chabad.org/library/bible_cdo/aid/9862, http://www.biblegateway.com/passage, New Heart English Bible and other sources.

- Be careful to do all things that I have said to you; and do not invoke the name of other gods, neither let them be heard out of your mouth. (Exodus 23:13)

- You shall not bow down to their gods, nor serve them, nor follow their practices, but you shall utterly overthrow them and demolish their pillars. (Exodus 23:24)

- But you shall break down their altars, and dash in pieces their pillars, and you shall cut down their Asherim (cult objects related to the worship); for you shall worship no other god: for the LORD, whose name is Jealous, is a jealous God. (Exodus 34:13-14)

- Then you shall drive out all the inhabitants of the land from before you, destroy all their stone idols, destroy all their molten images, and demolish all their high places. (Numbers 33:52)

- Lest you corrupt yourselves, and make yourself an engraved image in the form of any figure, the likeness of male or female. (Deuteronomy 4:16)

- There you shall serve other gods, the work of men's hands, wood and stone, which neither see, nor hear, nor eat, nor smell. (Deuteronomy 4:28)

- But you shall deal with them like this: you shall break down their altars, and dash their pillars in pieces, and cut down their Asherim, and burn their engraved images with fire. (Deuteronomy 7:5)

- I took your sin, the calf (idol) which you had made, and burnt it with fire, and stamped it, grinding it very small, until it was as fine as dust: and I cast its dust into the brook that descended out of the mountain. (Deuteronomy 9:21)

- And you shall break down their altars, and dash in pieces their pillars, and burn their Asherim with fire; and you shall cut down the engraved images of their gods; and you shall destroy their name out of that place. (Deuteronomy 12:3)

- And you shall stone him with stones so that he dies, because he sought to lead you astray from the Lord, your God, who brought you out of the land of Egypt, out of the house of bondage. (Deuteronomy 13:11)

- And has gone and served other gods, and worshiped them, or the sun, or the moon, or any of the host of heaven, which I have not commanded; and it be told you, and you have heard of it, then you shall inquire diligently; and look, if it be true, and the thing certain, that such abomination is done in Israel, then you shall bring forth that man or that woman, who has done this evil thing, to your gates, even the man or the woman; and you shall stone them to death with stones. (Deuteronomy 17:3-5)

- •But of the cities of these peoples, that the LORD your God gives you for an inheritance, you shall save alive nothing that breathes; but you shall utterly destroy them. (Deuteronomy 20:16-17)

- •They moved him to jealousy with strange gods. They provoked him to anger with abominations.... They have made Me jealous with that which is not God. They have provoked Me to anger with their vanities. I will move them to jealousy with those who are not a people. I will provoke them to anger with a foolish nation. (Deuteronomy 32:16, 21)

12.3.4 God's "Chosen" People

Judaism is a monotheistic and exclusivist religion. Jews believe in religious supremacy (they are God's "chosen" people). As per the Torah, the LORD God was for the sons of Abraham, Isaac, and Jacob. How realistic is it that God was playing favorites only to a small number of Jewish people in Arabia when there were millions of others human beings all over the world?

Here are verses showing God's preference for Jews over non-Jews:
- •I will establish my covenant between Me and you and your descendants after you throughout their generations for an everlasting covenant, to be a God to you and to your descendants after you. (Genesis 17:7)

- •The blood shall be to you for a token on the houses where you are and when I see the blood, I will pass over you, and there shall no plague be on you to destroy you, when I strike the land of Egypt. (Exodus 12:13)

- •Now therefore, if you will indeed obey My voice, and keep My covenant, then you shall be My own possession from among all peoples; for all the earth is Mine. (Exodus 19:5)

- •I will dwell among the sons of Israel, and will be their God. (Exodus 29:45)

- •Look, the LORD your God has set the land before you: go up, take possession, as the LORD, the God of your fathers, has spoken to you; do not be afraid, neither be dismayed. (Deuteronomy 1:21)

- •You shall be blessed above all peoples: there shall not be male or female barren among you, or among your livestock. (Deuteronomy 7:14)

•Only the LORD had a delight in your fathers to love them, and he chose their descendants after them, even you above all peoples, as at this day. (Deuteronomy 10:15)

12.3.5 Interfaith Marriages

The Torah has many stern warnings against interfaith marriages. A true believer in the Torah will want to solve this interfaith marriage problem by religious conversion of the non-Jewish fiancé(e). While in this day and age, many Jews might not ask for religious conversion they will almost certainly ask for the children of their interfaith marriage to be Jewish by bris and bar/bat mitzvah ceremonies. If one is looking for an interfaith marriage with equality for both faiths, keeping the child's religious "labeling" out and letting the child decide his or her own faith at an adult age may be an appropriate choice.

Here are the Torah's recommendations on interfaith marriages:

•The sons of Jacob answered Shechem and Hamor his father with deceit, and spoke, because he had defiled Dinah their sister, and said to them, "We can't do this thing, to give our sister to one who is uncircumcised; for that is a reproach to us. (Genesis 34:13-14)

•Be careful, lest you make a covenant with the inhabitants of the land where you are going, lest it be for a snare in the midst of you: but you shall break down their altars, and dash in pieces their pillars, and you shall cut down their Asherim; for you shall worship no other god: for the LORD, whose name is Jealous, is a jealous God. Do not make a covenant with the inhabitants of the land, lest they play the prostitute after their gods, and sacrifice to their gods, and one call you and you eat of his sacrifice; and you take of their daughters to your sons, and their daughters play the prostitute after their gods, and make your sons play the prostitute after their gods. You shall make no cast idols for yourselves. (Exodus 34:12-17)

•When the LORD your God shall bring you into the land where you go to possess it, and shall cast out many nations before you, the Hittite, and the Girgashite, and the Amorite, and the Canaanite, and the Perizzite, and the Hivite, and the Jebusite, seven nations greater and mightier than you; and when the LORD your God shall deliver them up before you, and you shall strike them; then you shall utterly destroy them: you shall make no covenant with them, nor show mercy to them; neither shall you make marriages with them; your daughter you shall not give to his son, nor shall you take his daughter for your son. For he will turn away your son from following Me, that he may serve other gods; so the anger of the LORD would be kindled against you, and He would destroy you quickly. But you shall deal with them like this: you shall break down their altars, and dash their pillars in pieces, and cut down their Asherim, and burn their engraved images with fire. (Deuteronomy 7:1-5)

12.3.6 Torah on Circumcision

Circumcision is not only a tradition but a central part of the Jewish identity. In an interfaith relationship with equality, one has to wonder if circumcision is science or superstition.[269]

- This is My (God) covenant that you shall keep, between Me and you and your descendants after you: Every male child among you shall be circumcised; and you shall be circumcised in the flesh of your foreskins, and it shall be a sign of the covenant between Me and you. He who is eight days old among you shall be circumcised, every male child in your generations, he who is born in your house or bought with money from any foreigner who is not your descendant. (Genesis 17:10-12)
- The uncircumcised male who is not circumcised in the flesh of his foreskin, that soul shall be cut off from his people. He has broken My covenant. (Genesis 17:14)
- When a stranger shall live as a foreigner with you, and will keep the Passover to the LORD, let all his males be circumcised, and then let him come near and keep it; and he shall be as one who is born in the land: but no uncircumcised person shall eat of it. (Exodus 12.48)
- In the eighth day the flesh of his foreskin shall be circumcised. (Leviticus 12:3)

12.3.7 Torah on Animal Sacrifices

As you can read in the Old Testament, it was common practice to sacrifice animals to wash off human sin. Later, Judaism did away with animal sacrifice completely. If you are a vegetarian or an animal lover, you may not want your children to read and follow these God's commandments.

- Every moving thing that lives shall be food for you. (Genesis 9:3)
- This is the law of the trespass offering. It is most holy. In the place where they kill the burnt offering, he shall kill the trespass offering; and its blood he shall sprinkle around on the altar. (Leviticus 7:1-2)

---

[269] Section 2.13.

- All the cattle for the burnt offering twelve bulls, the rams twelve, the male lambs a year old twelve, and their meal offering; and the male goats for a sin offering twelve; and all the cattle for the sacrifice of peace offerings twenty-four bulls, the rams sixty, the male goats sixty, the male lambs a year old sixty. This was the dedication of the altar, after it was anointed. (Numbers 7:87-88)

12.3.8 Torah on Cruelty to Others

Select verses from the Torah are listed here for information only, however we know that today's Jews do not follow it. Contemporary and progressive Jews are likely to interpret these verses in their historical context, not as mandates.

- You shall keep the Sabbath therefore; for it is holy to you. Everyone who profanes it shall surely be put to death; for whoever does any work therein, that soul shall be cut off from among his people. (Exodus 31:14)
- They warred against Midian, as the LORD commanded Moses; and they killed every male. They killed the kings of Midian with the rest of their slain: Evi, and Rekem, and Zur, and Hur, and Reba, the five kings of Midian: Balaam also the son of Beor they killed with the sword. The sons of Israel took captive the women of Midian and their little ones; and all their livestock, and all their flocks, and all their goods, they took for a prey. (Numbers 31:7-9)
- Now therefore kill every male among the little ones, and kill every woman who has known man by lying with him. But all the girls, who have not known man by lying with him, keep alive for yourselves. (Numbers 31:17-18)
- So the LORD our God delivered into our hand Og also, the king of Bashan, and all his people: and we struck him until none was left to him remaining. We took all his cities at that time; there was not a city which we did not take from them; sixty cities, all the region of Argob, the kingdom of Og in Bashan. All these were cities fortified with high walls, gates, and bars; besides the unwalled towns a great many. We utterly destroyed them, as we did to Sihon king of Heshbon, utterly destroying every inhabited city, with the women and the little ones. But all the livestock, and the spoil of the cities, we took for a prey to ourselves. (Deuteronomy 3:3-7)
- When you go forth to battle against your enemies, and the LORD your God delivers them into your hands, and you carry them away captive, and see among the captives a beautiful woman, and you have a desire

to her, and would take her to you as wife; then you shall bring her home to your house; and she shall shave her head, and pare her nails; and she shall put the clothing of her captivity from off her, and shall remain in your house, and bewail her father and her mother a full month: and after that you shall go in to her, and be her husband, and she shall be your wife. It shall be, if you have no delight in her, then you shall let her go where she will; but you shall not sell her at all for money, you shall not deal with her as a slave, because you have humbled her. (Deuteronomy 21:10-14)

12.3.9 Can One Read Torah in Its Context?

Your intended Jewish spouse may believe that the Torah is a direct message from God and has to be followed literally in your married life. Alternatively, your intended Jewish spouse may believe in interpreting the Torah in its context and believe it is not literally applicable today. The above listed points are to be discussed for its applicability to your planned marriage.

• You shall not add to the word which I command you, neither shall you diminish from it, that you may keep the commandments of the LORD your God which I command you. (Deuteronomy 4:2)

For an interfaith couple, it is not what is stated in an individual's scripture that is important but what an individual has learned from it.

Section 12.4: Bar Mitzvah for Hindus?

It is Jewish tradition to have their children participate in bris and bar mitzvah ceremonies. The bris (circumcision) is a religious ceremony performed on 8th day of childbirth. The Bar- (or Bat- for a girl) Mitzvah is a religious ritual performed at age of 12-13 years to announce the child as a Jewish adult (Coming of Age). The child has to commit to follow 613 mitzvoth (commandments) of the Torah for his/her life. The child becomes a son or daughter of the commandments, exploring what it means to live an ethical life, as they become a Jewish adult.

Is a Bar Mitzvah for children from a Hindu-Jew marriage with equality appropriate? It should be noted that if a Jew has married a non-Jew, he/she has already broken the covenant (#162) against marrying a non-Jew. Unless the Hindu is fully convinced and agrees that his/her children follow these mitzvoth, the Hindu probably should not commit to it for the following reasons: a) The Bar Mitzvah is not a hollow ritual devoid of meaning—without the intention to follow through you have created lies and deception as the foundation of your marriage, b) The Bar Mitzvah ceremony is not absolutely necessary by Jewish custom,[270] and c) Children of interfaith marriages may wish to decide his or her their own religion as an adult, like Barack Obama did, without having a religious label imposed on them.

Here the author has listed some of mitzvoth that may have potential conflicts with Hindu belief system or cultural values. The First and Second Commandments state that there is only one God and praying to "other" gods is not acceptable. Is LORD Krishna the "other" god? There are approximately 40 out of 613 commandments on "idol" worship and not praying to a Human form of God. Are Hindu Gods being worshipped as false gods? Approximately 25 out of 613 commandments deal with sex. In Indian culture, it would be uncomfortable to discuss sex with a 12-year-old child in public. There are also nearly 80 out of 613 commandments that address how to kill and eat animals. A Hindu may wish to replace all these with one simple one—Do not eat animal meat!

It is ultimately up to an interfaith couple to make a knowledgeable decision for their interfaith child.

---

[270] http://judaism.about.com/od/lifeevents/a/whatisabarmitzvah.htm.

A select number of mitzvoth relating to Hindus are listed here. The rest of the mitzvoth can be viewed at Wikipedia.[271]

Are Hindu Gods incarnations of the LORD God described in the Torah/Bible?

- •1: To know there is a God (*yes, but do LORD Krishna, Ganesh and Goddess Laxmi qualify as God/Devatas/Devis?*)
- •2: Not to think that there are other gods besides Him [*This is the second of the Ten Commandment.*[272]]
- •3: To know that He is One (*yes, but can She or He have different forms, like Hindu Gods?*)

Are Hindus Idol-worshippers?

- •31: Not to make human forms even for decorative purposes (*most Hindu Devis and Devatas are given human forms*)
- •33: To burn a city that has turned to idol-worship
- •39: Not to save the idolater
- •51: Not to bow down before a smooth stone (*most Hindu Gods, including Shiv Linga, are made of smooth stone*)
- •527: Press the idolater for payment
- •549: The courts must hang those stoned for blasphemy or idolatry

Are you comfortable talking about sex with your young ones?

- •139: Not to have sexual relations with your mother
- •155: A man must not have sexual relations with an animal
- •157: A man must not have sexual relations with a man
- •158: Not to have sexual relations with your father

Interfaith Marriage

- •162: Not to marry non-Jews (*why ask interfaith children to take this oath if their parents had an interfaith marriage?*)
- •164: Not to prevent a third-generation Egyptian convert from marrying into the Jewish people
- •166: Not to let a mamzer (a child born due to an illegal relationship) marry into the Jewish people

---

[271] http://en.wikipedia.org/wiki/613_Mitzvot.
[272] Read "The Torah on Hindus?" (Subsection 12.3.1).

Circumcision

•86: To circumcise all males on the eighth day after their birth

Marriage Contract

•122: To marry a wife by means of ketubah[273] and kiddushin (*is it a one-sided pre-nuptial agreement or a spiritual contract about their future life together and commitments?*)

Animal Killing

•168: Not to offer to God any castrated male animals
•176: To examine the signs of animals to distinguish between kosher and non-kosher
•187: Not to eat creatures that live in water other than (kosher) fish
•188: Not to eat the meat of an animal that died without ritual slaughter
•195: Not to cook meat and milk together
•203: To ritually slaughter an animal before eating it
•206: To send away the mother bird before taking its children
•351: Carry out the procedure of the sin offering
•354: Carry out the procedure of the guilt offering
•372: To offer two lambs every day
•443: Carry out the procedure of the Red Heifer (cow)
•490: Break the neck of a calf by the river valley following an unsolved murder

Miscellaneous Commandments

•208: Not to swear falsely in God's Name (*if you do not believe in all 613 mitzvoth, don't falsely swear to God*)
•214: Not to break oaths or vows
•579: Not to add to the Torah commandments or their oral explanations
•580: Not to diminish from the Torah any commandments, in whole or in part.

---

[273] Section 4.2.

Section 12.5: The Bible on Hindus?

All religious scriptures have shortcomings. The Lord Shiva and Lord God are portrayed as angry Gods, thought there may be justifications provided by believers. The Abrahamic (Jewish, Christian and Muslim) scriptures have spent a good deal of efforts criticizing others' belief systems.

For an interfaith couple, it is not what is stated in an individual's scripture that is important, but what an individual has learned from it, that is most critical.

The word "India" has been quoted twice, but there is no mention of the word "Hindu" in the Bible.[274] Here, select Biblical verses concerning 13 topics are quoted that a Christian-Hindu couple should be interested in knowing. By discussing these together, interfaith couples will better understand what these mean to their future marriage.

12.5.1 An Angry and Jealous God

The Abrahamic God is described as a "Jealous God" 31 times, as an "Angry God" 238 times and the word "fear" is used 455 times in the Bible. Many of these citations are by the God Himself. The Koran also has many stern warnings for unbelievers.[275] Two different viewpoints on the Jealous God concept are presented in Section 3.3.

12.5.2 Bible on the "Other gods"

Similar to Hindu Dharma, the Bible teaches that there is absolutely only one God or ultimate reality. However, the Bible has stern warnings for those who believe in "other gods." If so, are Lord Krishna, Rama, Ganesh, Goddess Laxmi, and many other forms of the God (Devas and Devis) as described in the Hindu scriptures, other gods? Likewise, Lord Krishna also said, "Those who are devotees of other gods and who worship them with faith actually worship only Me, but they do so in a wrong way."[276] Does it mean Christians are worshipping a wrong way? Like the author stated earlier, interfaith couples will have to learn to

---

[274] There are many versions of the Bible. The author has cited here most quotations from New Heart English Bible, but also has used The Holy Bible (The Gideons International), http://www.chabad.org/library/bible_cdo/aid/9862, http://www.biblegateway.com/passage, The Torah: The Five Books of Moses (The Jewish Publication Society), and information from many web sites.
[275] Section 12.6.
[276] Geeta 9:23 (also read Section 12.2).

interpret scriptures in their context. They should read these conflicting scriptures together and decide what it means to their planned married life.

• You shall have no other gods before Me. You shall not make for yourself a carved image—any likeness of anything that is in heaven above, or that is in the earth beneath, or that is in the water under the earth; you shall not bow down to them nor serve them. For I, the LORD your God, am a jealous God, visiting the iniquity of the fathers upon the children to the third and fourth generations of those who hate Me. (Exodus 20:3-5) [The Ten Commandments]

• He who sacrifices to another god, except to the LORD only, shall be utterly destroyed. (Exodus 22:20)

• Be careful to do all things that I have said to you; and do not invoke the name of other gods, neither let them be heard out of your mouth. (Exodus 23:13)

• And you shall break down their altars, and dash in pieces their pillars, and burn their Asherim with fire; and you shall cut down the engraved images of their gods; and you shall destroy their name out of that place. (Deuteronomy 12:3)

• And has gone and served other gods, and worshiped them, or the sun, or the moon, or any of the host of heaven, which I have not commanded;... then you shall bring forth that man or that woman, who has done this evil thing, to your gates, even the man or the woman; and you shall stone them to death with stones. (Deuteronomy 17:3, 5)

• I will utter my judgments against them touching all their wickedness, in that they have forsaken Me, and have burned incense to other gods, and worshiped the works of their own hands. (Jeremiah 1:16)

• They struck all the souls who were in it with the edge of the sword, utterly destroying them. There was no one left who breathed. He burnt Hazor with fire. (Joshua 11:11)

• And there is no God else besides Me, a just God and a Savior; there is no one besides Me. Look to Me, and be saved, all the ends of the earth; for I am God, and there is no other. By Myself have I sworn, the word is gone forth from my mouth in righteousness, and shall not return, that to Me every knee shall bow, every tongue shall swear to God. (Isaiah 45:21-23)

12.5.3 Bible on Idol-Worship[277]

Hindus are provided complete liberty to revere/worship and pray to God in any and every ways that works for them. For example, Mount Kailash, the river Ganges, the monkey God Hanuman, the elephant God Ganesh, the Sun and Moon, Mother Earth and many plants and animals are all sacred to Hindus. Not only sacred, they may be considered the earthly manifestations of God.

As one can read below, the Biblical God has absolutely no tolerance for some of Hindu ways of worshipping, what it terms as idol-worshipping.

- But you shall destroy their altars, break their sacred pillars, and cut down their wooden images (for you shall worship no other god, for the LORD, whose name is Jealous, is a jealous God), lest you make a covenant with the inhabitants of the land, and they play the harlot with their gods and make sacrifice to their gods, and one of them invites you and you eat of his sacrifice, and you take of his daughters for your sons, and his daughters play the harlot with their gods and make your sons play the harlot with their gods. You shall make no molded gods for yourselves. (Exodus 34:13-17)
- You shall make for yourselves no idols, neither shall you raise up an engraved image or a pillar, neither shall you place any figured stone in your land, to bow down to it: for I am the LORD your God. (Leviticus 26:1)
- Lest you corrupt yourselves, and make yourself an engraved image in the form of any figure, the likeness of male or female, the likeness of any animal that is on the earth, the likeness of any winged bird that flies in the sky. (Deuteronomy 4:16, 17)
- When you shall father children, and children's children, and you shall have been long in the land, and shall corrupt yourselves, and make an engraved image in the form of anything, and shall do that which is evil in the sight of the LORD your God, to provoke him to anger; ... There you shall serve other gods, the work of men's hands, wood and stone, which neither see, nor hear, nor eat, nor smell. (Deuteronomy 4:25, 28)
- You shall not make for yourself a carved image—any likeness of anything that is in heaven above, or that is in the earth beneath, or that is in the water under the earth; you shall not bow down to them nor serve them. For I, the LORD your God, am a jealous God, visiting the iniquity of the fathers upon the children to the third and fourth

---

[277] Also read Section 2.11.

generations of those who hate Me. (Deuteronomy 5:8-9) [The Ten Commandments]

- You shall burn the engraved images of their gods with fire. You shall not covet the silver or the gold that is on them, nor take it for yourself, lest you be snared in it; for it is an abomination to the LORD your God. (Deuteronomy 7:25)
- I took your sin, the calf which you had made, and burnt it with fire, and stamped it, grinding it very small, until it was as fine as dust: and I cast its dust into the brook that descended out of the mountain. (Deuteronomy 9:21)
- They moved Him to jealousy with strange gods. They provoked Him to anger with abominations.... They have moved Me to jealousy with that which is not God. They have provoked Me to anger with their vanities. I will move them to jealousy with those who are not a people. I will provoke them to anger with a foolish nation. (Deuteronomy 32:16, 21)
- You have even poured a drink offering to them. You have offered an offering. Shall I be appeased for these things? (Isaiah 57:6)
- "Only acknowledge your iniquity, that you have transgressed against the LORD your God, and have scattered your ways to the strangers under every green tree, and you have not obeyed My voice," says the LORD. (Jeremiah 3:13)
- Why have they provoked Me to anger with their engraved images, and with foreign vanities? (Jeremiah 8:19)
- Everyone is dull-hearted, without knowledge. Every metal smith is put to shame by the carved image. For his molded image is falsehood, and there is no breath in them. (Jeremiah 51:17)
- And have cast their gods into the fire; for they were no gods, but the work of men's hands, wood and stone. (II King 19:18)
- Let all them be shamed who serve engraved images, who boast in their idols. Worship him, all you gods. (Psalms 97:7)
- Their idols are silver and gold, the work of men's hands. They have mouths, but they do not speak. They have eyes, but they do not see. They have ears, but they do not hear. They have noses, but they do not smell. They have hands, but they do not feel. They have feet, but they do not walk, neither do they speak through their throat. (Psalms 115:4-7)
- You shall know that I am the LORD, when their slain men shall be among their idols around their altars, on every high hill, on all the tops of the mountains, and under every green tree, and under every thick oak, the places where they offered pleasant aroma to all their idols. (Ezekiel 6:13)

12.5.4 Bible on Temple Visits and Taking Prasad

Why not worship God with everyone, in whatever form they worship Her/Him? Why not take your Christian fiancé(e) to a Hindu temple and share prasad from Hindu Gods? Then why not reciprocate by going to his/her church and eat the bread-prasad (body of Jesus)? Is it not wonderful to share and enjoy each other's culture?

But this is what Bible has to say:
- You abstain from things offered (prasad) to idols. (Acts 15:29)
- Therefore concerning the eating of things sacrificed to idols, we know that no idol is anything in the world, and that there is no God but one. For though there are things that are called "gods," whether in the heavens or on earth; as there are many "gods" and many "lords;" yet to us there is one God, the Father, from whom are all things, and we for him; and one Lord, Jesus Christ, through whom are all things, and we live through him. (I Cornithians 8:4-6)
- For if anyone sees you who have knowledge eating in an idol's temple, will not the conscience of him who is weak be emboldened to eat those things offered to idols? (I Corinthians 8:10)
- But if anyone says to you, "This was offered to idols," do not eat it for the sake of the one who told you, and for the sake of conscience. (I Corinthians 10:28)

12.5.5 The Bible's Exclusivity over God

Christianity teaches that only their faithful will achieve salvation, and others will be condemned to hell on the Judgment Day, after the Second Coming of Christ in the future. Islam too has similar teachings. Does it mean your Hindu parents will go to hell?

- I will dwell among the sons of Israel, and will be their God. (Exodus 29:45)
- And that whoever would not seek the LORD, the God of Israel, should be put to death, whether small or great, whether man or woman. (II Chronicles 15:13)
- Jesus said to him, "I am the way, the truth, and the life. No one comes to the Father (God) except through Me. (John 14:6)
- The house which I build is great; for our God is great above all gods. (II Chronicles 2:5)
- So we shall be separate, your people and I, from all the people who are upon the face of the earth. (Exodus 33:16)
- Jesus therefore said to them, "Truly I tell you, unless you eat the flesh of the Son of Man and drink his blood, you do not have life in

yourselves. He who eats My flesh and drinks My blood has eternal life, and I will raise him up at the last day. For My flesh is food indeed, and My blood is drink indeed. He who eats My flesh and drinks My blood lives in Me, and I in him. (John 6:53-56)

- And there is salvation in none other, for there is no other name under heaven, that is given among men by which we must be saved. (Acts 4:12)

12.5.6 Bible on Baptism

An interfaith couple has to realize that baptism is not a hollow ritual devoid of meaning.

Baptism means formal acceptance of Christian doctrine, which as shown below, means abandoning anything that conflicts with it. One should not get baptized just for the sake of a marriage requirement. Accept baptism only if you truly believe in the Biblical teachings, and are really willing to renounce/denounce your current faith and cultural background as you are expected to do.

- He did that which was evil (baptism for a wrong reason), because he did not set his heart to seek the LORD. (II Chronicles 12:14)
- Assuredly, I say to you, unless you are converted and become as little children, you will by no means enter the kingdom of heaven. (Matthew 18:3)
- He who believes and is baptized will be saved; but he who disbelieves will be condemned. (Mark 16:16)
- But I have a baptism to be baptized with, and how distressed I am until it is accomplished. Do you think that I have come to give peace in the earth? I tell you, no, but rather division. (Luke 12:50, 51)
- Peter said to them, "Repent, and be baptized, every one of you, in the name of Jesus Christ for the forgiveness of your sins, and you will receive the gift of the Holy Spirit." (Acts 2:38)
- One Lord, one faith, one baptism. (Ephesians 4:5)
- By this you know the Spirit of God: Every spirit that confesses that Jesus Christ has come in the flesh is of God, and every spirit that does not confess that Jesus Christ has come in the flesh is not of God. (I John 4:2-3)
- Whoever goes on and does not remain in the teaching of Christ, does not have God. He who remains in the teaching, the same has both the Father and the Son. If anyone comes to you, and does not bring this teaching, do not receive him into your house, and do not welcome him. (II John 1:9-10)

12.5.7 Bible's Punishments to Unbelievers

Stern punishments are provided for those who do not follow Biblical commandments, including terror, wasting diseases, heaped coals of fire, fire of His wrath, utterly destroy that breathed, melting in their midst, stoning to death, torned open rib cages, hooks in their jaws, slaying, killing, burn houses, death, slay their sons, destroy first born, rivers turned into blood and more. It will certainly scare the faint of heart.

- I also will do this to you: I will appoint terror over you, even consumption and fever, that shall consume the eyes, and make the soul to pine away; and you will sow your seed in vain, for your enemies will eat it. (Leviticus 26:16)
- If your enemy is hungry, give him bread to eat; and if he is thirsty, give him water to drink; for so you will heap coals of fire on his head, and the LORD will reward you. (Proverbs 25:21-22)
- I will pour out my indignation on you; I will blow on you with the fire of my wrath; and I will deliver you into the hand of brutish men, skillful to destroy. You shall be for fuel to the fire; your blood shall be in the midst of the land; you shall be remembered no more: for I, the LORD, have spoken it. (Ezekiel 21:31-32)
- The city shall be devoted, even it and all that is in it, to the LORD. Only Rahab the prostitute shall live, she and all who are with her in the house, because she hid the messengers that we sent… They utterly destroyed all that was in the city, both man and woman, both young and old, and ox, and sheep, and donkey, with the edge of the sword… They burnt the city with fire, and all that was in it. Only they put the silver, the gold, and the vessels of bronze and of iron into the treasury of the LORD's house. (Joshua 6:17, 21, 24)
- So Joshua struck all the land, the hill country, and the Negev, and the lowland, and the slopes, and all their kings. He left none remaining, but he utterly destroyed all that breathed, as the LORD, the God of Israel, commanded. (Joshua 10:40)
- The assembly shall stone them with stones, and dispatch them with their swords; they shall kill their sons and their daughters, and burn up their houses with fire. Thus will I cause lewdness to cease out of the land, that all women may be taught not to do after your lewdness. They shall recompense your lewdness on you, and you shall bear the sins of your idols; and you shall know that I am the Lord GOD. (Ezekiel 23: 47-49)
- I will put hooks in your jaws, and I will make the fish of your rivers stick to your scales; and I will bring you up out of the midst of your

rivers, with all the fish of your rivers which stick to your scales. (Ezekiel 29:4)

- As for the head of those who surround Me, let the mischief of their own lips cover them. Let burning coals fall on them. Let them be thrown into the fire, into miry pits, from where they never rise. (Psalms 140:9-10)
- But bring those enemies of mine who did not want Me to reign over them here, and kill them before Me. (Luke 19:27)
- If anyone is to go into captivity, he will go into captivity. If anyone is to be killed with the sword, he is to be killed with the sword. (Revelations 13:10)
- Yet I am the LORD your God from the land of Egypt; and you shall acknowledge no god but Me, and besides Me there is no savior... I will meet them like a bear that is bereaved of her cubs, and will tear the covering of their heart. There I will devour them like a lioness. The wild animal will tear them. (Hosea 13:4,8)
- He turned their rivers into blood, and their streams, so that they could not drink. He sent among them swarms of flies, which devoured them; and frogs, which destroyed them. He gave also their increase to the caterpillar, and their labor to the locust. He destroyed their vines with hail, their sycamore fig trees with frost. He gave over their livestock also to the hail, and their flocks to hot thunderbolts. He threw on them the fierceness of His anger, wrath, indignation, and trouble, and a band of destroying angels. He made a path for His anger. He did not spare their soul from death, but gave their life over to the pestilence, and struck all the firstborn in Egypt. (Psalm 78:44-51)

12.5.8 Bible on Interfaith Marriages

The Bible has many stern warnings against interfaith marriages. Probably for this reason, a fearful Christian will want to solve this interfaith marriage problem with the religious conversion of his or her non-Christian fiancé(e) (or children by this marriage).

Here are the Bible's recommendations on interfaith marriages:
- And when the LORD your God shall deliver them up before you, and you shall strike them; then you shall utterly destroy them: you shall make no covenant with them, nor show mercy to them; neither shall you make marriages with them; your daughter you shall not give to his son, nor shall you take his daughter for your son. For he will turn away your son from following Me, that he may serve other gods; so the anger of the LORD would be kindled against you, and he would

destroy you quickly. But you shall deal with them like this: you shall break down their altars, and dash their pillars in pieces, and cut down their Asherim, and burn their engraved images with fire. (Deuteronomy 7:2-5)

- And they took their daughters to be their wives, and gave their own daughters to their sons and served their gods. The children of Israel did that which was evil in the sight of the LORD, and forgot the LORD their God. (Judges 3:6-7)

- Now king Solomon loved women, and he took many foreign women, together with the daughter of Pharaoh, women of the Moabites, Ammonites, Edomites, Sidonians, and Hittites; of the nations concerning which the LORD said to the children of Israel, "You shall not go among them, neither shall they come among you; for surely they will turn away your heart after their gods." Solomon clung to these in love. He had seven hundred wives, princesses, and three hundred concubines; and his wives turned away his heart. For it happened, when Solomon was old, that his wives turned away his heart after other gods; and his heart was not perfect with the LORD his God, as was the heart of David his father. (I Kings 11:1-4)

- Now therefore do not give your daughters to their sons, neither take their daughters to your sons, nor seek their peace or their prosperity forever; that you may be strong, and eat the good of the land, and leave it for an inheritance to your children forever. (Ezra 9:12)

- We have trespassed against our God, and have married foreign women of the peoples of the land. Yet now there is hope for Israel concerning this thing. Now therefore let us make a covenant with our God to put away all the wives, and such as are born of them, according to the counsel of my lord, and of those who tremble at the commandment of our God. Let it be done according to the law. (Ezra 10:2-3)

- They joined with their brothers, their nobles, and entered into a curse, and into an oath, to walk in God's law, which was given by Moses the servant of God, and to observe and do all the commandments of the LORD our Lord, and his ordinances and his statutes; and that we would not give our daughters to the peoples of the land, nor take their daughters for our sons. (Nehemiah 10:29-30)

- I contended with them, and cursed them, and struck certain of them, and plucked off their hair, and made them swear by God, "You shall not give your daughters to their sons, nor take their daughters for your sons, or for yourselves. Did not Solomon king of Israel sin by these things? Yet among many nations was there no king like him, and he was beloved of his God, and God made him king over all Israel. Nevertheless foreign women caused even him to sin. Shall we then

listen to you to do all this great evil, to trespass against our God in marrying foreign women?" (Nehemiah 13:25-27)
- The woman who has an unbelieving husband, and he is content to live with her, let her not leave her husband. For the unbelieving husband is sanctified in the wife, and the unbelieving wife is sanctified by the brother. Otherwise your children would be unclean, but now they are holy. Yet if the unbeliever departs, let there be separation. The brother or the sister is not under bondage in such cases, but God has called you to peace. (I Corinthians 7:13-15)

12.5.9 Bible On Women

In the western world, women's status does not reflect what is portrayed in the Bible! This is one good example where religious scripture and what people have learned from it are different. It is important to find out what your intended interfaith spouse has learned from his/her scriptures.

This is what the Bible has to say for women:
- But I would have you know that the head of every man is Christ, and the head of the woman is the man, and the head of Christ is God. (I Corinthians 11:3)
- For a man indeed ought not to have his head covered, because he is the image and glory of God, but the woman is the glory of the man. For man is not from woman, but woman from man; for neither was man created for the woman, but woman for the man. (I Corinthians 11:7-9)
- Let your women keep silent in the churches, for they are not permitted to speak; but they are to be submissive, as the law also says. And if they want to learn something, let them ask their own husbands at home; for it is shameful for women to speak in church. (I Corinthians 14:34-35)
- When you go forth to battle against your enemies, and the LORD your God delivers them into your hands, and you carry them away captive, and see among the captives a beautiful woman, and you have a desire to her, and would take her to you as wife; then you shall bring her home to your house; and she shall shave her head, and pare her nails; and she shall put the clothing of her captivity from off her, and shall remain in your house, and bewail her father and her mother a full month: and after that you shall go in to her, and be her husband, and she shall be your wife. It shall be, if you have no delight in her, then you shall let her go where she will; but you shall not sell her at all for money, you shall not deal with her as a slave, because you have humbled her. (Deuteronomy 21:10-14)

12.5.10 Bible on Circumcision[278]

The God the Father and Son Jesus have different take on circumcision.

- Every male child among you shall be circumcised; and you shall be circumcised in the flesh of your foreskins, and it shall be a sign of the covenant between Me and you. He who is eight days old among you shall be circumcised, every male child in your generations, he who is born in your house or bought with money from any foreigner who is not your descendant. (Genesis 17:10-12)
- The uncircumcised male who is not circumcised in the flesh of his foreskin, that person shall be cut off from his people. He has broken My covenant. (Genesis 17:14)
- Thus says the Lord GOD, "No foreigner, uncircumcised in heart and uncircumcised in flesh, shall enter into my sanctuary, of any foreigners who are among the children of Israel." (Ezekiel 44:9)
- Circumcision of No Avail [Jesus' message]: For circumcision indeed profits, if you are a doer of the law, but if you are a transgressor of the law, your circumcision has become uncircumcision. If therefore the uncircumcised keep the ordinances of the law, won't his uncircumcision be counted as circumcision? Won't the uncircumcision which is by nature, if it fulfills the law, judge you, who with the letter and circumcision are a transgressor of the law? For he is not a Jew who is one outwardly, neither is that circumcision which is outward in the flesh; but he is a Jew who is one inwardly, and circumcision is that of the heart, in the spirit not in the letter; whose praise is not from men, but from God. (Romans 2:25-29)

12.5.11 Bible on Friendship with Unbelievers

Why would a true Bible-believer get into a love relationship with a Hindu, other than to proselytize? Even if that is not the conscious intent, the doctrine makes conversion of the "other" imperative for the believer.

- You shall make no covenant with them, nor with their gods. They shall not dwell in your land, lest they make you sin against Me, for if you serve their gods, it will surely be a snare to you. (Exodus 23:32-33)
- You shall consume all the peoples whom the LORD your God shall deliver to you; your eye shall not pity them: neither shall you serve their gods; for that will be a snare to you. (Deuteronomy 7:16)

---

[278] Also read Section 2.13.

• But of the cities of these peoples, that the LORD your God gives you for an inheritance, you shall save alive nothing that breathes; but you shall utterly destroy them. (Deuteronomy 20:16-17)

• Do not be unequally yoked with unbelievers, for what fellowship have righteousness and iniquity? Or what fellowship has light with darkness? What agreement has Christ with Belial? Or what portion has a believer with an unbeliever? What agreement has a temple of God with idols? (II Corinthians 6:14-16)

• But as it is, I wrote to you not to associate with anyone who is called a brother who is a sexual sinner, or covetous, or an idolater, or a slanderer, or a drunkard, or an extortioner. Do not even eat with such a person. (I Corinthians 5:11)

• He who is not with Me (Jesus) is against Me, and he who does not gather with Me, scatters. (Matthew 12:30)

• If anyone comes to you, and does not bring this teaching, do not receive him into your house, and do not welcome him, for he who welcomes him participates in his evil works. (II John 1:10-11)

12.5.12 Bible on Animal Sacrifices

If you are a vegetarian or an animal lover, you may not want to endorse this history of the Bible.

• Every moving thing that lives will be food for you. (Genesis 9:3)

• King Solomon offered a sacrifice of twenty-two thousand head of cattle, and a hundred and twenty thousand sheep. So the king and all the people dedicated God's house. (I Kings 8:63; II Chronicles 7:5)

• They sacrificed to the LORD in that day, of the spoil which they had brought, seven hundred head of cattle and seven thousand sheep. They entered into the covenant to seek the LORD, the God of their fathers, with all their heart and with all their soul; and that whoever would not seek the LORD, the God of Israel, should be put to death, whether small or great, whether man or woman. (II Chronicles 15:11-13)

• The number of the burnt offerings which the assembly brought was seventy bulls, one hundred rams, and two hundred lambs: all these were for a burnt offering to the LORD. The consecrated things were six hundred head of cattle and three thousand sheep. (II Chronicles 29:32-33)

• One man has faith to eat all things, but he who is weak eats only vegetables. (Romans 14:2)

12.5.13 Bible's Final Words

- I testify to everyone who hears the words of the prophecy of this book, if anyone adds to them, God will add to him the plagues which are written in this book. If anyone takes away from the words of the book of this prophecy, God will take away his part from the tree of life, and out of the holy city, which are written in this book. (Revelation 22:18-19).

> *I like your Christ, I do not like your Christians. Your Christians are so unlike your Christ.*
> —Mahatma Gandhi

Section 12.6: The Koran on Hindus?

Christians and Jews are discussed in detail in several sections of Koran, but there is no direct mention of the word "Hindu" in the Koran.

You are an "unbeliever" or "disbeliever" if you believe in having the liberty to pray to multiple forms of God, associate other names of God with Allah (for example, Lord Krishna or Jesus, Son of God), are a worshiper of murtis or images, perform any kind of Hindu rituals (for example puja), do not believe that the heaven and earth were created in six days, do not believe in the Judgment Day, do not believe Mohammad as the "last" apostle or do not follow Islamic practices as cited in the Koran.

Selected verses from Koran about "unbelievers" are listed here as is,[279] without any commentary or interpretation for interfaith couples to read and discover what these will mean for their future marriage.

- 2:178 Believers, retaliation is decreed for you in bloodshed: a free man for a free man, a slave for a slave, and a female for a female. He who is pardoned by his aggrieved brother shall be prosecuted according to usage and shall pay him a liberal fine. This is a merciful dispensation from your Lord. He that transgresses thereafter shall be sternly punished. Men of understanding! In retaliation you have a safeguard for your lives; that you may enjoy security.
- 2:191 Slay then wherever you find them. Drive them out of the places from which they drove you. Idolatry is more grievous than bloodshed.
- 2:193 Fight against them until idolatry is no more and Allah's religion reigns supreme.
- 2:221 Marry not idolatrous women until they believe; even a beliving slave-woman is better than an idolatress, although she may highly please you. And give not believing women in marriage to idolaters until they believe; even a beliving slave is better than an idolater, although he may highly please you. (*This is the most critical*

---

[279] There are many interpretations of the Koran. The author has cited these quatations from: The Holy Quran - translated by Maulana Muhammad Ali; The Koran - translated by N. J. Dawood, Penguin Books; The Holy Quran with English Translation by Maulawi Sher Ali, Islam International Publications; and https://quran.com. The quoted verse numbers may be approximate. Readers are advised to read a few versions of the Koran to understand clear interpretations and full context for these verses.

statement for any one in an interfaith relationship with a Muslim. Ask that Muslim to explain you Koran 24:30)

- 3:117 O you who believe, take not for intimate friends others than your own people; they spare no pains to cause you loss. They love that which distresses you: Vehement hatred has already appeared from out of their mouths, and that which their hearts conceal is greater still.

- 3:150 We will cast terror into the hearts of those who disbelieve because they set up with Allah that for which He has sent down no authority, and their abode is the Fire. And evil is the abode of the wrong-doers.

- 4:56 Those who disbelieve in Our Messages, we shall make them enter Fire. As often as their skins are burned, We shall change them for other skins, that they may taste the chastisement. Surely Allah is ever Mighty, Wise.

- 4:91 You will find others who desire to be secure from you and secure from their own people. Whenever they are made to return to hostility, they are plunged into it. So if they withdraw not from you, nor offer you peace and restrain their hands, then seize them and kill them wherever you find them. And against these We have given you a dear authority.

- 5:33 The only punishment of those who wage war against Allah and His Messenger and strive to make mischief in the land is that they should be murdered, or crucified, or their hands and their feet should be cut off on opposite sides, or they should be imprisoned.

- 8:12 Allah revealed His will to the angels, saying: "I shall be with you. Give courage to the believers. I will cast terror into the hearts of those who disbelieve. Strike off their heads, strike off the very tips of their fingers!"

- 9:5 So when the sacred months have passed, slay the idolaters, wherever you find them, and take them captive and besiege them and lie in wait for them in every ambush.

- 9:23: O you who believe, take not your fathers and your brothers for friends if they love disbelief above faith. And whoever of you takes them for friends, such are the wrongdoers.

- 9:28 Believers, surely, the idolaters are unclean.

- 9:62 They swear by Allah to you to please you; and Allah as well as His Messenger has a greater right that they should please Him, if they are believers.

- 22:19-22 Garments of fire have been prepared for the unbelievers. Boiling water will be poured upon their heads, melting their skins and that which is in their bellies. They shall be lashed with rods of iron. Whenever, in their anguish, they try to escape from Hell, back they shall be dragged, and will be told: "Taste the punishment of burning!"

- •24:30 Say to beliving men to turn their eyes away from temptation and to restrain their carnal desires. (*Muslim men are not supposed to look at a woman with carnal desires. If they (Muslim boys) see a girl, they are supposed to lower their gaze.*[280] *Also read Islamic Khalwat (close proximity) law in Malaysia in Section 2.15.3. For a "true" Muslim, interfaith love relationship is not possible unless the objective is love-jihad. To ask for religious conversion for marriage after years of romantic relationship is an ugly form of proselytization.*)

- •36:8-9 Surely We have placed on their necks chains reaching up to the chins, so they have their heads raised aloft. And We have set a barrier before them and a barrier behind them, thus We have covered them, so that they cannot see.

- •42:23 I ask you only to love your kith and kin.

- •44:45-54 Like murky oil or molten brass, like scalding water, it shall simmer in his belly. A voice will cry: "Seize him and drag him into the midst of Hell Fire. Then pour out scalding water over his head, saying: 'Taste this, illustrious and honorable man! This is the punishment which you have doubted.'" As for righteous, they shall be lodged in peace together amid gardens and fountains, arrayed in rich silks and fine brocade. Even thus: and We shall wed them to dark-eyed houris (paradise of young attractive women).

- •47:4-6 So when you meet in battle those who disbelieve, smite the necks; then, when you have overcome them, make (them) prisoners, and afterwards (set them free) as a favour or for ransom till the war lay down its burdens. That (shall be so). And if Allah please, He would certainly exact retribution from them, but that He may try some of you by means of others. And those who are slain in the way of Allah, He will never allow their deeds to perish. He will guide them and improve their condition. And make them enter the Garden, which He has made known to them.

- •47:22 If you renounced the Faith, you would surely do evil in the land and violate the ties of blood.

- •47:23 Those it is whom Allah has cursed, so He has made them deaf and blinded their eyes.

---

[280] View an Islamic schlor Dr. Zakir Naik's video message: https://www.youtube.com/watch?v=foLbqR6fBf8.

- •48:29 Mohammad is the Messenger of Allah, and those with him are ruthless to the disbelievers but compassionate among themselves.
- •60:4: We are clear of you and of that which you serve besides Allah. We disbelieve in you and there has arisen enmity and hatred between us and you forever until you believe in Allah alone.
- •60:10 Do not maintain your marriage with unbelieving women.
- •66:5 Maybe, his Lord, if he divorce you, will give him in your place wives better than you, submissive, faithful, obedient, penitent, adorers, fasters, widows, and virgins.
- •72:14-15 And some of us are those who submit, and some of us are deviators. So whoever submits, these aim at the right way. And as to deviators, they are fuel of hell.

There's dogma and there's life.
Let's hope you will settle for life.

Section 12.7: The Koran on Christians and Jews?

One of the most important questions a Christian-Muslim couple has to address is if Jesus is a Son of God or one of the apostles. Readers are advised to read several chapters in the Koran on Christianity and Judaism. Here a brief summary is presented.

Christians believe that the Lord Jesus is a (Son of) God and that faith in Jesus is important to achieve salvation and to enter into heaven.[281] In contrast, the Koran teaches to have faith in Allah (God in Arabic). Jesus, son of Mary, was no more than God's apostle.[282] Allah forbids that He Himself should beget a son![283] Those who say: "the Lord of Mercy (Allah) has begotten a son" preach a monstrous falsehood.[284] Unbelievers are those that say: "God is the Messiah, the son of Mary"[285] and "God is one of three (trinity)."[286] Unbelievers will get "Hell Fire." Further, Allah said, "Believers, take neither Jews nor the Christians for your friends."[287]

Islamic Law permits a Muslim man to marry women from the People of the Book (that is, Christians and Jews) but all of the children must be brought up as Muslims. Muslim women are forbidden from marrying non-Muslim men.[288] In effect, all children of any interfaith marriage involving a Muslim must be raised as Muslims.

---

[281] I John 4:2-3.

[282] Koran 4:171. Also read Koran 4:157-160, 6:101, 9:30-31, 10:66-69, 17:111, 18:4-5, 21:26, 23:91, 25:2.

[283] Koran 19:34-35.

[284] Koran 19:88-92 (translated by Dawood; other translators used these terms: monstrous thing (Maulawi Sher Ali), atrocious thing (Sahih), disastrous thing (Pickthall), most monstrous (Yusuf Ali), abdominable assertion (Shakir), monstrous lie (Muhammad Sarwar), said a terrible evil thing (Mohsin Khan), something hideous (Arberry), etc).

[285] Koran 5:72.

[286] Koran 4:171, 5:73.

[287] Koran 5:51 (Dawood, Maulawi Sher Ali, Pickthall, Yusuf Ali, Shakir, Muhammad Sarwar, Mohsin Khan, Arberry).

[288] http://en.wikipedia.org/wiki/Interfaith_marriage_in_Islam.

Appendix A: Glossary

Abrahamic faiths: Judaism, Christianity and Islam. (Followers of Abraham, who received the first covenant of God in 1943 BC.)

Admin: The author of this book, Dr. Dilip Amin, who goes by this name at InterfaithShaadi.org.

Agnostic: A person who believes that nothing is known or can be known of the existence or nature of God or of anything beyond material phenomena; a person who claims neither faith nor disbelief in God.

Asherim: Cult objects related to the worship.

Atheism: A lack of belief in God or a belief that there is no God.

Ayat: Verse in the Koran.

Balvihar: Hindu Sunday school.

Baptism: The term "baptism" means ritual washing or cleansing, referring to washing away the "original sin," a central concept in Christianity. With such an oath, one agrees to cleanse from former practices and later live with Jesus Christ forever.

Bar (boy) **mitzvah/bat** (girl) **mitzvah:** Mitzvah means commandments. These are religious rituals performed at age of 12-13 to announce the child a Jewish adult (coming of age).

BBS: Baptism, bris/bar mitzvah, shahadah/sunat religious rituals of Abrahamic religions.

Bhagawan: Bhagawan is an epithet for God. Bhagawan also represents the concept of abstract God to Hindus who are religious but do not worship a specific deity.

Bhakti: Devotional service to the Supreme Lord.

Bible: The Christian scriptures, consisting of the 66 books of the Old and New Testaments.

Bindi: It is a red dot worn on the center of the forehead, commonly by Hindu and Jain women.

Brahman: The essence of the universe from which everything originates and to which it returns. It is the all pervading reality, the One Truth. It is eternal and infinite. "Godhead" is the closest English term.

Bris: Jewish circumcision on 8th day of birth and his formal entrance into the world of Judaism.

Burka: It is an enveloping outer garment worn by women in some Islamic traditions to cover their bodies when in public.

Darshan: Vision of the divine.

Deity: Divine character or nature, especially that of the Supreme Being.

Desi: Someone from back home country.

Derasar: A Jain temple.

Devas and Devis: They are specific energies or mundane manifestations of the Ultimate Supreme Brahman.

Dharma: Dharma is not the same as religion.[289] Dharma has the Sanskrit root *dhri*, which means, "that which upholds" or "that without which nothing can stand" or "that which maintains the stability and harmony of the universe." Dharma is often translated as laws and order by which this universe is sustained.

Dharmic faiths: Hinduism, Jainism, Buddhism and Sikhism.

Diwali: It is the "festival of lights." Diwali spiritually signifies the victory of light over darkness or good over evil, knowledge over ignorance, and hope over despair.

Dua: Prayer.

Easter: Easter is a holiday to celebrate Jesus' resurrection from the dead.

Eid: Eid al-Fitr is an important religious holiday celebrated by Muslims worldwide that marks the end of Ramadan, the Islamic holy month of fasting.

Exclusivist: A person whose mentality is characterized by the disregard for opinions and ideas other than one's own. Exclusivist asserts that only his/her way is true and all others are in error.

Garba: It is a form of folk dance that was originated in the state of Gujarat in India. The name is derived from the Sanskrit term Garbha (womb) and Deep (a small earthenware lamp). Traditional garbas are performed around a centrally lit lamp or a picture or statue of the Goddess Durga.

Geeta: Holy Bhagawat Geeta (or Gita) is one of Hindu scriptures. These are messages given by Lord Krishna to Arjuna on the battlefield of Kuruksetra.

---

[289] Read more on Dharma from Rajiv Malhotra at http://rajivmalhotra.com/library/articles/dharma-religion/.

Haram: Forbidden or proscribed by Islamic law.

Hijab: It is a veil that covers the head and chest, which is particularly worn by some Muslim women beyond the age of puberty.

Himsa: This word is derived from the Sanskrit root hims—to strike; himsa is injury or harm, a-himsa is the opposite of this, i.e. cause no injury, do no harm. Ahimsa is also referred to as nonviolence, and it applies to all living beings—including all animals—according to many Indian religions.

Hungama: Agitation, disturbance or irrational shouting in public.

Imam: An imam is an Islamic leadership position. It is most commonly in the context of a worship leader of a mosque and Muslim community.

Inclusivism: It is one of several approaches to understanding the relationship between religions, asserts that while one set of beliefs is absolutely true, other sets of beliefs are at least partially true. It stands in contrast to exclusivism, which asserts that only one way is true and all others are in error.

Ishvara: It is a representation of Brahman. It is a representation as icons with form (saguna sakara), such as Lord Ganesh. Different aspects of Brahman are represented by different icons.

Ishvara Allah Tero Nam: One God, different names. It was Mahatma Gandhi's favorite bhajan. It is also a polupar Bollywood devotional song sung by Mohammad Rafi and chorus for the movie Naya Raasta (1970).

Jihad: Jihad is an Islamic term referring to the religious duty of Muslims to maintain the religion. Jihad has two meanings: an inner spiritual struggle and an outer physical struggle against the enemies of Islam that may take a violent or non-violent form. Jihad is often translated as "Holy War," although this term is controversial.

Judgment Day: All people that have ever lived on the earth will be brought before the throne of God, and His glorious Son Jesus will judge each one of them.[290] Muslims believe that Allah will come to decide the destiny of believers and nonbelievers on the Judgment Day.

Kaaba: The kabah also referred as Kaaba Muazzama, is a building at the center of Islam's most sacred mosque, Al-Masjid al-Haram, in Mecca, al-Hejaz, Saudi Arabia. It is the most sacred Muslim site in the world.

---

[290] Matthew 25:31-33.

Kafir: A person who is an unbeliever in Islam or an infidel. It is used as a derogatory term.

Ketubah (written thing): It is a special type of Jewish prenuptial agreement. It is considered an integral part of a traditional Jewish marriage, and outlines the rights and responsibilities of the groom, in relation to the bride.

Khalwat: An Islamic law that forbids an unmarried Muslim from being alone (close proximity) with someone of the opposite sex.

Koran (or Qur'an): The Islamic sacred book, believed to be the word of God as dictated to Mohammad by the archangel Gabriel and written down in Arabic.

MNC: Multinational corporation.

Monotheism: A belief in one god.

Mushrik: Idolatresses or who ascribe God's attributes to other than Allah. (also see Shirk)

Murti: Literally it means any form, embodiment or solid object, and typically refers to an image, statue of a deity or person in Hindu culture. By the Prana (breath) Pratishtha (establishing) ceremony, the idol becomes identical with the deity.

Namasanskara: Hindu naming ceremony. It is one of 16 Sanskaras in Hindu Dharma and is performed around the 12th day. It is also spelled as namakaranam or naamsanskar.

Namaz: Muslim prayer (also known as Salah) is one of the five pillars in the faith of Islam and an obligatory religious duty for every Muslim. It is a physical, mental and spiritual act of worship that is observed five times every day at prescribed times.

New adult: Adults aged 18-30.

Nikaah: Islamic marriage contract. The bride and groom must be Muslim.

Pandit: A scholar and a (Hindu) teacher.

Parsi: It is a culture (Persian) followed by Zoroastrian (settled mainly in India).

Pheras: Hindu marriage ceremony involving elaborate rituals, one of the most important being the "saat phere" or the seven steps to marriage.

Pluralism: It denotes a diversity of views and stands rather than a single approach or method of interpretation. Pluralism is acceptance of all religious paths as equally valid and thus promotes peaceful coexistence.

Polytheism: The belief in or worship of more than one god.

Prasad: After food offering is made to God, the remnants are considered prasad or the Grace of God.

Proselytism: An attempt of any religion or religious individuals to convert people to their beliefs.

Puja: Worship ceremony, act of worshipping. Prayers and offerings (fruits, flowers, water, food) are offered to the image of Hindu deities.

Ramadan (Ramazan): It is the ninth month of the Islamic calendar, and is observed by Muslims worldwide as a month of fasting to commemorate the first revelation of the Koran to Mohammad according to Islamic belief.

Religion: An organized system of beliefs, ceremonies, and rules used to worship a person God or a group of Gods (based on Merriam-Webster). Literally it means re-align or connect again with divinity.

Roza: Fasting.

Salah: Namaz or prayer.

Satya Narayan Katha: It is the religious worship of the Hindu God Vishnu.

Secular: Denoting attitudes, activities or other things that have no religious or spiritual basis.

Shaadi: Wedding.

Shahadah:[291] Religious conversion to Islam. The shahadah is the first pillar of Islam. In Arabic, *lā 'ilāha 'il 'āllāh, muḥammadun rasūlu-llāh*, meaning, there is no god but God and Mohammad is the messenger of God.

Sharia law is the body of Islamic law. The term means "way" or " path;" it is the legal framework within which the public and some private aspects of life are regulated for those living in a legal system based on Islam.

---

[291] http://www.albalagh.net/kids/understanding_deen/Shahadah.shtml.

Shirk: In Islam, shirk is the sin of practicing idolatry or polytheism, i.e. the deification or worship of anyone or anything other than a singular God, i.e. Allah.[292]

Special Marriage Act 1954: A court marriage in India (Section 2.15).

Sunat/khitan/khafd (female)/**khatna:** Muslim circumcision ceremony.

Surah is a chapter of Koran.

Talaak: As per Sharia Laws, a Muslim husband can say talaak three times to announce a divorce from his marriage nikaah contract.

Taqiyya: It is a form of Islamic dissimulation or a legal dispensation whereby a believing individual can deny their faith or commit otherwise illegal or blasphemous acts while they are in fear or at risk of significant persecution. It is also used to describe deception and lying.

Ten Commandments: God gave the Ten Commandments to Moses on Mount Sinai (around 1593 BC).

Toleration/tolerance: It is defined as the practice of tolerating something. It could also have a negative meaning to "put up" with someone or "allowing someone to live."

Torah (laws): The holiest scripture of Jews and the first five chapters of the Bible.

Vedas: Vedas are oldest scriptures of Hinduism. Hindus consider the Vedas to be "not of a man, superhuman" and "impersonal, authorless."

Veil: A piece of fine material worn by Islamic women to protect or conceal the face.

Vivaha: Hindu wedding ceremony.

Zina: It is an Islamic law concerning unlawful sexual relations between Muslims who are not married to one another through a nikaah. It includes extramarital sex and premarital sex, such as adultery (consensual sexual relations outside marriage), fornication (consensual sexual intercourse between two unmarried persons), and homosexuality (consensual sexual relations between same-sex partners).

---

[292] Wikipedia.

Appendix B: Endorsements at InterfaithShaadi.org

The author has been providing guidance to new adults based on the theme of this book Interfaith Marriages with Equality at InterfaithShaadi.org under an alias "Admin." Below are some of unsolicited feedbacks from readers since 2009.[293] These positive comments encouraged the author to continue working on this complex subject matter. The author wishes to thank to all these bloggers.

Adi: Thanks for getting back to me Admin. As I was writing to you, it became clear to me that I had to pick my parents.

Aisha (Muslim)**:** I'm done… I understood his true color what he wanted … thank you so much.

Aishwarya: I now understand well what the video[294] is trying to say. I wish I had watched this video earlier in life, maybe 3-4 years back. This website is doing a very good job educating people, if only its message could reach youngsters at the age of 17-21 so that they know what they are getting into, before and not after so many years into the relationship, when it involves so much pain to both sides.

Amritesh: I read almost every post and blogs on this site… my feelings… I just can't express in words.

Angel (Christian)**:** Dear admin, Yeah I can understand your all points. Thank you for guidance.

Anushka: I wish I found this site earlier.

Aspi (Parsi)**:** Thanks Admin. Really appreciate it. (Section 10.2)

Bittu: Thank you for your questions and inputs—they got my head clearer because I was able to think aloud.

Chetna: I'm really thankful to Lord Shiva, Interfaithshaadi.org, Admin and Satyen and all the others who stood by me in this bad phase. I learnt another lesson about unconditional support and the core concept of

---

[293] *The names mentioned on these comments are preferred names by bloggers on the web site (or modified by the author for the book) and in most cases not their real names. The author has not authenticated the blogger's identities. Readers are advised to read details of referenced posts to find context for such endorsement at https://www.interfaithshaadi.org/blog/?p=4919.*

[294] https://www.youtube.com/watch?v=hlAuY85RlcE.

humanity. None of us know each other yet we have an unknown bond. (Section 5.33)

Chit: Dear Admin, I would say thanks for creating such a platform. I got overwhelming responses of my post. Thank you very much.

David (Christian): I do like your (Admin's) philosophy and train of thought. (Section 8.4)

Emily (Christian): Thank you so much! You have been a great help and encouragement!

Geet: Thanks a lot to this website. God bless you Admin, I got so much strength from this site. [Later] Admin once again after two years, I want to say you a big THANKs. I am glad I chose a right path. I am very happy, infact alone, but very happy. This site is very helpful.

Hareesh: Admin, you have brought up such an educative and informative piece which is really very appreciative and both men and women of the world should inculcate the message ingrained in it.

Jainab (Muslim): Dear admin, you are 100% right and your suggestions are very much useful to me. (a year later) Dear admin, asslam. First of all appreciate your courage and honesty. You always comment very wisely and your response on different blames is accurate. You are doing a noble job. I hope you will continue your work for guiding people like me inspire of all hurdles. Thanks a lot. Khuda Hafiz.

Jennifer (Christian): Thank you for this. This is what I was looking for. Thank you (Admin), it means a great deal to me. (Section 8.1)

Kartik: Thank you Admin for your advice. I was so confused with this matter too! It is because I don't want to convert. And now, I got some ideas because of you. Thank you very much Admin, really appreciated!

Kushagra: Admin, if you're a guy, I love you brother. If you're a woman, you're freaking awesome and hell yeah you rock.

Madhavi: Thank you so much for making me realize what horrible mistake I was going to commit. Thank you so much Admin, for holding on to me… and asking me to come back… thank you… for making me feel like a family. (Section 5.7)

Maria (Catholic): I feel extremely happy that I happened to visit this site at this right moment. Special thanks to Admin, your inputs gave me the courage to take my stand.

Maya: Dear Admin, thank you for giving me confidence to do the right thing. (section 3.14)

Narendra: 100% agree with your speeches on Message to Parents.[295]

Nisha: This website has opened my eyes. Thank you. (Section 5.20)

Noreen (Muslim): I just wanted to thank you for your support over the years. (Section 5.25)

Prabha: You've created a safe platform for people to express their worries and problems... and confront each other intelligently. It's amazing, really!

PSingh: Thanks again for your deep insight into the matter.

Rahul: I am very happy that I found this website to share my problem about my love.

Rima: I appreciate for your reply and your precious time for giving me such a good suggestion. This website is really good source of knowledge and you are doing good work. (Section 3.12)

Riya: I'm grateful to you for your constant support.

Sadia (Muslim): Dear Admin, thanks for your advice and thoughts that you shared. Thanks a ton anyway. (Section 8.5)

Samselvin (Christian): I agreed to your professional reply and liked it.

Sanket: I am so depressed... (3 days later) now I am feeling so positive, your advice helped me a lot.

Sara: Thank you for taking out time to reply, even the fact that someone out there is taking time out to help me brings joy to my heart. (Section 8.7)

Sarah: Thank you very much. You were a good help.

Satyen: I am indebted to the Admin for giving a platform to propagate the truth so that the predators may not victimize the innocents.

Shaniza (Muslim): It is always comforting to see that there are individuals that promote love and respect of all religions. You (Admin) and your co-authors are really doing something amazing. So congratulations and thank you for the support!

Shubham: Dear Admin, I salute you. Whoever you are, please keep on.

---

[295] https://www.interfaithshaadi.org/blog/?p=3510&cpage=1#comment-34354.

Smita: Thanks folks and Admin who actually took interest in my problem and not in religious fights.

Sofie (Christian)**:** Yeah, sounds fair. That was a beautiful advice Admin. I'm so thankful that I found this website. I'll follow both your advice.

Stacey (Catholic)**:** This is a very interesting website and thank you for your articles. (Section 8.3)

Sum (Muslim)**:** …voicing my thoughts here on this forum is a good idea to understand some challenges and benefits I would experience in an interfaith marriage.

Syeda: I really loved the response of the Admin, kudos. Couldn't think of any better suggestion than what you have given. This world needs to think in aspects of humanity more than religion.

Tanisha: Dear Admin, I am very excited and at peace now with all that has happened. I thank you for all help.

Tara (Muslim)**:** Your guidance helped me to decide well… i am so so so happy that I found you here because you helped me a lot. God bless you. I wish best rewards from God for you.

Bibliography

Bhagavad-Gita, As It Is, by His Divine Grace A. C. Bhaktivedanta Swami Prabhupada, Second edition (2016). Alachua, FL: The Bhaktivedanta Book Trust.

The Holy Bible - The Gideons International (1985). Nashville, Tennessee: Thomas Nelson, Inc.

The Holy Geeta - translated by Swami Chinmayananda (2006). Mumbai, India: Central Chinmaya Mission Trust.

The Holy Quran - translated by Maulana Muhammad Ali. Retrieved from https://en.wikisource.org/wiki/The_Holy_Qur%27an_(Maulana_Muhammad_Ali).

The Holy Quran with English Translation by Maulawi Sher Ali (2012). Silver Spring, MD: Islam International Publications Limited.

The Koran - translated by N.J. Dawood (2003). London, UK: Penguin Books.

The Koran - translated by Arberry. Retrieved from http://corpus.quran.com/translation.jsp.

The Koran - translated by Mohsin Khan. Retrieved from http://corpus.quran.com/translation.jsp.

The Koran - translated by Muhammad Sarwar. Retrieved from http://corpus.quran.com/translation.jsp.

The Koran - translated by Pickthall. Retrieved from http://corpus.quran.com/translation.jsp.

The Koran - translated by Sahih International. Retrieved from http://corpus.quran.com/translation.jsp.

The Koran - translated by Shakir. Retrieved from http://corpus.quran.com/translation.jsp.

The Koran - translated by Yusuf Ali. Retrieved from http://corpus.quran.com/translation.jsp.

Lerner, D.A. (1999). Celebrating Interfaith Marriages. New York, NY: Holt Paperbacks.

Latner, H. (1998). The Everything Jewish Wedding Book. Avon, MA: Adams Media Corporation.

New Heart English Bible. Retrieved from http://studybible.info/NHEB.

Srimad Bhagwad Geeta - translated by Prabha Duneja (1998). Delhi, India: Publisher Govindram Hasanand.

The Torah: The Five Books of Moses (1992). Philadelphia, USA: The Jewish Publication Society.

Index

About the Author

The author has a doctorate degree in Pharmacology and is a lifelong (42 years) researcher in the medical field. Dr. Dilip Amin has earned 6 patents and authored 23 scientific publications. He was born in Gujarat, India and is now settled in America. Dr. Amin has travelled to 27 countries to learn of different cultures and religions. He was a President of Plymouth Balvihar, Blue Bell, Pennsylvania, USA, and is a founder of the Balvihar at Sanatan Mandir, San Bruno, California. Dr. Amin is a Director of Peninsula Multifaith Coalition in the San  Francisco Bay area. He is a certified speaker at Islamic Networks Group, San Jose, California. He is a Dharma Ambassador with Hindu American Foundation. He co-authored the book Vivaha Samskara: The Hindu Wedding Ceremony. Dr. Amin founded a Forum for Interfaith Marriage with Equality (InterfaithShaadi.org) in 2009 where he guided more than 900 youths in their interfaith love relationship issues. He has been happily married for past 38 years and has two children born and raised in America. Dr. Amin's email address is InterfaithShaadi@gmail.com.